LOVE AND THE CARIBBEAN

Love and the Caribbean

TALES, CHARACTERS AND SCENES OF
THE WEST INDIES

By Alec Waugh

PARAGON HOUSE
NEW YORK

First Paperback edition, 1991

Published in the United States by

Paragon House Publishers
90 Fifth Avenue
New York, NY 10011

Library of Congress Cataloging-in-Publication Data

Waugh, Alec, 1898–
Love and the Caribbean ; tales, characters and scenes of the West
Indies / by Alec Waugh. — 1st pbk. ed.
p.   cm. — (The Armchair traveller series.)
Reprint. Originally published: New York : Farrar, Straus and Cudahy,
1959. c1958.
ISBN 1-55778-351-9 : $12.95
1. West Indies—Descriptions and travel. 2. Waugh, Alec, 1898—
Journeys—West Indies. I. Title. II. Series.
F1611.W374   1991
917.2904′52—dc20   90-7220
CIP

Manufactured in the United States of America
10 9 8 7 6 5 4 3 2 1

Contents

Foreword

IN THIS BOOK I have collected the various pieces that I have written about the West Indies in travel books and magazines. They tell of my own love for the islands and of love in the islands. Hence, the title. I have been visiting the islands for thirty years. Several of them are very different now from what they were in 1928; several of my prophecies have not been fulfilled; on several points I have changed my mind; but I have not tried to bring this book up to date. The whole point of a travel book is that it should be dated.

Travel books are not a profitable form of writing; their sale is usually small but they have for the author the satisfaction of possessing reference value. They hold their place on library shelves and are consulted by the student and the traveller long after novels that enjoyed a brief bright summer are utterly forgotten. I do not suppose that it would pay a publisher to reissue today Froude's *English in the West Indies*, Treeves's *Cradle of the Deep*, or Rutter's *If Crab No Walk*, but those three books provide indispensable research material. It is of value to learn how certain places struck certain people twenty, fifty, eighty years ago. I have therefore left these pieces as I wrote them except for a few excisions. One or two repetitions will still be found, because I felt that the individual pieces would lose their identity if I pruned them too severely. I have dated each chapter, adding an occasional note and including a few interpolations explaining how I got my material. The interpolations are printed in italics.

On no issue has the situation changed more rapidly during the last few years than that of color. It will change even faster in the future. Racial discrimination is practically at an end, but color itself has not ceased to be a problem; and though it may cease to be a problem, it will remain, in my opinion, a consideration. The roots have gone very deep. I have inserted an occasional note to the effect that a certain situation would not exist today, but I have left untouched most of the paragraphs that dealt with color, because I believe that it will help the student of the future who turns these pages in a library, as I myself have turned those of Froude, to be able to say, "This is how it struck a certain kind of Englishman in 1928, '38, '48, and '58."

The name Eldred Curwen appears often in these pages. He died in London in September 1955 at the age of fifty-two. He had a peculiar upbringing. His family—its country seat was Workington, in Cumberland—was referred to in a gossip paragraph as "old enough to make the Plantagenets seem parvenus." His mother died when he was young, his elder brother was killed in the First War and his father never recovered from the shock, becoming a recluse and taking no interest in his younger son. Eldred had no real education. He was superannuated from Shrewsbury, and was allowed from the age of sixteen to wander about Europe on a monthly allowance of thirty pounds. (A pound was a respectable sum of money in 1919, in terms of dollars and in actual purchasing power.) He spoke colloquially French, German, Spanish, and Italian, but never grasped the grammar of any language. He would, for instance, spell the contraction of "did not" "dident." "People understand what I mean," he would retort. At the age of twenty-one his allowance was raised to a thousand pounds a year. A little later he broke the entail on Workington in favor of his sister's children in return for an annuity of two thousand pounds. In 1931, on his aunt's death, he inherited a charming Victorian villa in Antibes, which he made his base.

He was short, red-haired, well-built; he was a keen skier and a good tennis player. Though he was basically uneducated, he was a man of sound, practical common sense. He never did a day's work but he organized his own life effectively. Whereas most men are concerned with the earning of an income, he was concerned with the spending of one. His problem was how to get the most out of an income, first of thirty pounds a month, later of a thousand and, finally, of two thousand a year. He never got into debt.

As a friend he was affectionate and loyal. And if he was selfish, as leading such a life it was inevitable that he should have been, he was sensitively considerate of other people; tasks and feelings. For me, as for many others, the world is a different place without him.

B A C K G R O U N D : Gateway to the West Indies

Martinique

The Buccaneer

The Black Republic

An Historical Synopsis

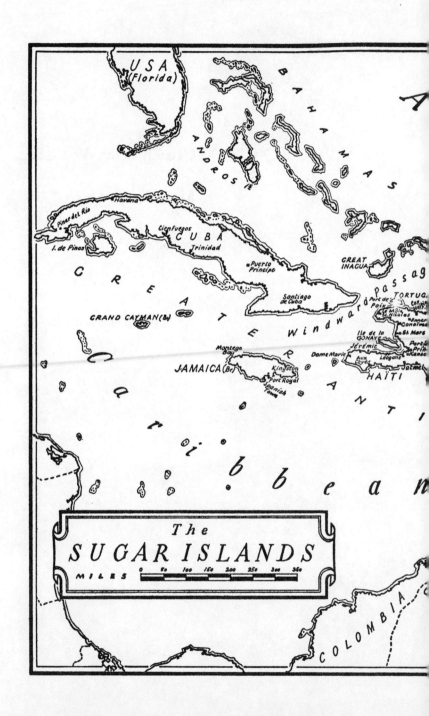

USA
(Florida)

BAHAMAS

ANDROS I?

•Havana

Pinar del Rio•

Cienfuegos

CUBA

Trinidad

I. de Pinos

•Puerto
Principe

GREAT
INAGUA

CREATER

GRAND CAYMAN (Br)

Santiago
de Cuba

Windward Passage

TORTUG.

Port de
Paix

St. Mar
St. Nicolas

Anse
Gonaïves

Cape

St Mars

Ile de la
GONAVE

Jérémie

Port
Prince

Dame Marie

Montego
Bay

Léogane

JAMAICA (Br)

Aux
Cayes

Jacmel

Kingston
Port Royal
Spanish
Town

HAÏTI

ANTI

Caribbean

The
SUGAR ISLANDS

MILES 0 50 100 150 200 250 300 350

COLOMBIA

Gateway to the West Indies

from THE SUGAR ISLANDS

WRITTEN IN 1947

SOMETHING ALWAYS REMAINS out of a love affair. Usually the last thing one would expect. A year ago, a man whom I have known for a quarter of a century, with whom for five or six years I was on terms of quite close friendship and with whom, nowadays, in the course of most years I arrange at least once to lunch or dine, asked me if I had been surprised the first time he invited me to dinner.

It had been in the early "twenties." I was four or five years younger than he was. We had nothing very obvious in common. He was a Treasury official. He was not a footballer or a cricketer. As members of the Savile Club, we met casually two or three times a month. There was no particular reason why he should have invited me to a dinner which marked—we could recognize it now in retrospect—the start of our real friendship. Had I been surprised when he invited me? "Yes," I said. "I suppose I was."

He smiled. "You'll be more surprised when I tell you why I did. I had heard that you were a good friend of Phyllis's. I had just fallen for her, crazily. I thought it might do me good to have you saying nice things about me to her. I read in *The Times* this morning that she is a grandmother. I don't suppose I've thought of her ten times in the last fifteen years. It's strange to reflect that our friendship, yours and mine, is the only thing that survives now out of all that emotional disturbance."

5

We have most of us had, I fancy, an equivalent experience. And when an interviewer recently asked me what it was that had first attracted me to the Caribbean, I was forced to remind myself, a little ruefully, that this interest of mine in the West Indies is all that is left alive now in my life of an entanglement on whose account at the end of the nineteen-twenties I travelled many thousand miles.

It was incidentally, without premeditation, as part of a quite different plan, that I saw the West Indies first.

In the spring of 1926 I went round the world. I travelled by the Messageries Maritimes. And in view of the difficulty and cost of travel now, it is pertinent to recall that a ticket that sent me first-class round the Mediterranean touching at Greece, Turkey, and the Levant; thence from Port Said via Colombo to Malaya; from Singapore, calling at the Dutch East Indies, to the Australian ports; from Sydney northwards across the Pacific to the New Hebrides, Tahiti, Panama, the West Indies, and finally Marseilles; a ticket that included twenty weeks' board and lodging, cost 166 pounds.

For a writer with no responsibilities or overhead expenses, who was able to earn a thousand pounds a year, large-scale travel was, in the "twenties" and "thirties," a definite economy. When I have mentioned the places I have been to, I have often been asked incredulously how on earth I could have paid the passage. My answer has been that it was only because I was travelling half the time that I was able to run a flat and entertain my friends in London. During my round-the-world trip I spent during nine months, without being austerely economical, under five hundred pounds.

I have described that journey in another book, *Hot Countries*, telling how, like so many travellers before me, I decided at the first sight of Tahiti to let my ship sail on without me; telling in the form of fiction how gradually I came to realize that Tahiti, whatever it may have been in the days of Melville, was no place in the nineteen-twenties for a young man of ambition to take root in; telling how I decided suddenly, in an afternoon, to get back to England by the quickest and shortest route across America, not waiting for the French boat by which I had a ticket. I did not tell, however, in *Hot Countries*, how on the way up to San Francisco all my plans for settling permanently in England became reversed

and how in the smoke-room of the *Manganui* I made a rendezvous for August in Tahiti.

Six months later I started back for the Pacific in the *Louqsor*, a
converted seven-thousand-ton French troopship which carried
about sixty mixed-class passengers. She sailed from Marseilles. She
was bound for New Caledonia, through the Panama Canal. Tahiti
was six weeks away. At the head of the gangplank a small black
board announced that we would leave at 11:30 for Pointe à Pitre.
"Where's Pointe à Pitre?" I asked.
"Guadeloupe. It's the chief port there."
But I was not interested in Guadeloupe. I barely knew of its
existence. I remembered it vaguely from history lessons as one of
the islands that kept changing hands during the French wars of
the eighteenth century. Guadeloupe, like Colon, was a station
upon a six weeks' journey. When the notice board announced
eighteen days later that we would dock on the following afternoon,
such anticipation as I felt was no more than the corollary to eighteen landless days. I wanted to feel my feet on concrete, I wanted
to loiter before shop windows, to "consult" a menu, to patronize
a "dancing." It was in that mood that I went ashore; and appropriately enough, the only recordable incident that I can recall
about the next ten hours is that I first drank Lanson then.

The next day we docked at Martinique.
It was a cloudless July morning. The sky looked very blue
against the gray-green tamarinds. The shrubs lining the road down
which we sauntered from the quay were studded in pink and
white with the bell-mouthed hibiscus. There was a broad, grass-
grown savannah flanked with mango trees. In its center was a
white statue set about with palms, with royal palms that stood
straight and tall like sentries. On two sides of the savannah was
the irregular broken skyline of two- and three-storied buildings;
clubs and hotels and shops and cafés; some wooden and some
brick; some with fresh-painted shutters; others with blistered wood-
work and warped frames. On the edge of the grass a succession of
one-man stalls offered soft drinks and biscuits.
The tourist season for the Caribbean ends in April. The summer
is popularly supposed to be made as intolerable by heat as is the
autumn by rain and wind. But I do not remember it as being

particularly hot. Everything was bright and gay; there was color
and animation along the streets. Many of the women wore the
native dress, wide-skirted about the ankles, tight-bodiced, with a
silk handkerchief about the shoulders and a smaller silk handkerchief knotted in the hair, with the ends pointing upwards. The
French officials looked very dapper and self-important in their
white ducks and high-crowned, mushroom-like sun helmets; the
mulatto men, very elegant, in their silk shirts and gaudy ties and
tightly waisted suits. There was a great deal of noise. Cars were
honking at every corner. Range after range of jagged mountains,
indented with the pale blue of bay and estuary, rose like a bastion
behind the harbor. Over the porch of the Hotel de France [*the
Hotel de France has been displaced by a large Odeon-lighted
cinema. The savannah at Fort de France would not affect the
modern traveller in the same way today. Too many cars are parked
round it. It looks like a garage.*] the tricolor was flying. There was
an air of the Midi about it all. And across the grass, the white
statue in its circle of guardian palms gave a dignity and significance to the scene. Whom was it to? I asked.

My question was greeted with a laugh. Had I forgotten that
Josephine was born here?

I strolled across to it.

So many pens have described the details of that statue—the
long, flowing robes of the First Empire, the high waist, the bare
arms and shoulders, the hand resting on a medallion that bears
Napoleon's profile, the head turned southwards to the place of
her birth, Trois Ilets—so many magazine articles have been
adorned with its illustration that it is hard for the modern traveller
to assess its intrinsic value as a work of art. It is hard to dissociate
it from its subject: it is hard not to react against its overpraise; it
is easy to dismiss it scoffingly as "the kind of thing that you would
see in half a hundred cemeteries." Moreover, it is set upon so high
a pedestal that it is impossible to get a level and close-up view of
it. I have never seen a photograph that did it justice; and it is possible that if you were to see that statue in a London gallery, you
would consider it of small account. Seen, though, in Martinique,
in its own setting, from a distance of forty yards, it is not easy to
be unmoved by it. As I saw it on that first July morning, white
against the green of the tamarinds and mangoes, it seemed to
stand there on its pedestal, in the center of the savannah, in the

circle of its palms, as a symbol, as a tribute to the romantic destiny not only of a woman, but of an island's life. "This must be a real place," I thought.

The *Louqsor* was to sail at four. It was close upon six before she did. No French cargo boat, I was told, has ever sailed punctually from Fort de France or made full speed next day. No French sailor, however he may be warned, can appreciate that a liquid which is served as a *vin de table* at five francs [*The value of the franc at this time was a hundred and twenty to the pound*] the bottle can have the potency of rum. The police have a busy afternoon on boat days rounding up the crew.

We leaned, the purser and I, against the taffrail watching the stragglers being brought in one by one, while the women who had coaled the ship—the *charbonnières*—stood beside their baskets roaring with laughter, their teeth showing very white against their soot-grimed faces.

The purser shrugged.

"La Martinique," he said. "There is no place like it."

"How about Tahiti?"

He shrugged again. "Tahiti is, how shall I say, *hors concours*. You can make no comparison. There is only one Tahiti. But La Martinique. She is special too. Yes; she is very special."

Fifteen months later I was to remember that conversation. I was in need of an impersonal period, a pause in which to think and write, to refresh and recreate myself. Martinique might prove, I thought, a sister island to Tahiti. It was French and in the tropics, as far north of the line as was Tahiti south of it. She was special in her own way, the *commissaire* had said. It might be amusing to try to discover where the difference lay. I might write an article, or even a book, comparing the two islands. Early in December I started off.

That first trip of mine, in the company of Eldred Curwen, lasted five months. Starting from Martinique, we went northwards to Dominica, Guadeloupe, Antigua, staying long enough in Dominica and Antigua to become identified with the way of life there. Then we made for Barbados, pausing at St. Lucia on the way. From Barbados we went to Trinidad, from Trinidad to Ja-

maica. In those days there were no airplanes and it was an eight days' journey by ship via Panama. From Jamaica we crossed to Haiti, then returned by a slow and friendly French ship that stopped at Puerto Rico, St. Martin and St. Barthélemy. I used this trip as the framework for my first travel book, Hot Countries.

The book opened with a chapter on Tahiti; it went on to describe Martinique.

Martinique

from HOT COUNTRIES

WRITTEN IN 1928

It was while I was on my way to Panama, on my second visit to the South Seas, that I first saw Martinique. Out of a blue sky the sun shone brightly onto a wide square flanked with mango trees, onto yellow houses, onto crowded cafés. And here I thought, maybe, is another and a less far Tahiti. An island in the tropics, under French rule, as far north of the line as was Tahiti south of it. I shall come back here one day, I told myself.

Now, having returned, I am wondering whether it would be possible for two islands to be more different. Their very structure is unlike. They are both mountainous, but whereas the interior of Tahiti is an unpathed, impenetrable jungle, every inch of Martinique is mapped. Nor is West Indian scenery strictly tropical. In Martinique the coconut and the banana are not cultivated systematically. The island's prosperity depends on rum and sugar. And as you drive to Vauclin you have a feeling, looking down from the high mountain roads across fields, green and low-lying, to hidden villages, that you might be in Kent were the countryside less hilly. The aspect of the villages is different. Whereas Tautira is like a garden, with its grass-covered paths, its clean, airy bungalows, its flower-hung verandas, it is impossible to linger without a feeling of distaste in the dusty, ill-smelling villages of Carbet and Case Pilote, with their dirty, airless cabins, their atmosphere of negligence and squalor. In Tahiti the fishing is done for the most part at night, by the light of torches, on the reef, with spears. In

11

Martinique it is done by day with weighted nets. In Martinique most of the land is owned by a few families. In Tahiti nothing is much harder to discover than the actual proprietor of any piece of ground. Proprietorships have been divided and redivided, and it is no uncommon thing for a newcomer who imagines that he has completed the purchase of a piece of land to find himself surrounded by a number of claimants, all of whom possess legal right to the ground that their relative has sold him. Scarcely anybody in Tahiti who derives his income from Tahiti has any money. In Martinique there are a number of exceedingly wealthy families. On the other hand, whereas the Tahitian is described as a born millionaire, since he has only to walk up a valley to pick the fruits and spear the fish he needs, the native in Martinique, where every tree and plant exists for the profit of its proprietor, lives in a condition of extreme poverty.

The Tahitian woman lives for pleasure. She does hardly any work. By day she lives languidly on her veranda, and by night, with flowers in her hair, she sings and dances and makes love. The woman of Martinique is a beast of burden. When the liner draws up against the quay at Fort de France you will see a crowd of grubby midgets grouped round a bank of coal. [*The ships that call at Martinique now are oil-burners and this practice has consequently ceased.*] When the signal is given they will scurry like ants, with baskets upon their heads, between the ship's tender and the bank of coal. The midgets, every one of them, are women. They receive five sous for every basket that they carry. When there is no ship in port they carry fish and vegetables from the country into town. There is a continual stream of them along every road: dark, erect, hurrying figures bearing, under the heavy sun, huge burdens upon their heads.

In Tahiti there exists a small, formal, exclusive French society, composed of a few officials and colonial families who hold occasional receptions, to which those who commit imprudences are not received. But the average visitor is unaware of its existence. It is uninfluential. In Martinique, too, there is such a society composed of a few Creole families. It is very formal and very exclusive. Its Sunday *déjeuner* lasts, I am told, till four o'clock. It is also extremely powerful and holds all the power, all the land, and most of the money in the island.

Tahiti is a pleasure ground; Martinique is a business center. The

atmosphere of Tahiti is feminine; of Martinique masculine. In
Fort de France everyone is busy doing something: selling cars,
buying rum, shipping sugar. Whereas social life in Papeete is
complicated by the ramifications of amorous intrigue, in Fort de
France it is complicated by the ramifications of politics and commerce. "Life here is a strain," a young dealer said to me. "One
has to be diplomatic all the time. One has business relations of
some sort with everybody." In Papeete it is "affairs" in the English sense; in Fort de France in the French sense. No one who has
not lived in a small community, each member of whom draws his
livelihood from the resources of that country, can realize the inter-
dependence of all activities, the extent to which wheels revolve
within one another. Everyone has some half-dozen irons in everybody else's grate.

   In Tahiti the only people who are in a position to spend money
are the tourists who stay over between two boats and the English
and Americans who come to spend a few months on the island
every year. In Tahiti there is accommodation for the tourist. In
Moorea there is a good hotel. There are bungalows to be let by
the month within some two and a half miles of Papeete. In the
country there are several places where you can spend a few days
in tolerable comfort. In Martinique there are no tourists. Between
January and March some dozen English and American liners stop
at St. Pierre. Their passengers drive across the island to Fort de
France, where they rejoin their ship. That is all. There is no
accommodation for the tourist. In Fort de France there is no hotel
where one would spend willingly more than a few hours. [*There
are now at least two hotels, the Lido on the beach and the Vieux
Moulin in the foothills. Both are about six miles out of Fort de
France.*] In the country there is no hotel at all. As far as I could
discover there was not in the whole island a single foreign person
who lived there out of choice.

   Finally, the native population of Tahiti is freeborn; that of Martinique has its roots in slavery. You have only to walk through a
native village to realize the difference that that makes. In Fort de
France, which is cosmopolitan, you do not notice it. But in the
country, where day after day you will not see one white face, you
grow more and more conscious of a hostile atmosphere; you feel
it in the glances of the men and women who pass you in the road.
When you go into their villages they make you feel that they

resent your presence there. You are glad to be past their houses. They will reply to your "Good mornings" and "Good evenings," but they do not smile at you. Often they will make remarks to and after you. They are made in the harsh Creole patois. You do not understand what they say. You suspect that they are insulting you. They are a harsh and somber people. They do not understand happiness. You will hear them at cock-fighting and at movies, shrieking with laughter and excitement, but their faces, whenever they are in repose, are sullen. Their very laughter is strained. They seem to recall still the slavery into which their grandparents were sold. It is only eighty years since slavery was abolished. There are many alive still who have heard from their parents' lips the story of those days. They harbor in their dull brains the heritage of rancor. They are exiles. Under the rich sunlight and the green shadows their blood craves for Africa. They are suspicious with the unceasing animosity of the undeveloped. They cannot believe that they are free. In their own country they were the sport and plunder of their warlike neighbors. It was the easy prey that the pirate hunted. They cannot believe that the white strangers who stole them from their dark cabins have not some further trick to play on them. They cannot understand equality. They will never allow you to feel that you are anywhere but in a land of enemies. In vain will you search through the Antilles for the welcoming friendliness of Polynesia.

[*This is, it must be remembered, a first impression. I do not feel in that way now in Caribbean villages and, of course, in thirty years great changes have taken place in West Indians themselves, mentally as well as materially. They have acquired self-confidence. At the same time, even now there is a basic difference between a freeborn people and one that has been subjected to foreign domination. I felt this very strongly on a recent visit to Thailand (1957). The Thais have a light-heartedness that I have not found in India or Malaya. Prince Chula in* The Twain Have Met *referred to the "colonial neurosis" to which his fellow-countrymen had been exposed.*]

In Martinique there is no accommodation for the tourists. If you are to stay there you have to become a part of the life of its inhabitants. Within two hours of our arrival Eldred Curwen and I had realized that.

"We have got," we said, "to set about finding a bungalow in the country."

I am told that we were lucky to find a house at all. Certainly we were lucky to find the one we did. A little over four miles out of town, between Case Navire and Fond Lahaye, a minute's climb from the beach, above the dust of the main road, with a superb panorama of coastline, on one side to Trois Ilets, on the other very nearly to Case Pilote, it consisted of three bedrooms, a dining-room, a wide veranda over whose concrete terrace work—the hunting ground of innumerable lizards—trailed at friendly hazard the red and yellow of a rose bush and the deep purple of the bougainvillea. The stone stairway that ran steep and straight towards the sea was flowered by a green profusion of trees and plants; with breadfruit and with papaia; the great ragged branch of the banana; the stately plumes of the bamboo; with, far below, latticing the blue of the Caribbean, the slender stem and rustling crest of the coconut palm. [*The villa was still standing in 1952, but I had great difficulty in finding it, so built over was the hillside surrounding and below it.*] It was the kind of house one dreams of, that one never expects to find. Yet nothing could have been found with less expense of spirit.

It was the British Consulate that found it for us.

"You want a house," they said. "That is not easy. We will do our best. If you come tomorrow afternoon we will tell you what we have been able to manage."

It was in a mood of no great optimism that we went down there. Everyone had shaken their heads when we had told them we were looking for a house.

"Nobody will want to let his house," we had been told. "A house is a man's home. Where would there be for him to go? And for those who have a house both in the country and the town— well, that means that he is a rich man, that his house in the country is his luxury. There are not many luxuries available in the colonies. He would not be anxious to deprive himself of it."

It sounded logical enough. And when we found two men waiting for us in the Consulate, it was with the expectation of being shown some sorry shack that we followed them into the car. The sight of the house upon the hill was so complete and so delightful a surprise that we would have accepted any rent that its proprietor demanded of us. We were prudent enough, however, to conceal our elation. And three days later we were installed in the bungalow with three comic-opera servants, the sum of whose monthly wages in francs can have exceeded only slightly the sum of their united ages.

Our cook, Armantine, received eighty francs. Belmont, the guardian, whose chief duty was the supervision of the water supply and the cutting of firewood, fifty francs. His wife, Florentine, who ran errands, washed plates, and did the laundry, had forty francs. It does not sound generous, but it is useless to pay Negroes more than they expect. American prosperity is built on a system of high wages. The higher the worker's wages, the higher his standard of living, the higher his purchasing capacity, the greater is the general commercial activity. But the Negro in the French Antilles has no ambition; he is quite content with his standard of living. He does not want it raised. If you were to pay him double wages, he would not buy himself a new suit. He would take a month's holiday. A planter once found that, however high the wages he offered to the natives, he could not induce them to work. In despair he sought an explanation of an older hand.

"My dear fellow," he was told, "what can you expect with all those fruit trees of yours? Do you think they are going to work eight hours a day when at night they can pick enough fruit to keep them for half a week?"

In the end, at considerable cost and inconvenience, the planter cut down his fruit trees. Then the natives worked.

Our staff considered itself well rewarded with a hundred and seventy francs a month. And it not only made us comfortable but kept us constantly amused.

Armantine was the static element. She was a very adequate cook, considering the limited resources at her disposal. Meat could only be obtained in small quantities twice a week. Lobster was plentiful only when the moon was full. The small white fish was tasteless. There are only a certain number of ways of serving eggs. And yam and breadfruit, the staple vegetables of the tropics, are uninteresting even when they are flavored with coconut milk. It says much for her ingenuity that at the end of six weeks we were still able to look forward to our meals. She was also economical.

I have little doubt that our larder provisioned her entire family. But no one else was allowed to take advantage of our inexperience. Resolutely, sou by sou, she contested the issue with the local groceries. I should be grateful if in London my housekeeper's weekly books would show no more shillings than Armantine's showed francs. She was also an admirable foil to Florentine.

Florentine was quite frankly a bottle woman. She was never sober when she might be drunk. Amply constructed, I have never seen a person so completely shapeless. Her face was like a piece of unfinished modelling. With her body swathed in voluminous draperies it was impossible to tell where the various sections of it began. When she danced—and she was fond of dancing—she shook like an India-rubber jelly. Very often after dinner, when we were playing the phonograph, we would see a shadow slinking along the wall. On realizing that its presence had been recognized it would quiver and giggle, turn away its head and produce a mug sheepishly from the intricacies of its raiment. We would look at one another.

"Armantine!" Eldred would call out. "Here!"

In a businesslike, practical manner Armantine hurried round from the kitchen.

"How much," we would ask, "has Florentine drunk today?"

Armantine's voice would rise on a crescendo of cracked laughter.

"Too much," she would reply.

We would look sorrowfully at Florentine and shake our heads, and she would shuffle away like a Newfoundland dog that has been denied a bone. On other evenings Armantine would be lenient.

"Yes," she would say, "you may give her some tonight."

So the bottle was got out, the glass was quarter filled. Florentine never looked at the glass while the rum was being poured. She preferred to keep as a surprise the extent of her good fortune, in the same way that a child shuts its eyes till a present is within its hands. And in the same way that a child takes away its present to open it in secret, so would Florentine, with averted face, hurry round the corner of the house. A minute later she would return, a shiny grin across her face.

"Now I will dance for you," she would say.

Sometimes she would become unruly as a result of visits to the village. And Armantine would come to us with a distressed look.

"Please," she would say, "give Florentine some clothes to wash. She earned five francs yesterday. Unless she is employed here, she will go down into the village and get drunk."

So we would make a collection of half-soiled linen, and sorrowfully Florentine would set about the justifying of her monthly wage.

A grotesque creature, Florentine. But a friendly, and a good-natured one. Once I think she may have been attractive in a robust, florid, expansive way; the kind of attraction that would be likely to wake a last flicker of enterprise in an ageing heart. For Belmont was very many years her senior. Now he has passed into the kindly harbor of indifference. He does not care what she does. He observes her antics with the same detachment that one accepts the irritating but inevitable excursions of a mosquito. He remains aloof, behind an armor of impressive dignity.

He was one of the most impassive and the most dignified figures that I have ever met. He never hurried. Under the shadow of such a straw hat as one associates with South America he moved at a pace infinitely slower than that of a slow-motion film. He possessed a pair of buttonless button boots which can have served no other purpose, so perforated were they, than the warming of his ankles. One day he would wear the right boot. On the next the left. Every fourth or fifth day he would wear neither. Only once did I see him wearing both. That was on New Year's Day. To our astonishment he appeared at breakfast-time in both boots, a straw hat, a flannel shirt buttoned at the neck, and a clean white suit. In his hand he carried a bunch of roses. He was going into Fort de France, he explained, to wish the proprietor of the house a happy New Year.

"C'est mon droit," he said, "comme gardien." No Roman praetor could have boasted more proudly of his citizenship.

Indeed, there was a Roman quality in Belmont. There was something regal about the way he would lean completely motionless for a whole hour against the concrete terrace work, looking out over the sea, and then at the end of the hour walk across to the other side of the veranda to lean there for another hour, motionless. And as he slowly climbed the steep stairway from the beach, a long, straight cutlass swinging from his wrist, he looked

very like some emperor of the decadence deliberating the execu-
tion of a stubborn courtier.

There are two ways of forming an impression of a country. In
a few weeks one can only hope to gain a first impression. Very
often, if one stays longer, the vividness of that first impression
goes. The art of reviewing a book is, I am told, not to read the
book carefully. Accurate considered judgment of a book within
twenty-four hours of reading it is not possible. A rough idea is all
that can be got. And it is usually to one's first impression that
ultimately one returns. At the end of ten days in a place I have
often felt that I should know no more of it if I were to stay ten
years, but that were I to stay ten months the clarity of that first
impression would be gone. My sight would be confused with detail; I should be unable "to put anything across."

The tourist has to rely on first impressions. The question is how
is that first impression best obtained? There are two ways. Either
you are the explorer, who leaves no corner unexamined, who hur-
ries from place to place collecting and codifying facts; or else you
are the observer. From a secluded spot you watch the life of one
section of it pass in front of you. From the close scrutiny of that
one section you deduce and generalize. Each way has its merits
and demerits. It is a matter of temperament, I suppose. Myself, I
have always chosen to let life come to me. And in the mornings
as I sat on the veranda of our bungalow I would watch the life
of the island pass in review before me.

Northwards and southwards, over St. Pierre and Fort de France,
there is a rainbow curving, for the rainless is as rare as the sunless
day; westwards, on the horizon beyond "the bright blue meadow
of a 'bay,'" ships are passing: the stately liners of the Transatlan-
tic, with their twin funnels and their high white superstructures;
the smaller boats of three or four thousand tons, the innumerable
and homely cargoes, broad, black, low-lying, with only the white
lookout of the bridge above their high-piled decks. Whither are
they bound? Northwards for New York, for Jacmel and the dark
republics? Southwards for Cristobal, for the silent wizardry of
Panama? Afterwards in the blue Pacific will they turn southwards
to Peru and Ecuador, or northwards to the coffee ports of Mexico
and Guatemala; to Champerico, where they haul you in baskets
up onto the long iron pier that runs out into the sea; to Puerto

Angeles, where the lighters are loaded by hand, by natives who splash through the waves, their broad shoulders loaded; to Manzanillo, where for three intolerable days I sat in the shadow of a café among squabbling Mexicans, while the *City of San Francisco* discharged an oil tank; Salvador, Guatemala, Mexico? In six weeks' time, who knows, these broad beams may be swinging through the Golden Gate; there may be passengers there who six weeks from now will be looking down from the high window of the *St. Francis* onto the lights and animation of the little square. Whither are they bound, those nameless cargoes? Hour after hour I would watch them pass and repass upon the horizon.

Sometimes, in a state of high excitement, Armantine would come rushing from the kitchen. *"Regardez! Touristes Américains!"* Slowly, in the majesty of its twenty thousand tons, the vast ship would be moving southwards. Shortly after breakfast it discharged its passengers at St. Pierre. For a little they wandered among the ruins; then in a fleet of cars they hurried over the southern road to Fort de France. For an hour or so they will assume control of it. With cameras in their hands they will stroll through the town as though it were an exhibition. They will peer into private houses. They will load themselves with souvenirs, with shouts of laughter they will call each other's attention to such sights as will appear to them remarkable. They will consider fantastically humorous their attempts to make themselves understood in pidgin French. For an hour, buying, examining, commenting, they will parade the town. Then, with a sigh of relief, they will consider their educational duty to themselves acquitted. It is time the fun began.

"Let's go some place and enjoy ourselves," they say.

As likely as not they will choose the Café Bédiat. It is lunchtime. But they do not bother about food. You can eat anywhere. You can eat in Ogden and Omaha and Buffalo. You do not come all the way to Martinique to eat.

"Rhum, compris? Rhum, beaucoup," they will tell the waitresses.

There is no nonsense about their drinking. They do not spoil good liquor with ice or lime or syrup. This isn't bootleg gin. [*The U.S.A. was in the clutches of Prohibition at this time.*] They know how to treat the real stuff when they meet it. They take it straight. A port glass of neat rum in the one hand, a tumblerful of ice water as a chaser in the other, they set about the serious

business of their trip. By the time the last siren of their steamer
goes, half the men and three-quarters of the women are drunk.
In a country where you can drink all you want for two francs and
as much as you can carry for four, they toss their hundred-franc
notes upon the table.

"Ah, don't bother about that," they say, as the waitress fumbles
in her pocket. "If you can find any use for that flimsy pink stuff,
you cling on to it."

Laughing and shouting, arm in arm, they sway towards the ship,
having in one small section of the globe done their country's name
more damage in four hours than her statesmen and engineers and
artists can do it good in as many years. Tomorrow they will pass
the day comparing "hang-overs." Who are these people, what are
they, where do they come from? In America itself one never sees
them.

Far on the horizon the large ships pass; the liners, the tourists,
and the cargoes. Nearer the shore is the little tug that plies between St. Pierre and Fort de France. It carries mail and cargo and
a few passengers, stopping at Belfontain and Carbet and Case
Pilote. At Carbet there is a little pier against which the tug is
wharfed. But at Belfontain and Case Pilote and St. Pierre small
boats row out to it. A fierce conflict is always staged about the
ladder. The boat that gets its cargo and passengers discharged first
will get back to the shore in time for another load. No sooner has
a boat got into position beside the ladder than another boat en-
filades it, creeping closer to the side of the ship; it tries to elbow
it out into the sea. It is a form of aquatic spillikins: the object of
the game being to displace the other boat without upsetting
its passengers and cargoes into the water. The sailors shriek at each
other like baseball players. It is a damp and noisy game. The last
time I made such an excursion I offered our boatman double fare
if he would wait till last. He shook his head. The game was greater
than the reward.

Four or five times a day the little tug passes across the bay.
And between it and the shore are always a number of fishing
boats. For the most part in Martinique they fish with nets. The
nets are long and about ten feet deep. One side of the nets is
strung with cork, the other is weighted. Two canoes, rowing
outwards from one another, swing the net into a circle. To bring

the fish to the surface they throw stones into the circle and beat
the water with their oars. Then gradually, foot by foot, they draw
in the nets.

They are small fish for the greater part and most of them are
sent into the market at Fort de France. From my veranda in the
morning, I watch the girls coming over the hill from Fond Lahaye,
carrying baskets of them upon their heads. In one of his loveliest
essays Lafcadio Hearn has described the life of *La Porteuse*: the
girl who is, in comparison with the *Charbonnière*, as is the race-
horse to the cart-horse; who for thirty francs a month travelled her
thirty miles a day, who was trained from childhood to her pro-
fession, whose speed was so fast that a good average walker could
not keep pace with her for fifteen minutes. In those days all the
trade of the island was in her hands. But it was forty years ago
that Hearn lived under the shadow of Mont Pelé; today the
truck and the lorry have taken the place very largely of *La
Porteuse*. The big plantations have no need for her. It is only
from the small estates and the fishing villages that morning after
morning the young island women are sent out, their heads laden,
into Fort de France. In a few years *La Porteuse* will have vanished.
But the sight of those slim, upright, exquisitely proportioned girls
moving in a smooth, fast stride under their heavy loads is still
one of the most picturesque features of the island.

Now and again one or other of them pauses in the roadway
below the bungalow.

"Armantine!" she calls out. "I have fish."

We sign to her to come up, and without the least appearance
of effort she climbs the long, steep flight to lay down her charge
on the top step of the veranda. Usually it is a basket of small fish.
And nothing is more deceptive than the small fish of the tropics.
There they lie, an infinite variety of shapes and colors. In appearance not one of them is the same; but in taste they are identical.
And their taste is that of dry bread that has been soaked in water.
When the moon is full or waxing, however, it is the *langouste*
that she brings. Then the entire bungalow is stirred into interest.
We all gather round the veranda steps: Eldred, myself, Armantine,
and Florentine. Even Belmont now and again, with a small three-
months' pig trotting at his heels. We stand in a semicircle, looking at the basket.

"How much?" says Eldred. "That, the little one."

For here, as in Europe, the taste of the small *langouste* is delicate.

The girl lifts it up by it tendrils. She examines carefully its flicking tail. "Five francs," she says. We roar with laughter. "Five francs!" we say. "We bought a far better one than that for four francs yesterday." The girl turns away her head and the inevitable bargaining begins. Sou by sou we approach a central figure. In the end we get the lobster for four francs fifty. The days are few on which somebody does not bring us something: breadfruit or coconut or bananas. Once there was a rabbit and once a hare.

Sometimes, sitting quietly on my veranda, I felt that in the course of a day I had seen the whole life of the island pass in front of me. Far on the horizon there are the big ships, the liners and the cargoes that maintain contact between it and the world, that bring to it the blood that feeds it: the fabric and machinery it needs; that in exchange carry away the rum and sugar that make it rich. And, closer, there is the little tug plying between St. Pierre and Fort de France, that maintains contact between the various island villages that hill and stream separate from one another. And still nearer, between the tug's path and the shore, are the fishing boats on which rests the prosperity of those villages, and along the road there are the young girls carrying that produce to its consumer, and on my veranda there is the salemanship and the unit of exchange.

The whole life of the island in a day.

"I suppose," said Eldred at the end of our second day at Case Navire, "that sooner or later we shall find the snag to this."

We never did. Day after day life followed its happy and unexacting course. No routine could have been simpler. In the tropics it is light by six. And before the tug that leaves Fort de France at daybreak had turned the headland beyond Fond Lahaye I was drinking my morning coffee. By seven I was at work. I remained there for four hours. In London, where one is surrounded by distractions, by the noises in the streets, by telephones, by the morning's post, by one's conversation of the previous evening, by the thought of the party one is going to that night, it is only by the most rigid seclusion that one can hope to concentrate upon one's work. But in the tropics, where there are no distractions, where there are no telephones, no letters, no conversations to remember or look forward to, you welcome the casual interruptions of an island day. You are content enough to hear a phonograph playing behind your shoulder, to discuss in the middle of a paragraph the menu for the day's meal and the extent of Armantine's weekly books; to exchange gossip with Belmont and join in the friendly bargaining round the lobster basket.

At eleven I would put away my books, shave, and go to join Eldred Curwen, who would be sunbathing on the beach. It was in a very secluded, shut in and unobserved section of the beach that we bathed; so secluded that we thought bathing clothes unnecessary. It cannot, however, have been as secluded as we thought, for one morning we found chalked upon our cabin: "They are bathing necked just like worms. Dirty peoples!" We left the writing there, and one evening, a few days later, we found a studious half-caste standing in front of it turning the pages of a pocket dictionary. His face wore a puzzled look.

At half-past twelve we lunched. And with lunch the bad period in the tropical day has started. It is very hot. One's eyes are dazzled by the glare. Most people prefer to go to bed. If you have eaten heavily and taken alcohol at lunch no power on earth can keep your eyelids open if you lie out on a long chair. Most Europeans do siesta, but myself, I have never felt anything but the worse for one. [*I was thirty years old when I wrote this passage. The siesta is now an essential part of my day's pattern, not only in the tropics.*] You wake as you do after a heavy night. Even a shower does not put you straight. And invariably that hour or so of sleep ruins your night's rest. Myself, I have always found that it is better to lunch lightly, to avoid alcohol till sundown, and after lunch to write letters, play chess or patience; at any rate, to choose an occupation that demands the sitting erect on a hard chair. By three o'clock the worst is over. One is ready for a walk.

I am told that it is dangerous in the tropics to take much exercise. But I have been told that so many things are dangerous in the tropics. I have been told that unless I wore colored glasses I should get sunstroke through the eyes and that without a sun helmet, through the head. I have been told that if I ate lettuce I should get dysentery; that if I did not eat green vegetables I should catch scurvy. I was told that I should catch elephantiasis by going barefoot. I have been told that unless I wore underclothes I should catch a skin complaint called *dobiage*. I have been

told that alcohol is poison, and that whisky is the only antidote
to malaria. Each particular part of the tropics has its particular
fad. The French wear sun helmets eighteen degrees north of the
Equator; the English wear underclothes on the Equator. We all
have our fads. Mine is, I suppose, the refusal to take a siesta after
lunch. Anyhow, I have always felt better on the days when, in
addition to two good swims, I have done an eight-mile walk.

And there are good walks in Martinique. Even if the roads are
appalling the countryside is varied. One section of it is pasture
ground. Another is laid out in sugar. There are coconut groves
by Carbet. In the extreme south there is practically a desert, where
you can find the prickly pear. While high on Balata, in imitation
of Montmartre, there is the Sacré Cœur of Martinique, a vast
white church that you can see from half the island. There is no
lack of walks in Martinique. And by the time that one is back
the best hour of the day has started. The sun is low in the sky;
there is no glare from the sea nor from the red stone of the
veranda; the green of the hills takes on a deeper, almost an unreal,
green: though really it is for that hour only during the day that
you see their true coloring. When the sun is high their burnished
surfaces are no more than mirrors. It is only in that last hour of
daylight that you can realize the incredible deepness of their
coloring.

And later, after we had bathed, after the sun had sunk, a rapid
red descent into the sea, we would lie out on the veranda in deck
chairs, with the violet of the sky darkening and the crickets and
lizards beginning to murmur from the hills. We would not talk
a great deal. We would be listening with strained ears for the
sound of a Rugby's horn. Our only means of communication with
Fort de France was a car, a kind of private bus garaged in Case
Navire, that carried a passenger or two each morning, ran errands
in town, and in the evening brought out a load of passengers and
such provisions as might have been ordered by its clients. It was
on this car that we relied for our ice, for our bread, and for our
butter. We never knew when the car would arrive nor how much
would have been forgotten. The ice usually appeared. The bread
two days in three; the butter perhaps one in four. It was like
waiting for rations to arrive during the war. And till the ice had
arrived, till the decanter of rum and sugar had been set out, we
could not settle down to the peace of a tropic evening, than

which I have found nothing in the world more lovely and serene.

Sometimes friends from Fort de France would join us. Suddenly, at about seven o'clock, there would be the hooting of a horn, the flash of lights along a drive, and up the steps a shouting of "We've brought some ice; and some new Sophie Tucker records. So we're hoping that we'll be welcome."

These visits were always unexpected; such visits always are in Martinique. During our first weeks we invited people for fixed days, made preparation and kept meals back for them. But we soon learned that in Martinique, when people say "We will come out on Wednesday," they usually mean "some time in the middle of the week." So after a while we said, just vaguely, "Come out when you'd like a swim." And sometimes they did and sometimes they didn't. And when they did it simply meant the adding of an egg or two to the omelet or the opening of another tin. And we would bathe and chatter and play the new Sophie Tucker records and dance on the balcony in a moon-silvered dusk. But whether friends came out or not, by half-past ten the bungalow was quiet and asleep.

Into Fort de France we went as rarely as possible. For that is about the first thing that travel teaches one: that life in a town is just not possible. Of the many tropical towns that I have visited, Penang is the only one in which I should be happy to make a home. It would be surprising, indeed, if it were otherwise. The population of every tropical town is either commercial or administrative. Everyone has a definite reason for being there. There is no leisured class to create an interior world that exists for its own amusement. Since the majority of such towns are of recent growth, there are no interesting buildings, no picture galleries to be seen. In consequence, there is absolutely nothing for the unoccupied tourist to do till offices close at five o'clock and companionship is again at his disposal.

Fort de France was no exception. It is a pretty town. From the balcony of the club you look out over the green stretch of the savannah. On your left is a flanking of yellow houses; to your right the blue water of the harbor, the masts of schooners, the red funnels of cargo boats and liners. In front of you, circled by sentinel palms, is the white statue of Josephine, her face turned southwards to the Trois Iles, where she was born. Fort de France is easily the prettiest town in the Leeward and Windward groups, and it was charitable of fate to divert northwards the cyclone that in the autumn of 1928 raged over the Antilles.

At Guadeloupe there was little that cannot be rebuilt. And over Guadeloupe the cyclone raged mercilessly.

"Heaven knows how we shall get into port tomorrow," said the captain of the *Pellerin* on the eve of our arrival. "I don't know what there'll be to recognize it by."

Yet, when we did arrive, Pointe à Pitre seemed very little different from the picture that my memory had formed of it. I had only spent a day and a night there on my way towards Panama, but those few hours had left an ineffaceable impression of dejected squalor. With its straight, puddle-spotted streets, its wooden and tin houses, garnished with slipshod balconies, it always looked as though it were about to fall to pieces. It reminded me of the kind of small town in an early Keystone comedy, that was destined every inch of it to be knocked down in the last hundred feet of film. The cyclone, instead of altering Pointe à Pitre, seemed to have put it in harmony with itself. In the same way that when you set side by side a photograph of a landscape and a modern painting of it you say of the photograph "That's what it looks like," and of the painting "That's what it really is"; so, as I walked through Pointe à Pitre, remembering Pointe à Pitre as it had been sixteen months earlier, as I paused before the battered houses, the piles of masonry and iron, the spread-eagled balconies, the uprooted trees, the twisted bandstand, the unroofed and unclocked cathedral, onto whose floor, through innumerable apertures, the rain was pouring; "Yes," I kept saying to myself, of this melancholy provincial town through which the business of life in market and shop and office was continuing in unaltering indolence, "this is how it really is."

It was not till we got out of Pointe à Pitre into the country that we realized what the cyclone had really meant. The effect there was extraordinary. The countryside, with its coconut palms lopped and uprooted, gave the impression of a face that has not been shaved for several days. Like a blunt razor the cyclone had passed over it. As I drove through the wrecked landscape towards Basse Terre I thanked Heaven very humbly that it had spared the green savannah, and the white statue and the palm trees guarding it; that in all its beauty and friendliness Fort de France should be waiting there untouched to welcome me.

And yet, lovely though it is, Fort de France is intolerably hot. Set in a basin of hills, its very excellences as a harbor make it the less habitable. Not a breath of air reaches it. Everyone who can afford to, lives out of town, in the cool and quiet of the hills. Not only is Fort de France extremely hot; it is also very noisy. The streets are narrow, the cars are many. The chauffeurs drive with the recklessness, but not the skill, of Parisian taximen. When cars were introduced into Northern Siam the sense of speed was so intoxicating to the Laos that in Chiengmai artificial bumps were raised in the main streets to force the chauffeur to drive slowly. I have often wished, as I have seen disaster approaching me at every corner, that the authorities in Fort de France would take the same precautions. But it is doubtful if it would have much effect. If the roads were as bumpy as the scenic railway in San Francisco, I think the Martiniquais would continue to rush their fences, trusting blindly in the immunity of one-way streets and a hand rhythmically pressed upon a horn. All the time horns are honking. It is one's last, it is one's first, impression of Fort de France. Long before evening one's head has begun to ache.

The casual traveller, with nothing definite to occupy him, finds his attention concentrated exclusively on the incessant noise. Only during the week ends is there systematized entertainment.

Every Sunday morning there was cock-fighting. It was worth seeing once. The Gallodrome was a circular wooden building, arranged in five galleries. On the top gallery there was a piano and a bar. You paid five francs at the door. The pit was about twenty feet across. For the first minute and a half a fight is thrilling. The cocks are introduced to one another by their owners: they are placed on the edge of a circle five feet apart. The instant they are let loose they fly at one another. Quite often in that first leap, with a single blow, one of them is killed. For a moment or two it is a whirlwind of blows and feathers. But after that minute it grows uninteresting. The cocks do not, as in the North of England, wear spurs. They peck wearily at the back of each other's necks. The chief interest is in the audience: in the half-castes and Negroes who bounce excitedly in their seats, who shriek encouragement to the animals, who shout their odds across the pit.

Nominally the fight is to the death; actually it is as long as the cocks will fight. After a quarter of an hour or so they stand, blind and weary, gasping and indifferent, the fight forced out of them. Their owners take them by the wings and place them at the edge of the circle, facing each other, five feet apart. They make no movement. Inside that circle there is a smaller circle. Again the animals are lifted by their wings. They are within a few inches now of one another. They do not move. The crowd yells fiercely. Then suddenly one pecks forward. The other turns away its head. The fight is finished. Pandemonium is released. The Negroes jump in their seats and shriek with excitement, waving the francs that they have lost or won, while the owners carry away the cocks, scrape the skins of their heads and legs with a small pocket knife, slit the congested flesh about the neck and crown, pour lemon juice over the wounds, and hope for equal or greater fortune in the following week.

Within five minutes another fight has started.

Cock-fighting is the chief sport in Martinique. Every district has its fight on Sunday.

In the villages there are no cockpits. The Negroes form a rough circle round the cocks, and as the fight moves the circle follows up and down the length of the village street. From a distance it looks like a scrum in Rugby football. Children perch themselves on verandas and on the roofs of cabins; they shriek with laughter when the cocks fall into a gutter or stumble over a more than ordinarily misplaced cobblestone. It is a hilarious business. But to see cock-fighting at its best you have to see it at the three big centers, at Trinité, St. Pierre, and Fort de France. In the same way that, although there is a *festa* of some sort in every village on the six or seven Sundays before Lent, to see carnival at its best you have got to go to Fort de France. [*I wrote this before I had seen films of the carnival in Trinidad.*]

For the actual carnival I was at Dominica. And there it was a subdued affair. Two years earlier there had been trouble; a police officer had been beaten very nearly to death. Dominica is a curious place. Once a French possession and geographically a French possession still, it is in feeling more French than English. It is Roman Catholic. The natives speak Creole. Smuggling, that the police are powerless to check, is constantly carried on between

Martinique and Guadeloupe. Dominica is the Ireland of the
Antilles. It is the loveliest of the islands and it is the most difficult
to manage. It should be prosperous but blight after blight has
fallen on the crops. First coffee was destroyed. Then when the
lime industry was established—Dominica is the center of Rose's
lime juice—a disease struck that. The country is very mountainous. When Columbus was asked to describe the island he crum-
pled up a sheet of paper and tossed it on the table. The roads are
so bad that fruit cannot be profitably marketed. Dominica is a
constant drain on the Imperial Government's exchequer. The
more money that is spent there, the less settled does life become.

Anything might have happened in Roseau during that wild
week of carnival had not a gunboat providentially and unexpectedly arrived in harbor. Many stories are told in explanation of
that gunboat's presence. It is said that an admiral expressed a
wish for grapefruit. There was no grapefruit, he was told. Where
could grapefruit be got? Nowhere nearer than Dominica. Could
any excuse be devised for sending a gunboat there? Papers were
consulted; an American courier had passed two days before. There
might be a mail there. That was sufficient excuse when an admiral
was hungry. And so, at the very moment when Roseau was in the
hands of the rebels, a gunboat appeared in the harbor. There was
no fighting. The crowds dispersed; the sailors were not even aware
that there had been any trouble. The sight of the gunboat was
enough. In five minutes order had been restored. That evening the
admiral ate grapefruit before *consommé*.

Probably the story is untrue. But the arrival of the gunboat was
no less providential on that account. In the following year the
carnival was forbidden. And when I was there, though the carnival
took place, no sticks were carried, and at six o'clock the streets
were cleared. It was an orderly affair. It lasted for two days. In the
morning from the hour of nine the streets were patrolled by
small groups of men and women with masks and costumes, a
drum at their head, at their back a crowd of ecstatic urchins. The
costumes were as various as the local store and local wit permitted. There were pierrots and pierrettes; there were sailors and
there were cowboys; there were men dressed as women, padded
with footballs to give their skirts the effect of a Victorian bustle.
Some tried to make themselves appear attractive; the majority
tried to make themselves as plain as possible. In Fort de France

there were occasional satirists. One afternoon a group of men, dressed up as women in skirts five inches long, had paraded the streets singing "*Malpropre baissez la robe.*" Most of the songs that are sung at carnival are impromptu references to some local event. The chief song at Roseau commemorated an attempted suicide.

> "Sophia drink wine and iodine
> Why, Why, Sophia?"

During the afternoon Roseau echoed the name Sophia. Every shop was shut. Half the population was "running mask." The stray groups that had shouted down the streets during the morning had joined up into a solid phalanx, seventy yards in length, that marched backwards and forwards, singing and dancing, cracking whips; while separate bands of twenty to a dozen girls, dressed uniformly, marched with small orchestras to solicit alms. Each band represented something. One band dressed in yellow represented Colman's mustard; another *Tit-bits*; a third, hung with red, white, and blue, carrying plates of oranges and maize and breadfruit, "Dominica Produce." It was the Martinique carnival on a small scale, surpassed by it in the same way that in its turn Martinique is surpassed by Trinidad. If you want to see street carnival go to Port of Spain. But if you want to see that of which street carnival is the symbol you will stay in Fort de France. In white-run sections of the world I never expect to see a more astounding exhibition than the Bal Lou-Lou. [*The Bal Lou-Lou exists no longer.*]

Twice a week, on Saturdays and Sundays, there is a ball, or rather there are several. There is the Palais and the Casino. But it is at the Select Tango that you will see it at its best. There is nothing to tell you that you are to see anything extraordinary. At the end of a quiet street facing a river there is a large tin building. You pay your twelve francs and you are in a long room hung with lanterns and paper streamers. A gallery runs round it, on which tables are set, and at each end of which there is a bar. It is rather like a drill-hall. And as you lean over the balcony you have the impression that you are at a typical provincial *palais de danse.* You see the kind of people that you would expect to see. On the gallery there are one or two family parties of white people. The white women will not dance. They will look on, and they will leave early. In the hall below are a certain number of young Frenchmen of good family with their dusky mistresses. There will be some white policeman and white soldiers; but for the most part it is a colored audience of shop assistants, minor officials, small proprietors; a typical provincial dance hall. And at first, in the dance itself, there is nothing that you would not expect to see in such a place. The music is more barbaric, more gesticulatory; but that you would expect to find. As the evening passes, as the custom at the bar grows busier, the volume of sound increases, but that, too, you would expect. That you have seen before. You grow tired and a little bored. You begin to wonder whether it is worth staying on. Then suddenly there is the wail of a clarinet. A whisper runs round the tables: "*Danse du pays.*" In a moment the galleries are empty.

It is danced face to face. The girl clasps her arms round the man's neck. The man holds her by the hips. The music is slow and tense. "*Le talent pour la danseuse,*" wrote Moreau St. Méry, "*est dans la perfection avec laquelle elle peut faire mouvoir ses hanches et la partie inférieure de ses reins en conservant tout le reste du corps dans une espèce d'immobilité.*" The couples appear scarcely to move. In a dance of twenty minutes they will not make more than one revolution of the room. They stand, close clasped and swaying. The music does not grow louder or more fast. It grows fiercer, more barbaric. The mouths of the dancers grow lax; their eyes are clouded, their movements exceed symbolism. "*La danseuse arrive et bientôt elle offre un tableau dont tous les traits d'abord voluptueux deviennent ensuite lascifs. Il serait impossible de peindre la* chica *avec son véritable caractère et je me bornerai à dire que l'impression qu'elle fait est si puissante que l'Africain ou le Créole de n'importe quelle nuance qui le verrait danser sans émotion passerait pour avoir perdu jusqu' aux dernières étincelles de la sensibilité.*" [*The actual* chica *is a slightly different dance, somewhat similar to the hula-hula. The couples do not touch each other as they dance.*]

That is on ordinary evenings. During carnival it is fantastic. A stranger arriving at the Select Tango at one o'clock in the morning would imagine himself mad. He would not believe it possible that in a white-run community the payment of twelve francs at a public turnstile would admit him to such a bedlam. He would imagine that such spectacles were held behind doors as rigidly

guarded as those of the Bal des Quatre Arts. The noise is deafen-
ing. The galleries and hall are crowded. Most of the girls are
masked. They wear gloves and stockings so that not an inch of
dark skin appears. Some of them, it is whispered, are white women
in disguise. They might well be. It is a dance in which caste and
blood are alike forgotten. Everyone is drunk; not with alcohol but
with music. People are dancing by themselves. They shriek and
wave their arms. They seize a partner, dance with her for a moment, then break away. A girl will be dancing by herself. *"Un
danseur s'approche d'elle, s'élance tout à coup et tombe au mesure
presque à la toucher. Il recule. Il s'élance encore, et la provoque
à la lutte la plus séduisante."* The young Frenchmen in the arms
of their mulatto mistresses will parody and exaggerate the antics
of the Negroes. A woman embraced between two men will be
shrieking to friends up on the gallery. In the thronged center of
the ball couples close-clasped will stand swaying, their feet and
shoulders motionless, a look of unutterable ecstasy upon their
faces.

But it is not possible to describe the Bal Lou-Lou. The only
phrases that would describe it are incompatible with censorship.

Once every five days or so we went into Fort de France, and
it was always with a feeling of excitement that we began the day.
It was fun after five days of bare legs and open throats to put on
trousers and arrange a tie. The four mile drive assumed the proportion of high adventure; which in point of fact, with a chauffeur
such as ours, it was. We felt very like country cousins coming up
for a day's shopping as we deposited with the head waiter of the
Hôtel de la Paix a list of groceries and a vast wooden box in which
to store them. There was the excitement of discovering at the
photographer's how many of the snapshots we had taken during
the previous weeks were recognizable comments on the landscape.
And by the time that was finished it would be half-past eleven.

"The club," Eldred would remark, "will probably not be empty
now."

There was a delightfully welcoming friendliness about the club.
There would certainly be four or five of our friends on the wide,
airy veranda looking out over the savannah. We would draw our
chairs up into the circle. Hands would be clasped, decanters would
be set upon the table. There would be silence while the waitress

performed the ritual of mixing a Creole punch: quarter of a
finger's height of sugar, two fingers' high of rum, the paring of a
lime, the rattling of ice. Then talk would begin, friendly, unexacting gossip, the exchange of comment and reminiscence, till the
hands of the clock were pointing at half-past twelve, with the
world, after a couple of rum punches, appearing a pretty companionable place.

"We ought to come into town more often," we would say as
we hurried lunchwards, down the Rue Perignon. And after five
days of eggs and lobster and native vegetables it was fun to eat a
chateaubriand that you would certainly not be grateful for in London, and drink a *vin ordinaire* with which even in a New York
speakeasy the management would hesitate to serve you. And, "Certainly, we must come in more often," we would say as we sat over
our coffee afterwards on the terrace of the hotel. But it would be
no more than half-past one when we would be saying that. And
the sun was beating fiercely upon the corrugated iron of the roof.
In the street below the cars were honking merrily. For three and a
half hours the club was certain to be empty. There was nothing
for us to do. We could go to the phonograph shop, of course, and
play some tunes. But you cannot stay more than an hour in a shop
where you are only going to buy one record and the last two numbers of "*La Sourire.*" And even an hour leaves you with two and a
half hours to be killed. There is the library, of course, and it is a
good library. But the heat and the noise make concentration difficult. Usually it ended in a visit to the Délices du Lido.

"At any rate," we'd say, "it'll be cool and quiet there." Whatever the Délices might not be, on days when there was no boat in
it was that.

The actual town of Fort de France is about half a mile from
the coaling station; a road shadowed by a tent of trees curves
round an inlet of the bay to the savannah; on the left of the road,
on boat days, are innumerable vendors of fruit and cakes; on the
right a collection of two-story wooden houses. It is to this that
sailors refer when they tell you that Martinique is the loveliest
island they have ever seen. It is the only part of the island that
most of them ever do see. It is the red-light district.

And it is, beyond question, the most picturesque part of the
town. [*A wall has now been built in front of the Délices du Lido
and the section is a very squalid one.*] At sunset the view across

the bay is the loveliest thing I have seen this side of the canal.
And in the afternoon even, the Délices du Lido was about the
most pleasant place in the town to sit about in. By the time we
left the island we had come to know the majority of the girls
there. They were mulattoes—when they were not pure Negroes
—simple, smiling, friendly, and improvident; laughing and chattering, quarrelling and crying. The kind of girls that one would
expect to find in such a place. There was one girl, however, whose
presence there was inexplicable. She was one of the ten loveliest
women that I have ever seen. She was very young; she could not
have been more than twenty. Seeing her in Martinique, one knew
that she must have colored blood in her; but if one had met her
in Paris or London one would not have suspected it. She was of
the Spanish type. Her features had genuine refinement. Good
clothes and a good hairdresser would have made her the kind of
woman whose entrance into a London restaurant would have
meant the turning of twenty heads. I do not see how in any big
town a girl with her appearance would not have been a big success. Yet, here she was in this wretched stew, the associate of no
matter whom.

What was she doing there? How had she got there? Why was
she staying there? They were questions to which I could find no
answer. As long as she remained there she was futureless. No man
would run the risk of taking her away from such an atmosphere.
Sometimes I wondered whether she did not enjoy the sense of
superiority that she could exert in such a place. She was by no
means an agreeable person. She was arrogant and disdainful; she
never hid her contempt for the other girls, about whom she was
constantly making cruel and cutting remarks. Such a one might
relish the sense of empire that such a setting gave her. Probably,
though, that is too involved an explanation. Probably her presence in that one-way street meant nothing more than that she
was lazy. It was a problem with a fascination that led us most
afternoons to the ordering of a series of lime squashes in the Délices du Lido. But though Fort de France could offer no better
entertainment to the tourist, it was an unsatisfactory one.

For soft drinks do you no more good than rum does in the
afternoon. You are better without either. I have never spent an
afternoon in Fort de France without envying those who had offices
and telephones, letters to be dictated and strings of agents trying

to ship their sugar crops. I have never at the day's end, without a feeling of unutterable relief, looked down from the climbing road on to the lighted streets and the lights of the ships at anchor.

One such day in particular I remember. We had come into Fort de France one afternoon, in the mistaken belief that a friend of Eldred's was on the *Flandre*. We had spent a hot and profitless half-hour walking round an oven-like ship. Coaling was in progress and the coal dust had blown into our eyes and mouths. We were hot, fractious, and uncomfortable. "Let's go and have an orangeade and then get out of this as quickly as possible," we said. On the steps of the club, however, we ran into the son of its President, Edouard Boulenger.

"What, you fellows here?" he said. "You're just in time. Jump in quick. We're going up to the pit. There's a fight on. A snake and a mongoose."

It was the first time that I had seen such a fight. There is not actually a great deal to see. It is darkish inside the building, the pit itself is netted over, and through the mesh of wire it is hard to distinguish against the brown sanded floor the movements of the small dark forms. You see a brown line along the sand and a brown shadow hovering. Then suddenly there is a gleam of white; the thrashing of the snake's white belly. For a few moments the brown shadow is flecked with the twisting and writhing of the white whip. Then the brown shadow slinks away. The *fer de lance*, the most hostile small snake in the world, is still. There is not a great deal to see. But it is thrilling. There is a taut, tense atmosphere, not only through the fight but afterwards, when the snake has been lifted out of the pit while its head is cut open and the poison poured into a phial. During a cockfight there is an incessant noise. Everyone shouts and gesticulates. But there is complete silence during the snake's silent battle. It has a sinister quality. And it is with a feeling of exhaustion and of relief that you come out into the street, into the declining sunlight. You are grateful for the sound of voices.

Longer than usual that evening we sat on the veranda of the club. It was completely dark when we came down its stairs into the savannah. Never had the cool and quiet of the hills been more welcome. Never had a swim seemed a more complete banishment of every harassing circumstance that the day had brought. Low in the sky there was a moon, a baby moon. As we swam it was

half moonshine and half prosphorus, the splintered silver that
was about us. And even in the north of Siam, after a day of march-
ing over precipitous mountain paths and above flooded paddy
fields, I have known no greater peace than the lying out on the
veranda after dinner, watching the moon and the Southern Cross
sink side by side into the sea, hearing from every bush and shrub
the murmur of innumerable crickets.

Once we went to St. Pierre.

From Fond Lahaye it is a three hours' sail in a canoe, along a
coast indented with green valleys that run back climbingly through
fields of sugar cane. At the foot of most of these valleys, between
the stems of the coconut palms, you see the outline of wooden
cabins. So concealed are these cabins behind that façade of greenery that were it not for the fishing nets hung out along the beach
on poles to dry you would scarcely suspect that there was a village
there. Nor, as you approach St. Pierre, would you suspect that in
that semicircle of hills under the cloud-hung shadow of Mont
Pelé are hidden the ruins of a city for which history can find no
parallel.

At first sight it is nothing but a third-rate, decrepit shipping
port, not unlike Manzanillo or La Libertad. It has its pier, its
warehouses, its market; its single cobbled street contains the usual
dockside features. A café or two, a restaurant, a small wooden
shanty labelled "Cercle," a somewhat larger shanty labelled "Select Tango." A hairdresser, a general store. At first sight it is one
of many thousand places. It is not till you step out of that main
street into the tangled jungle at the back of it that you realize that
St. Pierre is, as it has always been, unique.

Even then you do not at first realize it. At first you see nothing
but greenery, wild shrubbery, the great ragged leaves of the banana
plant, with here and there the brown showing of a thatched roof.
It is not till you have wandered a little through those twisted paths
that you see that it is in the angles of old walls that those thatched
cottages are built, that it is over broken masonry, over old stair-
ways and porticoes, that those trailing creepers are festooned; that
empty windows are shadowed by those ragged leaves. At odd corners you will come upon signs of that old life: a marble slab that
was once the doorstep of a colonial bungalow; a fountain that
splashed coolly through siestaed summers; a shrine with the bronze

body broken at its foot. Everywhere you will come upon signs of
that old life; *"le Pays des Revenants"* they called it. With what
grim irony has chance played upon the word.

But it is not till you have left the town and have climbed to
the top of one of the hills that were thought to shelter it, till you
look down into the basin of the amphitheatre that contained
St. Pierre and, looking down, see through the screen of foliage
the outline of house after ruined house, that you realize the extent
and nature of the disaster. No place that I have ever seen has
moved me in quite that way.

Not so much by the thought of the twenty-eight thousand
people killed within that narrow span: to the actual fact of death
most of us are, I think, now a little callous. Nor by the sentiment
that attaches itself to any ruin, the sentiment with which during
the war one walked through the deserted villages of Northern
France, the feeling that here a life that was the scene of many
lives has been abandoned; that here, at the corners of these streets,
men had stood gossiping on summer evenings, watching the sky
darken over the unchanging hills, musing on the permanence, the
unhurrying continuity of the life they were a part of. It is not that
sentiment that makes the sight of St. Pierre so profoundly solemn.
It is the knowledge rather that here existed a life that should be
existing still, that existed nowhere else, that was the outcome of a
combination of circumstances that now have vanished from the
world for ever. Even Pompeii cannot give you quite that feeling.
There were many Pompeiis, after all. Pompeii exists for us as a
symbol, as an explanation of Roman culture. It has not that personal, that localized appeal of a flower that has blossomed once
only, in one place: that no eye will ever see again.

St. Pierre was the loveliest city in the West Indies. The loveliest
and the gayest.

All day its narrow streets were bright with color; in sharp an-
glings of light the amber sunshine streamed over the red-tiled
roofs, the lemon-colored walls, the green shutters, the green verandas. The streets ran steeply, "the breaking into steps as streams
break into waterfalls." Moss grew between the stones. In the run-
nel was the sound of water. There was no such thing as silence in
St. Pierre. There was always the sound of water, of fountains in
the hidden gardens, of rain water in the runnels, and through the
music of that water, the water that kept the town cool during the

long noon heat, came ceaselessly from the hills beyond the murmur of the lizard and the cricket. A lovely city, with its theatre,
its lamplit avenues, its *Jardin des Plantes*, its schooners drawn
circlewise along the harbor. Life was comely there; the life that
had been built up by the old French *émigrés*. It was a city of
carnival. There was a culture there, a love of art among those
people who had made their home there, who had not come to
Martinique to make money that they could spend in Paris. The
culture of Versailles was transposed there to mingle with the Carib
stock and the dark mysteries of imported Africa. St. Pierre was
never seen without emotion. It laid hold of the imagination. It
had something to say, not only to the romantic intellectual like
Hearn or Stacpool, but to the sailors and the traders, to all those
whom the routine of livelihood brought within the limit of its
sway. "Incomparable," they would say as they waved farewell to
the *Pays des Revenants*, knowing that if they did not return they
would carry all their lives a regret for it in their hearts.

History has no parallel for St. Pierre.

And within forty-five seconds the stir and color of that life had
been wiped out.

The story of the disaster is too familiar, has been told too many
times to need any retelling here. The story of those last days when
Pelé was scattering cinders daily over Martinique; when the vegetables that the women brought down from the hills to market
were dark with ashes; when the Rivière Blanche was swollen with
boiling mud; when day after day was darkened by heavy clouds:
it has been told so often, the story of that last morning that
dawned clear after a night of storm for the *grande fête* of an As-
cension Day: of the two immense explosions that were heard
clearly in Guadeloupe, of the voice over a telephone abruptly si-
lenced, of the ship that struggled with charred and corpse-strewn
deck into the harbor of St. Lucia, the ship that two years later was
to be crushed by ice: of the voice that cried back to the questioner
on the wharf, "We come from Hell. You can cable the world that
St. Pierre exists no longer." It has been told so many times.

At eight o'clock a gay and gallant people was preparing on a
sunlit morning busily for its *jour de fête*. Forty-five seconds later,
of all that gaiety and courage there was nothing left. Not anything.
Certain legends linger. They say that four days later, when the
process of excavation was begun, there was found in the vault of

the prison a Negro criminal, the sole survivor. They say that in a
waistcoat pocket a watch was found, its hands pointing to half-
past nine, a watch that had recorded ninety useless minutes in a
timeless tomb. And there are other stories. The stories of fishermen who set sail early in the morning to return for their *déjeuner*,
to find ruin there; of servants whom their mistresses had sent out
of the town on messages; of officials and business men who left
the town on the 7th or 6th of May for Fort de France. They are
very like the war stories you will hear of men who returned after
a five minutes' patrolling of a trench to find nothing left of their
dugout nor the people in it. They are probably exaggerated when
they are not untrue. And yet it was these stories, more than even
the sight of St. Pierre itself, that made that tragedy actual to me.

"We were," I was told, "twenty-four of us young people one
Sunday on a picnic. We would have another picnic on the following Sunday, we decided. When that Sunday came there were only
three of us alive."

A European cannot picture in terms of any tragedy that is likely
to come to him what that tragedy meant for the survivors of
Martinique. It did not mean simply the death of twenty-eight
thousand people; the loss of property and possession; the curtain
for many years upon the prosperity of the island. It meant the
cutting of their lives in half more completely than would mean
for me the destruction of every stone and every inhabitant in
London. It meant the loss of half their friends, half their families,
half their possessions, half their lives.

"I left St. Pierre on the seventh," a man told me. "I was to be
married on the ninth. I had come into Fort de France, leaving
my fiancée behind to make some last arrangements. I cannot ex-
press the excitement with which I woke on that morning of the
eighth. I was twenty-four. She was three years younger. It was
the first time that either of us had been in love. And that was the
last whole day, I told myself, that I should ever spend alone. It
was so lovely a morning, too. Bright and clear. And after one of
the worst nights that there can have ever been. Thunder and lightning and unceasing rain. The sunlight was a happy omen. Never
had I known, never shall I know, anything like the happiness with
which I dressed and bathed and shaved that morning. And then,
just as I was finishing my coffee, there came those two explosions.
They were terrific. They shook the entire island. But I wasn't

frightened. Why should I be? What was there to connect them with Pelé? I went on, as the rest of us did, with what we had to do.

"For a while that morning life went on in Fort de France in its ordinary way. But soon you had begun to notice a worried look on people's faces. The sky was dark; a thin dust in which pebbles were mingled was falling over the town. Rumor had started. There was no news coming through from St. Pierre. The telephone line had been cut suddenly in the middle of a message, at the instant of the two explosions. Since then there had been silence.

"You know how it is when a rumor starts in a small place. The most fantastic stories get about. A *porteuse* from Carbet had reported that a fisherman had seen flames behind St. Pierre, and no one asked themselves how even a *porteuse* could have done the more than seventeen miles from Carbet in two hours.

"I tried not to feel frightened. It was absurd to be frightened. No one had been frightened in St. Pierre the afternoon before, when I had left it. Earlier they had been frightened, yes; when those cinders had been falling in the streets, when lightning was flickering about the crater's mouth; when the day was dark with clouds; when the sugar factory by the Rivière Blanche was being swept away by boiling mud. They had been frightened then. But the scientists had told them there was no need to be afraid. The Governor and his wife had come out there themselves. The cinders had practically stopped falling. It was only old Pelé amusing himself again.

"That was what I told myself. But you know how it is when panic catches hold of a place. By eleven o'clock our nerves had gone. Three hours and still no news, with the wildest rumors flying round, not one of us could work. We sat in the club, forgetting our rum punches, one thought only in our minds. I shall never forget that morning: the suspense, the terror, the uncertainty. Midday and still no message had come through. The boat that had been sent out to make inquiries had not returned. We sat and waited. It was not till one o'clock that we knew."

He paused and shrugged his shoulders.

"It's twenty-six years ago," he said. "That's a long time. One can forget most things in that time. One thinks one's heart broken. But it mends. One thinks one's life is over. But it isn't. One goes on living. One makes the best out of what's left. I've not had a bad best, either. I've had a happy marriage. I'm proud of my children. I've made a position. But," he again shrugged his shoulders, "I don't know that since that day I've felt that anything mattered in particular."

I think that in that anecdote is expressed what life has been for the whole of Martinique, for the whole of his generation of Martinique. The carrying on with life in face of the feeling that nothing really matters.

The Buccaneer

from TROPIC SEED

Hot Countries *was published in 1930. In England it had a warm reception from the Press, but very few members of the public invested fifteen shillings in it. In the U.S.A., however, it was a Literary Guild choice. This lucky break reorientated my life and writing. For the next few years my time was divided between New York and London.* Hot Countries *did not, however, sever my link with the West Indies. It brought me a commission to write, in the form of a novel,* A History of Piracy, *showing how the pirates of Tortuga became the gangsters of Chicago. It was published in 1932 in England under the title* No Quarter. *In the United States it was called "Tropic Seed." It did not do very well; in fact it did rather badly. It suffered from a fatal deficiency; it had no continuity of interest. It covered three hundred years and the only link between one set of characters and the next was one of blood. But I think that the first section—the story of how a seventeenth-century Frenchman became a buccaneer—can stand by itself, and that its historical background helps to interpret the West Indian scene.*

WRITTEN IN 1930

She WAS COMELY after the manner of Provençal women in the third decade of the seventeenth century.

Her figure under the blue-laced bodice was firm and supple. The black hair was heavy under the knotted handkerchief. A morning's labor in the terraced vineyards had flushed her cheeks. Her breath came slowly between lips that parted over straight white teeth. The dark eyes were bold and bright as they met the glance, casual at first, then searching, of the young gallant who

43

cantered by, the buckles and buttons of his green doublet a-glitter in the April sun, down the mountain pathway to Marseilles.

The young man made no particular bones about his courtship. When the nature of its success became apparent, her father shrugged his shoulders. Then, as an example to her sisters, unhitched his belt and thrashed her soundly. Her mother wept and supposed that she might just as well now marry François. François lifted his eyebrows and said, "What would you?" anticipated thirty sous of his betrothed's dowry, stood treat uproariously at Gustave's cabaret, murmuring as his guests escorted him homewards up the sun-parched gutter that was the village's main street: "Farm hands. One can always do with another farm hand. I'll find good use for him some day. You wait."

He was long in waiting.

From the start the bastard son of the Chevalier de Monterey, whose name in the parish register was entered as Roger Vaisseau, proved intractable. As an infant he howled at all such times as his howling was certain to be a nuisance; howled not with the querulous bleating of the weak, but with the full-lunged indignation of the wronged. His howls were a protest, not a plea; they were an assertion of independence. His parents caressed him, and he bellowed. They beat him and his bellowing achieved a lustier note. They ignored him and his screams were jubilant.

"If only one could find out what he wants," his mother said.

"He doesn't want anything," grumbled his foster-father, "that's the trouble. A fellow with a chip on his shoulder, that's what he is."

As an infant he was a pest. As a small boy he was little better. On Sunday after the morning service when the village worthies assembled for their discussion of tithes and taxes, when the young matrons in their bright, padded clothes and flower-girdled hats sauntered back towards their houses, when the young people danced, wrestled, and played ball, he would sit apart, a surly disdainful look in his brown eyes. Only occasionally would he join in the games of the other children, and when he did it was illtemperedly. They would be playing "*monsieur le curé*": it would be his turn to pay the forfeit: "Of three things you must do one," they would demand of him. "You must fly in the air, or you must take the moon between your teeth, or you must kiss Lisette." As likely as not he would turn away with a curled lip and a contemptuous "No, thank you, not Lisette."

One evening as he sat in the shadow of the house looking out over the blue Mediterranean, he overheard his mother and grandmother discussing him.

"He's different from the others," his mother said. "I suppose you couldn't expect him not to be, seeing who his father was."

His grandmother nodded her head.

"Blood always comes out," she said. "He's got his father's eyes. He has your mouth, but it looks as though he was going to have his father's nose. However you bring him up, he'll be his father's son."

Eagerly the small boy listened.

On the following Sunday his lips curled haughtily when the other children invited him to play.

"The son of the Chevalier de Monterey does not play with the sons of laborers."

He was greeted with a derisive laugh.

During the week he had rehearsed and re-rehearsed the scene. He had pictured in proud detail the flattering hush that would follow his announcement. They would be humble and abashed. They would understand and be respectful of his aloofness. They would admit his superiority. Yet here they were, grinning at him with their monkey faces. The son of the Chevalier, they mocked. And who had told him that he was that?

His cheeks flushed scarlet. Angrily he stamped his foot.

"I am," he cried. "I know I am."

They laughed the louder, as the scarlet deepened in his cheeks, and tears glittered in his eyes. It was the first time that they had seen Roger Vaisseau at a disadvantage. They were resolved to make the most of it.

In a circle they stood taunting him. So he was the son of a chevalier. Would he like them to kiss his hand? Should they kneel before him? Would he deign to place the sole of his foot upon their necks? Where were his rings, they jeered, his feathered hat, the jewelled cross about his neck?

His fists clenched tightly.

"You don't believe me, then we'll ask my father."

In a group outside the church François Vaisseau was discussing with the worthies of the village such local matters as came under

the jurisprudence of their weekly gatherings. They had no great
authority. The inspectors from Paris regulated the settlement of
their taxes. But they liked to talk; they liked to sit around in their
best clothes, solemnly agreeing or disagreeing with one another.
Every Sunday for a couple of hours or so they would deliberate.
Their deliberations were respected. Wives did not dare disturb
them. In the village annals there was no precedent for the irrup-
tion into the sacrosanct circle of a hot-cheeked, wild-eyed infant,
with a crowd of sniggering children at his heels; for the full-
volumed thunder of infant lungs: "Father, tell them whose son
I am.

"These children wouldn't believe that I'm the son of the Chevalier de Monterey. Will you please, Father, tell them that I am."

It is not often that the members of a village assembly laugh.
Laughs are out of place in that austere atmosphere. And it was
less a laugh than a snigger that rippled through those venerable
beards. François had boasted appropriately about his four months'
son. But there had been whispers. There had been suspicions. Now
they knew.

For a moment François Vaisseau did not realize what exactly
lay behind this demand. His brain moved slowly. When it had
travelled far enough for him to understand, he took three swift
steps across the sward, swept Roger beneath his arm and staggered
up the sun-parched gutter that led towards his home.

Under a steady rain of blows Roger, rolled into a ball, his knees
drawn high into his stomach, his arm wrapped round his head, lay
without sound or movement. When his father with a kick and a
last curse left him, he rose to his feet, shook himself, hobbled over
to the fire, and knelt on one knee before it. There was not an inch
unbruised upon his body. For days sleep would be an agony to
him, but his head was held high, his lips were firm and his eyes
bright.

His father had not denied that he was the Chevalier's son.

Never again was he to make any reference to his father. Like a
stored heirloom the knowledge of his birth remained shut within
his heart. It gave him a sense of superiority over his surroundings
and a distaste for them. As boyhood passed his contempt deepened for his home and for the life his parents and their neighbors
were content to lead.

§

It was a hard and rugged life. The days of the kindly monarch who had wished for every peasant a fowl in his pot on Sundays were at an end. The era of the Sun King had dawned; Richelieu and Mazarin were preparing the way for Colbert and for Vauban. France and her possessions were to be bled so that Paris might impose her culture on the world. Through every district the flock of inspectors swarmed like bees over a garden, carrying away the honey of their spoils. The peasant bound to the soil, laboring under the caprice of chance, dependent upon favorable or unkindly seasons, upon the sun that ripened and the frost that withered the early grapes and the tender shoots, accepted mutely and uncomplainingly the demands made upon him first by the *seigneurs* and later by the centralized officialdom of Paris; accepted them as he would accept a succession of bad harvests, adopting the same protective measures. In summer you laid away the stores that would see you through the dark days of winter. You let the good harvest insure you against the bad. When the demands of the inspector grew oppressive you concealed your profits, hiding them in a stocking beneath the bed for the day when taxes would be increased. You were not going to invest your profits in any improvement of your property when these improvements would only be accepted by the intendant as a proof of increased prosperity, and as an excuse for heavier taxation.

Right through his boyhood Roger listened to talk of tithes and taxes; listened to it contemptuously knowing that for his father and his half-brothers on the hill there were no such taxes, that their lives were free and unfettered of such cares.

They called him a ne'er-do-well. He was; as resolute a ne'er-do-well as was to be found in a village well-stocked with ruffians. Whenever the chance came his way he would escape down the steep mountain roadway to Marseilles, to linger in the taverns beside the quay as long as his pennies and the charity of the sailors lasted. He was nowhere happier than in those dark little rooms, ranged on either side of the narrow, mounting streets, in which sailors would spend in five hours the labor of five months. With avid interest he would listen to the talk of ships and seamen. It was more romantic than any fairy-tale. To think that the carved and painted poops of the high galleons that rested so quietly now against the quay should have breasted and overcome the hostile seas; that those bags which bare-shouldered laborers were unloading from the holds had come from the lands of sunshine; that it was from Alexandria those spices came; from Cairo those rugs and feathers; that Persia had sent opium and rhubarb; Constantinople her wool and sheep; Venice her casks of wine; Algiers her leatherwork.

Seated beside the sailors in those taverns he could not believe that these ordinary-looking men, with their rough clothes, hard faces, and slow voices, had encountered the innumerable perils of the sea: the hurricanes that lashed across the gulf of Lyons, the pirates of the Barbary coast, the hidden rocks of the Grecian Archipelago. As he stood on the quay when the ship sailed, with its volley of cheers and waving flags, he found it hard to believe that those dangers of which he had heard seamen talk were waiting behind the outline of the Château d'If, that those very sailors who cheered so light-heartedly from the decks might be seeing for the last time the high cliffs, the narrow streets, the mounting houses.

"Soon," he would think, "quite soon."

He had no doubt but that destiny would transport him into an ampler world. By that belief the despondency of his boyhood had been consoled. He was confident of fame and fortune. One day his father would be proud of him. Under his father's eyes he would cover himself with glory. In different settings he had seen the moment. Sometimes it had been in battle; sometimes upon the sea; sometimes in some local brawl. But always the end had been the same. There had been that dignified figure pausing with a look of interest in his eyes, saying, "What is your name, young man?" and himself replying, "They call me Vaisseau, but I am your son."

The road would stretch straight before him then. Men honored their natural sons, when they were worth honoring. He would be sent as an officer to the wars, or to Paris as a courtier, with fine clothes and money in his purse. There would be an end to the long, dull days, to the monotony and drudgery of the vineyards and the terraced slopes.

That was how he dreamed in boyhood.

The same dream that had sustained him then was with him on

the brink of manhood. An arrogant, surly figure he waited for his chance.

§

It came on the occasion of the biannual fair that was held a mile or two northwards of Marseilles. Like other fairs it was the commercial monopoly of the priesthood; and in their eyes it was a commercial transaction simply; the means of marketing profitably the merchandise their ships had brought from the Levant. From all sections of the Midi and Provence came buyers to that fair, for the patrolling of lonely villages or the replenishing of city stores. But to the local peasantry the fair was a fair simply. They came to display their best dresses to their neighbors; to exchange gossip with their neighbors; to laugh and dance; to see the sideshows; the marionettes; the camel with the head of a horse and the eyes of a tiger; the two-trunked elephant; the three-footed monkey; the bearded dwarf; the woman who was too fat to cross her legs; the tattooed Negress; the Abyssinian with distorted nostrils; the Arab with a ring hung from his lower lip. For three days and nights the fair continued; three days of bargaining, of drinking, of love-making, of quarrelling. The homes were few that did not at its close number one broken crown.

It was on the second day that Roger got his chance. He was standing with some twenty others round the roped circle from which a bare-backed, sunburned sailor, his hands upon his hips, the muscles standing high upon his arms and shoulders, was challenging anyone at the rate of twenty-five sous to five to stand up in the ring against him for five minutes. He was strong and brutal; with his nose squashed back like a Negro's upon his cheeks and his lips drawn thinly and tightly over toothless gums. There was not an ounce of fat on him. He weighed fourteen stone.

"Come on, you yellow bellies," he called out. "I'm not asking you to beat me, to knock me down. Merely to stand on your feet here for five minutes. Just to protect yourselves; that's all I'm asking you. And I'm offering twenty-five sous against five to the man who's fit to do it."

With a hoarse, arrogant voice he bawled out his challenge.

It was answered by a smooth, precise, and slightly mocking voice.

"They've seen you here too often, Victor, I'm afraid. They've seen too many of their friends lose their five sous to you. It's only strangers that'll run the risk."

Roger turned at the sound of the voice; turned and gave a start. There, two yards away from him, was the tall, elegant figure, lined and stoutened a little now by middle age, but graceful enough still with its haughty manner and brocaded clothes, round which so many of his thoughts had centered. His father, and two yards away from him!

And stepping over the ropes, he tossed the coppers into the ring.

From behind him there was a murmur of surprise. Then a laugh. It was for this that the peasantry had waited.

The boxer, his hands upon his hips, laughed too.

"So this is what I get, this," he cried. "No, I'm sorry, but I really can't. You take back those five sous of yours. You'll go down so easily that you'll discourage the others. I'd rather you went out of the ring; I really would."

It was the strategy that he invariably adopted. He would madden his opponents by his jibes till they would rush hot-blooded at him, to be the victims of his science. But his taunts went so near the truth this time that they might well have been accepted literally.

Roger, tall, well-built and straight though he might be, looked weak and puny beside this rough-hewn giant. A fact that he himself knew well enough as he stood there in the ring, with the peasants tittering behind and the burly boxer straddling in front. He had not the slightest doubt that within three minutes he would be stretched senseless on the ground. He knew that he did not stand a chance.

"All the same, I'll make a show of it," he thought. "I'll show them that I'm worth something."

His father's eyes emboldened him.

With an angry haste he tore off his jerkin and flung it on the ground.

"Now," he said, and swung a right hook at his opponent's jaw.

A second later he was floundering on his hands and knees upon the grass, with the giant in assumed good nature laughing uproariously above him.

Roger had not realized that so heavy a man could be so quick upon his feet. His opponent stepped back quickly. The swing had missed by a full foot. Its impetus had half swung him off his feet.

While he was off his balance, the boxer had pushed him lightly but shrewdly on the shoulder.

"Come now, come now," the boxer laughed, "that isn't the way to fight. Don't you think you'd better take that offer of mine, pick up those coins and run back with them to Mammy? You still can, you know. I don't want to rob a baby."

His mind a mist, Roger stumbled to his feet. To be hurt, to be struck senseless, for that he had been prepared; but to be pushed over, to be laughed at, for that he had not bargained. "I'll show him," he thought. "I'll show him."

This time he was ready for his opponent's speed. He knew that Victor, with his love of the crowd's laughter, would try to repeat his effect. Once again Roger swung at his opponent's jaw. Once again the boxer stepped back to dodge; but this time the swing had been no more than a feint. And as Victor stepped back, Roger came forward and crashed his left fist into the toothless, noseless face. It was a hard blow; hard enough to bark his knuckles. But it did not make Victor stop. It merely wiped from that brutal face the look of assumed geniality. Victor had not meant to be hit; he had not expected to be hit. He had planned to play with this raw stripling; to amuse the crowd at his expense; to make an exhibition of his own skill. It was his self-esteem that that blow had hurt. The thin lips set tighter over the toothless gums. A hard light came into the narrow eyes. "So that's it, is it?" he muttered. "Well, we'll see."

He swayed forward, low-bent, his fists moving before his eyes. He half hit with his left, then with his right; then with unforeseen swiftness his left fist landed on the bridge of Roger's nose. It was a stinging blow that brought the tears involuntarily into Roger's eyes. Roger groped forward with his left. As he did so, Victor jolted his right fist into his side, three inches below the heart.

It was the greatest agony that Roger had ever known. Every ounce of breath had been knocked out of his body. He lay on the ground, completely conscious, completely impotent. He could see with blurred eyes the grinning face of his opponent, could hear the peasants laughing and chatting together, could hear his father's carefully cadenced, exquisitely bored voice: "That was too easy a job for you, I'm afraid"; he could hear his own moans and whimpers as breath by agonizing breath the air fought its way back into his lungs. Of that of all things he was most ashamed. If only he had been hit senseless to the ground, to lie like a log till people flung water over him. There would have been some glamor about such a beating. But to lie on the ground, gasping and whimpering like a baby, in complete control of his senses. If only he could stop those groans. But he could not. They were wrung from him involuntarily. There was nothing to do but lie there, the brutal, mocking face of his conqueror clear before his eyes, the sound of his conqueror's voice ringing in his ears.

"Come on, now, I've had enough of this," said Victor finally. "He's spoiling my market snivelling there. Take him away, some-one."

So they helped him up, some half-dozen of them, and carried him, still gasping and groaning, to the outside edge of the ring. He was too weak, too weary to protest. In limp silence he listened to their condolences, surrendering himself to their restoratives. Then, when breath had returned to his body and strength to his knees, he lifted himself from the ground and slunk slowly away to a booth where they sold drink.

Dejectedly he sat upon a bench, a glass of wine beside him, gazing at the ground. So that was that, then. He had had his chance, and he had made himself ridiculous. He had been laughed at by a low prize-fighter, by ignorant, uncouth peasants, and in his father's presence. He had not even given a creditable display of courage. He had just lain on the ground, whimpering like a baby. He had won his father's contempt rather than respect. He had had his chance and he had missed it.

It was while he sat there brooding, that a group of young men and women came up to him.

"We're just going to start a dance," they told him. "Come and join us."

He shook his head.

"I'm sorry," he said. "I'm tired."

But the party was not to be put off lightly. They were young, they were gay, they had been drinking.

"No, no," they insisted, "you must come with us."

And when he again refused, one of the girls, a dark-eyed buxom wench, stepped forward. "You wait. I think I know how to make him." Her voice had a mischievous pitch to it.

Seating herself upon Roger's knee, she put an arm about his

neck, ran her fingers through his hair and with her cheek close against his ear began to whisper.

But Roger was in no mood for gallantry. Impatiently and roughly he pushed her away.

"Oh, so it's that way, is it?"

With the drinker's quick change of front she swung over to ill-humor. Her hands on her hips, her legs straddled, her eyes fiery, she stood before him.

"I suppose you're too high and mighty. You didn't look half so grand half an hour ago when you were sprawling on the grass."

From behind her went up a shout of laughter. Delighted and emboldened by the applause she tossed her head back haughtily.

"I suppose you think you're a man because you can go into a ring and fight. You didn't look much of a man there, I can tell you. You looked a baby blubbering on the ground."

It was more than Roger was prepared to stand. The crowd of gibbering young men and women swam before him. By his side there was a stool. He grabbed it up.

"Child?" he shouted. "I'll show you," and flung the stool into the grinning crowd.

There was a crack like splintered glass as the stool, flung straight and hard, landed in the group; a startled cry of agony; a gasp; a moan or two; then silence. After the silence there was a sudden buzz of whispering from down-peered faces, with the man in charge of the booth hitting Roger warningly on the shoulder.

"Quit; quit fast before there's trouble."

"What's happened?"

"Don't you wait to see what's happened. Run while you still can. Through there, behind that row of tents."

Roger had not the mental vigor to resist.

Three hours later in a small inn half-way down one of the dark, narrow, winding Marseilles streets, he leaned back against the wall a head whose throbbing grew every second more intolerable.

At his side a sailor, incapable with drink, was lying on the floor, his head rested in the lap of a blowsy but pleasant-faced young woman who stroked his hair and looked down commiseratingly at him.

"It's his last night here," she explained. "His ship sails at dawn."

He was young, at the most nineteen. His large eyes were wide with misery. With his arms clutched round the girl's knees, he sobbed imploringly.

"I don't want to go," he said.

The girl looked moodily at Roger.

"It's after seven," she said. "In an hour or so they will be coming after him. They know where he is. He's been nowhere else since his ship came in. He's spent every penny here. That's why he's signed on again. He never meant to. It's best to help him to forget."

She poured him out a neat glass of cordial and held it to his lips. At one gulp he swallowed it, shuddered a little, began to talk wildly, then incoherently, finally subsiding into sleep.

She looked down at the drooped blond head. "And the funny thing is that as like as not there're plenty of people in the town who'd be ready to change places with him. People in trouble who'd like to get away from it."

"I guess."

As he looked at the tumbled figure, he wondered what trouble he had brewed for himself back there in the hills, and asked himself what point there was in waiting to find out.

"What's the ship called?" he asked.

"The *Bordelais*."

"Where's she bound?"

"For the South Seas."

To Roger the word symbolized romance; adventure; an escape from the smug, the conventional, the prudent; from the memory of disgrace.

"What's his name?"

"Renal."

"I think I'll borrow it for a little. Let's get his clothes off."

And so in the small, damp, ill-lit bar Roger Vaisseau stripped himself of his smart jerkin, pulled on the yarn stockings, the blue shirt, the cotton waistcoat, the canvas breeches, the blue neckcloth, the striped shaggy cap, and walked out into the narrow street.

He had no difficulty in finding the *Bordelais*. She stood in the November dusk, an imposing shadow, with her sail-filled masts and cannon-charged flanks and ornately embellished poop. From the deck came the sound of singing. There was a group gathered by the quay. At the head of the ladder a large-chested, large-thighed mariner was standing.

"So it's you, is it?" he called out at the sight of Roger. "We didn't expect to see you at this hour, nor sober either. We were just going to send the boys out for you."

In silence Roger began to climb the ladder.

"Come alone, too, have you?" the man called out. "Quarrelled with your love-bird?"

Roger made no reply. The man whose clothes and name he bore had spoken with a Breton accent. He was not going to invite detection.

"Grown sullen, have you!" his cross-examiner continued. "Or perhaps you can't speak for choking. Let's see if there are any tears."

At the head of the ladder a lamp was swinging. The first mate peered down into the face that approached his rung by rung. He drew back as Roger stepped aboard the ship.

"Now what's his little game?" he said. "You're no more Renal than I am."

"These are Renal's clothes, and all that you want is strong limbs within them."

"That's as may be. What have you done with Renal?"

"What's that to do with either of us. I'm here."

The first mate pushed his head forward. It was a young man's face, but heavy drinking and the long night watches at the helm had drawn hard lines between the nose and mouth. Across the forehead a Spanish quarrel had traced a long wide furrow. It was a hard, weather-beaten face.

"So you want to be a sailor, do you? Well, let's see if you are fit to be one."

Without warning he jabbed his left fist at Roger's face. Roger was unprepared and in the uncertain light of the swinging lantern it was by chance mainly that he warded off the blow. As it was the blow staggered him, sending him off his balance unguarding him for the right swing that lifted him off his feet and flung him dazed and shaken against a pile of ropes.

The first mate wiped his hands together.

"You'll do," he said. "You stopped the first blow, and you'll know who's master here."

§

In addition to Renal's name and clothes, Roger acquired a musket, a knife, a cutlass, some clothes, and a third share in a hammock slung from two beams in a narrow cabin, down whose center ran a long deal table, and which housed the entire crew with the exception of the four officers. It was ventilated by a narrow shaft, and by the stairway which led from the kitchen to the hold. In the cold weather it was draughty. In the warm weather it was stifling. In all weathers it smelt intolerably. Luckily one was only in it when one slept.

His day was divided into shifts: eight hours on, four hours off. Of the eight hours a day that one was off duty, two were occupied with meals, cleaning, and inspections. The captain believed that hard work alone could keep a crew out of mischief.

"He's a swine," one of the sailors informed Roger. "Every inch of him. He's a good sailor. That's all that can be said for him."

More than his share of work seemed to come Roger's way. It was his business both to sweep out the cabin and to fetch the food from the kitchens. The crew ate twice a day: in the morning at ten o'clock; in the evening shortly before sundown. It was for the evening meal that meat was served. Roger would be roused from his sleep to fetch it. The slab of salted meat would be laid upon the deck. To one man would be given the task of dividing it into portions. So that the portions might be accurate one of the sailors stood with his back to the carver. "Whose piece is this?" the carver would ask as each piece was severed. And the sailor would call out whatever name came into his mind.

It was Roger's job to fetch and take away the platter of food for every meal.

"Why should I always have to do that job?" he asked. "Why shouldn't it be taken in turns?"

"It will be," they answered, "when you have proved yourself a sailor."

"And how am I to prove myself?"

"By swarming to the end of the mainmast yard-arm."

With steady eyes Roger looked up at the mainmast as it towered a hundred feet above him. The day was rough; the canvas sails were stretched; the ship was keeling over in a steady fifteen degrees roll. There were drops of rain in the wind. "Very well," said Roger.

The beginning was simple. Though the ladder swayed beneath him and the roughness of the cold rope cut against his feet, he clambered swiftly to the division of the spar. Then he paused. Below he could see the upturned faces of his comrades. In front of him the yard-arm stretched, greasy and cold and wide. He had not realized as he stood on the deck how much the ship was rolling. It seemed to him that by no means within his power would he be able to save himself from sliding headlong down that slippery surface into the sea. He paused, but he did not for one second consider the possibility of returning to the deck. It was simply that he preferred to face his fate before he went to meet it. He looked down the long straight spar, then leaning over and clasping it to his stomach, he began to swarm towards the end.

If he had not realized as he had stood upon the deck the extent to which the ship was swaying, neither had he realized as he had rested against the juncture of the spar how, as the ship swayed downwards, it would seem as though the whole ship were diving into the sea, so that he would seem to be clinging to the prow of some vast airship that was plunging into the green churned waters that heaved below him; so that he would think, with the yard-arm pressed against his stomach, his arms and hands numb, his feet tingling and his head singing, how much more simple it would be to let go and drop into that chill greenage and be engulfed; so much easier than fighting his way inch by precarious inch to the yard-arm's end.

To the watchers below, however, no sign of this irresolution was apparent. They saw the young man creep slowly but steadily down the yard-arm's length, then slowly and steadily work his way back to the juncture and with a laugh swing down the rope ladder to the deck.

"Well," he said, "have I proved myself a sailor now?"

§

It was for a rough life that he had proved himself.

The captain had been described to him as a bully.

He was.

Of the last thirty years of his life twenty-eight years had been spent at sea. He had no ties, no family, no friends. The sea was the one thing he loved. He loved it on cold, rainswept days when the ship was jerked by short gusty wavelets; loved it on days of storm when the huge gray wall of the sea rose above the yard-arm and the ship pitched and rolled in the quicksand-bottomed troughs of water; loved it on the calm, blue, windless days, when the sails hung slack upon the masts and the crossing of the deck was like hot iron beneath his feet; loved it on the days of wind and sun, when the ship, heeled slightly over with the masts full-rigged, cut through the sea's blue carpet with the soft swish of tearing silk.

For long hours he would lean over the larboard taffrail, gazing out to the gray or blue horizon. Then he would go back to his cabin and pore over charts that he alone on that ship understood completely; on one side of him the instruments he guarded jealously; on the other a glass of grog.

For his sailors he had no personal regard. They were the slaves of the ship, the servants of the sea. Every morning he read prayers to such of the crew as were not on duty. Wet or fine he would keep them standing or kneeling on the deck while he read in a rum-roughened voice the exhortations to virtue that thundered from that lined, bearded face like Hadean menaces.

"If I hear any of you using the name of Our Blessed Saviour in blasphemy," he would conclude, "I'll string him up against that mast and thrash him."

The crew knew that he was not threatening idly. He was a strict, a brutally strict, disciplinarian. He appeared to be disappointed when there was no excuse for punishment. A man who was late for duty, or was found smoking after sunset, was ducked three times without discussion from the bowsprit. Once he saw a man throw overboard the red contents of a mug. "Hi there," he shouted out. "Who's that wasting wine? String him up, you men."

"But they were the dregs," the sailor pleaded. "They were the end of a barrel."

"Who are you to say that the dregs aren't good enough? They're wine. They're wet. If you prefer water there's the sea and plenty of it. Over with him, boys."

Once he came across a sailor sparring with a drawn knife. The sailor protested that it was in fun, that he was not fighting.

"Fun," roared the captain. "I'll have no fun of that sort on my ship. I know that kind of fun. Up against the pole with him."

On another occasion he found two men really fighting. He made no inquiries into the rights and wrongs of it. "Strip them," he shouted. "Ropes round their wrists and ankles, weights round their bellies."

Savagely he looked the naked and manacled figures up and down.

"You ought to be grateful to me for this," he snarled. "If I hadn't interfered one of you would have been killed for certain. As it is you both *may* live." With an incredibly sinister hiss his voice underlined the "may." "Over with them, boys."

By heels and wrists they were lowered from the bowsprit, the weight drawing down their bellies in a curve.

They sank the instant they touched water. The men holding the ropes walked away, the one to the larboard, the other to the starboard; they pulled till they found resistance. Then, still pulling, they struggled their way to the stern, dragging their comrades' bodies along the barnacle-knotted keel. At the stern, they dragged up and flung upon the deck the half-drowned, mangled creatures.

There was not much unblemished. Their backs and arms and legs were torn and bruised; raw, bleeding, tattered flesh. It would be days before they could wear a shirt. The captain surveyed his handiwork with satisfaction. "That will be a lesson to you others," he said. "Get about your jobs quietly."

One evening there was an ugly quarrel: knives were drawn; a man lay motionless on the deck.

There was silence round him as he lay there; silence as the captain strode down from his bridge towards the prostrate body; lifted an arm; dropped it with a thud upon the deck; straightened himself and looked between the eyes the hard-breathing sailor who stood by with naked and stained knife.

"Dead," said the captain. "You know what that means. Tie them up."

It was the law of the sea no man questioned. Two sailors bent, lifted the dead body, stood it back to back against its late antagonist, tied ankle to ankle, wrist to wrist, then gave a heave and wrench.

There was a cry as the two bodies struck the weed-covered, oily water. There was a second or two of splashing as the live man tried to keep himself afloat, threshing with his fettered limbs,

treading with his labored feet. Then the weight of the other body
pulled him down. With a gurgling cry he sank. The ripples swayed
sluggishly against the scattered seaweed, then sluggishly the banks
of seaweed swung back and closed again. The crew, leaning over
the side, waited for the drowned bodies to rise; waited in vain.

That evening the men grumbled over their salt fare. "He
needn't have done that," they said. "It's the law, we know it.
But he needn't have done that."

Contemptuously Roger listened to their grumbling. "If you
feel like that, why don't you do something?" he asked.

"What can we do?"

"He's one, you're many."

The bearded seamen looked at him with shocked surprise.

"I shouldn't let the first mate hear you talk like that," they
said. "You know what the penalty is for mutiny."

"Talking's not mutiny."

"Near enough, my son, on a ship like this."

So Roger held his peace as the ship raced its way through
mounting seas towards the Straits of Magellan.

To him it was incredible that the blue lake whose gentle washing of the gold Mediterranean coast he had watched from his
village square, could achieve such turbulent effects of terror. It was
magnificent; it was terrible. At times the ship would plunge between waves so high that they would feel themselves becalmed,
with not a breath of air blowing on them, and the sails hanging
slack upon the masts. Then a second later they would be shot
skywards so that they would have the sensation of standing on
the edge of a turreted battlement. At their back would be the
wail of the wind against the canvas, and streaming over the bows
a river of crested foam. For days they were battered, driven,
drenched, and shaken. For days they shivered in wet clothes in
the fetid fo'castle. The cold of the Antarctic was upon them.
Even the fiery rum that burnt their throats only momentarily
warmed their veins. With numb and frozen fingers they clawed
at the hard ropes, swarmed over the slippery masts. Their heads
ached with noise and want of sleep. There were set, sullen looks
upon the seamen's faces. "We were better off ten days ago," they
said. "At any rate we were warm then."

Their meals had ceased to be of pleasure to them. They just

wolfed their stew hurriedly before a lurch of the ship should spill a valued morsel. Provisions were running short. They had eaten, during the days of doldrums, the food that they had shipped from the Guinea coast. Their biscuits were maggoty. There were two kinds of maggots. The gray maggots were tasteless and could be ignored. The white maggots had a bitter flavor. When white maggots emerged from the biscuit they knew that all that was nourishing in the biscuit had been consumed. They made no more bones about the eating of the maggots than would their relatives in Europe over a ripe cheese. In the Sargossa they had finished their last jar of butter. It had melted in the heavy heat. As they approached the last half-pound the yellow cream was filled with hair. At the bottom of the jar they found a dead mouse, completely bald, that had fallen into the jar, sunk, and been suffocated. They put the mouse into a stew; Roger had the luck to draw it. It tasted excellent. "As it should do," he answered, "considering the good stuff it has been nourished in." It was indeed the general view that the mice and rats were the best food upon a ship since they had fattened upon the ship's provisions. They were hard to catch, however. Two or three a day would be a whole ship's catch. More days than not the crew went hungry.

In shivering, surly clumps they would huddle together grumbling.

"We're pretty fair fools, aren't we?" they would say. "Letting ourselves be led out here, just so that some merchant in Marseilles can buy himself another house. We're treated like slaves. We are slaves with a captain such as ours."

Every day the cold grew more intense; the soaked clothing seemed a frailer protection against the wind; the food grew scantier; the crew grumbled more. There was water to drink now; and they were no longer afraid of the thirst that strong liquor woke in them. But the liquor was running short. The captain on his bridge learned of this with a wry face.

"Warm liquor's more important than warm clothing. We shouldn't have relied on our getting plunder in so soon."

The outlook was difficult and he knew it. But he was not showing any sign of nerves before the men. In his detached, indifferent fashion he would stand upon his bridge, his hands clasped upon the balcony. Then he would turn back to his cabin, and with a

glass of grog beside him study his maps and charts. To the men
he betrayed no sign of doubt.

All the same there were rumors below decks that things were
not well. The other officers, it seemed, had been trying to persuade the captain to round the Horn instead of sailing through
the Straits. The Straits were dangerous and uncharted; they were
narrow, with strong tides and uncertain anchor-ground, with
contrary winds and sudden gales blowing from the snow-bound
mountains. Nor could they be sure that were they forced to land
they would be kindly treated by the native Indians, who had
starved where they had not slaughtered the garrison with which
Spain had attempted to block up the passage to other nations.
The rounding of the Cape was a tough business, they maintained,
but it was safe. And, once in the South Seas, the rich coasts of
Peru would be at their mercy, and there would be the Manila
galleons to be plundered on their way to Acapulco.

Unmoved the captain listened.

"My men want food," he said. "The ship needs to be careened.
I can't run the risk of waiting."

Though these deliberations were staged in the secrecy of the
captain's cabin, rumors of them reached the crew. By every man
below decks it was known that the officers and the captain were
divided.

§

The entrance to the main bay of the Straits of Magellan is less
than a mile across. It is set about with mountains so high that
the sun rarely shines on them. It is beyond speech cold; snow
falls; the nights are long. There are harbors, however, with good
water and trees of an aromatic essence, whose bark smells like
pepper shoots and whose green wood burns in the fire as though
it were dry; there are rivers and pleasant streams. In the center of
the Straits the tides of the Atlantic and Pacific meet with a
prodigious shock and noise. The floods rise to a great height
from which they will subside so suddenly that there is a danger
of the ship's being stranded on dry ground. The rise and fall of
the tides is a matter of four-fathom depth. There is no piece of
water in the world that demands more delicate navigation. As
that they were cold and hungry, sang as they labored at the ropes.
the ship passed through the high lane of rock, the sailors, for all

Soon they would have food and fruit; their course would be set northwards to the blue seas, blue skies, and heavy sunlight.

They were still singing when a sudden shock passed through the entire ship, when there was a scraping, rending noise, and the ship, for all that there was wind behind it, came to a sudden halt. There was a silence. Then a pandemonium of voices through which rang loud and menacing the captain's voice. "Quiet there. There is nothing to be frightened over."

Nor was there, for the moment. The ship had become wedged between two rocks that held it firmly.

"Down into the hold," the captain shouted. "See if there's a leak."

There was no leak. The fabric had stood the strain. The ship was imprisoned but it was safe. The captain gathered the crew together.

"There is no danger," he said. "In a little while when the tide subsides we shall be on dry ground. We shall then careen the ship, loosen it, and when the tide rises, float it. In the meantime I shall send the pinnace in search of a harbor where Indians may be met and gifts exchanged with them."

Roger was one of the sailors chosen. They took with them bangles, glass jewelry, and other such gimcrack objects as would be likely to appeal to the simple Indian. They rowed upwards of ten miles to a bay on the north side of the second narrow, where a ship could ride in clear, sandy ground.

The Indians had gathered on the shore to meet them. They were of middle stature, well-limbed with round faces, low foreheads, little noses, small black eyes and ears, black hair of an indifferent length. Their teeth were white; their faces were of an olive color, daubed with spots of white clay and soot; their bodies were painted with red earth and grease. After the fashion of a Highland plaid they wrapped round them the skin of seals; they made caps for themselves with the skin of chickens to which the feathers remained attached; their feet they protected with skin sandals. The women wore no caps but instead surrounded their arms with shell bracelets. They were active and nimble and, in spite of the cold, went naked. Their language was guttural and slow. They displayed the highest satisfaction over the trinkets that the sailors showed them. In exchange they gave such fish and fruit as they possessed, promising to bring more on the next and

following day. That night, for the first time for many days, there
was revelry and song aboard the *Bordelais*.

At the same time there was a feeling of discontent. There
might be fresh fish and fruit upon the table, but the ship was
wedged between two rocks. The captain in whom they had trusted
had wedged it there.

"The officers were right," the seamen said. "He should have
taken us round by the Cape. It's mere chance that there's one
of us alive."

For the first time doubt of their captain's seamanship had come
to them. Roger, lying back in his hammock, his hands crossed
behind his head, listened with a sardonic smile upon his lips.

"Yes, yes," he said, "and you talk like that, and you say that
he's a swine, that he's not even a good sailor, yet you'll show up
quietly while the ship's refloated and set off through the Straits.
You'll trust your lives to a man you hate, whom you've no faith
in. You don't know where you're going. You'll be starved; you'll
be cold; you'll go short of wine; and all so that some rich man in
Marseilles shall grow more rich. You'll grumble, but you'll submit."

In years of experience of the sea Roger was the junior man
aboard. And though he was broad-shouldered and well-built, there
were half a dozen men whose fists could have settled a quick account with him. But his voice had a note of authority that no
other man's had got. His fellows listened to him uneasily.

"What else is there for us but to submit?" they said.

Roger made no direct reply. His eyes were fixed on the
blackened roof.

"There's plenty of time. There's no hurry yet," he said.

He did not let the matter drop. He had learned much in the
taverns of Marseilles of the sea's life and of the ships that sailed
it. "We're told that we've come to trade in the South Seas," he
said. "We haven't. We're privateers. We're looking for a ship
to plunder, a town to sack or ransom. We're at war with the
world, English, Spaniards, Dutch; they are free, any one of them,
to attack us. We're no better off than the filibusters of Tortuga."

In the cafés of Marseilles he had heard often of that strange
group of derelicts from St. Christopher, who had banded themselves against the hazards of Spanish tyranny on the small turtle-

shaped island to the north of San Domingo. From all countries they had come. There were Protestants from La Rochelle and Dieppe; soldiers unemployed after the religious war and by the disappearance of the Prince's party; Scottish Puritans and English Catholics; cadets of Gascony, Normandy, and Flanders; sailors who had mutinied or deserted; *engagés* who had broken from their servitude to the white planters in San Domingo. Inoffensive settlers to begin with, but driven by oppression to realize that they must fight or die, they had levied war in their long boats against the world. "No prey, no pay" had become their motto. There was no West Indian captain whose spy-glass did not nervously sweep the horizon for signs of the Brethren of the Coast.

"If we were one of them, we should be in no worse danger than we are now," said Roger. "And we should be free, we should be working for ourselves."

The crew listened, suspicious but impressed.

In the shadowed room, lit by the wavering lantern light, he looked strong and purposeful, with his broad shoulders, his proud, high-held head, his long-beaked nose, and the scar that ran along his cheek-bone.

"We are slaves," he repeated, "and we needn't be. Not so many miles away there is an island where we could live freely, as we chose, fighting whom we chose, when we chose, sharing our spoil among us."

He paused, and when he spoke again his voice had a ringing, imperious quality, a quality that made each sailor recognize the power of leadership.

"We are many, he is one."

§

Two mornings later the *Bordelais* was driving fast and straight through the second narrows. That night the first mate was roused in his sleep by a foully smelling hand pressed on his mouth and the point of a dagger rested against his throat. Through the rusk of the cabin he could not recognize the faces that peered down into his; nor was the voice that whispered into his ear familiar.

"You will make no sound or you will be killed," the voice was whispering. "You will get up, and you will walk to the captain's cabin. You will knock on the door and ask him to let you in. What follows is not your affair."

Drowsy with sleep and wine, the first mate stumbled from his hammock. With the point of the knife pressed close against his side he felt his way down the passage to the captain's cabin. He beat with his fist on the studded door. There was silence, then a voice, angry, rough, resentful:

"Who's that? What is it? I'm asleep."

"It's I, Dargot."

"I can hear it is. What in hell's name do you want?"

"To see you."

"What about?"

He hesitated. The point of the knife was pressed tighter into his side.

"About something very important," he called back.

"Ah, very well, then."

There was the sound of a shot bolt, the creaking of a hinge. The door swung open. As it did so the first mate received a push in the back that flung him face downwards on the cabin floor. Lying there in the corner he saw what happened; saw stride into the room a young sailor, tall, lithe, broad-shouldered, with long-beaked nose and a scar below the eye, with after him a half-dozen or so of sailors, three of whom pinioned the captain's arms behind the head. That he saw with his head singing, with a hand gripped upon his throat, with the cold blade of a cutlass laid against his neck; saw it, and seeing, heard the astounded, indignant boom of the captain's voice: "Now what in hell's name does this mean?"; heard that and heard ringing on it the reply of the young sailor: "What does it mean? Not more than this. That the ship's head is going to be set south; then, when the Horn is rounded, to the north."

The captain glared with wild, rage-filled eyes.

"And after that?" he asked.

"After that we will decide with the filibusters of Tortuga what use is to be made of her."

Roger flicked with the tip of his finger at the long blade of his knife.

"I shall stand beside you," he said. "There is no one else on this ship qualified. I shall see that you steer her right."

The captain made no reply, but the first mate, sprawled there on the floor, knew from the way the lips set over the ragged and blackened teeth that the last word had not yet been spoken.

That night Roger moved into the captain's cabin. The crew, trained in subservience, accepted his leadership with the same meekness that they had their captain's. They knew that they were powerless of themselves. They yielded to those who could control them. There were no prayers next morning. Roger spoke to them instead.

"We are bound," he said, "for an island where men are free; where they share equally the profits of their work. In a few weeks' time we shall be there. We shall join the brethren on such terms as their brotherhood ordains. Till then, however, so that the ship's running may be smooth, it is best that the former discipline of the ship be maintained."

As far as the actual seamen were concerned, the mutiny involved little change. If anything, there was rather more work for them to do. Three men were required to guard the captain; and the officers who had been transferred below decks were indifferent substitutes. Roger saw to it, however, that the ration of rum was increased to a tumbler and a half a day.

And so the ship swung south into the Antarctic tempests. And for days, with the sails screaming and the ship plunging, the mutineers fought their way round the Horn, till at last their head turned northwards. And it was on their right that the sun rose, lilac and lavender out of a morning sky, and on their left that it drowned in a foam-churned, tawny-red horizon. And the wind became gentle gradually, and the seas less fierce. The days lengthened and grew warm. Over the pale water the white flying-fish would quiver. And at night the sailors would sit out under the stars singing the songs of their own country.

They were happy. The supply of fruit was nearly finished. Scurvy would soon be once more on them. There was only a barrel of rum left. They knew that. But they were happy. They were bound for an island where men were free, where men could make riches quickly and return with them to their parents, their wives, their sweethearts; to the friends that awaited them. The songs that they sang by starlight were the songs of yearning: of a homesickness for the white houses and the gray-green terraces of the south; for the long bare cliffs of Brittany; the thatched cottages, and the fields, green-brown in the mild spring light.

Roger, at the captain's side, listened to their singing with a mind detached. He was not yet twenty. He had been less than a year at sea. Yet already the familiar faces and the familiar scenes of his boyhood had grown unreal. He imagined that he would see them again one day. But he did not dream, as these others did, of returning one day rich to the village that had despised him in his youth. He did not think about the village much. He did not look ahead. The present sufficed for him. He felt complete. And as the days passed he became aware, as primitive people are aware, of a kinship of loneliness between himself and the hard, weather-beaten sailor he had enslaved, who had not in any port in the world a human tie; who existed for himself, within himself, in his love for the sea and for his ship.

They rarely spoke during the long weeks of their journey northwards. Taciturn as ever the captain buried himself over his charts; walking from time to time on the bridge to sweep the horizon with his spy-glass; the beaker of grog unceasingly replenished was at his side. He might have been captain still except that he never cast a look towards the crew. He made no reference to the mutiny. He gave instructions to Roger as though Roger had been his officer. He did not ask whether or not those orders had been carried out. He made no attempt to speak with his former officers or with any of the men. He accepted his position. Occasionally he would fix a slow searching glance on Roger. Once he asked him a question.

"When and how did you join this ship?" he asked.

When Roger told him he nodded his head.

"I seem to remember them telling me," he said. "I didn't hear till we had left Marseilles. They should have told me. I don't suppose if I had seen you I should have let you sail."

That was the only reference he ever made in Roger's presence to the mutiny. With the quiet efficiency that had won him the respect of merchant owners he steered the ship along the Brazilian coast, rounded the outposts of Venezuela, passed between the narrow straits that separate Trinidad and Tobago, sailed into the calm waters of the Caribbean that had held for a century past, and was for two centuries yet to hold, the West in fee; was to be the symbol of romance; the Eldorado of beglamored youth; the background against which the courage and skill of British seamen, Drake, Nelson, Rodney, Howe, were to flame through history; that had sent, first gold and silver from its mines; and later from its fertile soil was to pour sugar, rum, coffee, cocoa into Europe, till the phrase, "rich as Crœsus," should be displaced by "rich as a Creole." Green and high and fecund they circled jewelwise this tropical Mediterranean, the islands for whose sake so much blood and money should be spilt; Trinidad, Jamaica, Cuba, San Domingo.

As the *Bordelais* swung through Trinidad's northern channel, Roger standing upon the bridge had a sense of entering a kingdom.

"How many days away is Tortuga now?" he asked.

"Seven or eight maybe."

"Have you ever been there before?"

"I've been there."

And the old man turned his eyes back to the shimmering white-blue horizon. In silence they sailed on across that unruffled lane. There is no land between Trinidad and San Domingo.

High and green the mountains of San Domingo rose out of the sea. As the ship cruised along its southern coast, turning northwards round Dame Marie, then eastwards from the Môle St. Nicholas by the same route Columbus took, the crew laughed and sang about their work, happy in the knowledge that in a few hours' time there would be fresh food for them and wine. They had asked no questions as to what would happen when they arrived. Had they done so Roger would have been uncertain how to answer. He had himself the haziest idea of what would happen. But he lacked the imagination that would have caused such haziness to worry him. His heart was restless with excitement.

At his side the captain was more taciturn, more withdrawn than ever. His lips were set tight upon his ragged teeth. His eyes shone brightly. He answered abruptly with his face fixed on the horizon such questions as Roger asked.

"Harbors," he said. "There is only one harbor."

"Is the coast rocky?"

"Very."

"I suppose that's why the buccaneers chose it. They thought it would make them safe against invasion."

"I suppose so."

And indeed it would have been hard to picture anything more barren and bleak and inaccessible than the high-humped island that grew clearer hour by hour. Along its dark-green coast there was no sign of life; roots and trees grew on its rocky face, like ivy against a wall.

Through the spy-glass Roger gazed closely at the approaching beach. "This is where my life starts," he thought.

Though the sun was shining fiercely out of a blue sky there was a keen wind blowing. The water in the narrow channel was churned and choppy. The ship, as each wave hit against it, pitched to such an extent that Roger at first took for no more than the impact of a larger wave the sudden jolt that flung him off his feet and sent the ship heeling over to a twenty degree angle. It was not till the ship, as he struggled to his feet, did not right herself, that he realized that it was not water that had caused that jolt.

"What's that?" he cried.

The captain fixed on him a look of triumph and cunning. The old man's eyes were bright. There was a glow of color in his lined, rum-roughened cheeks. He spoke slowly and proudly, on a note of self-vindication.

"You thought," he said, "that you could frighten me into steering my ship into an enemy harbor, and making a present of her to pirates at the bidding of mutineers."

"What's happened?"

The old man took no notice of the interruption. "You could force me to bring my ship into the Caribbean. But you couldn't make me surrender my ship to pirates. You can kill me now. But no pirate's hand is ever going to touch this wheel. My ship is hit hard upon a reef of rock. If she's afloat in an hour's time I'll be surprised."

Roger made no answer. There was none to be made. There were other matters to be seen to. Already the crew had begun to gather on the lower deck, terrified and complaining, waiting for instructions. As Roger stood looking down on them from the quarter-deck he had a comforting feeling of superiority to them all. He was responsible for their lives. He had led them to mutiny. He had brought them to this pass. Yet he could feel no particular sense of guilt, nor any particular pity for them. They were poor sheep. They should be grateful to him for having shepherded them so long.

In the shortest possible words he told them what had happened. "We've gone aground. In half an hour in all human probability we shall be five fathoms deep in the Caribbean. The land's a league and a half off. We're sixty. The pinnace will hold twelve. You had best draw lots for it."

Had he made a long speech the men might have had time to recover from their astonishment and start protesting. He did not give them time for that. With pieces of string he set them to the task of drawing lots.

In a few moments it had been decided which ones were to be granted places in the pinnace. Twelve men had stepped forward from the rest.

"Very well," said Roger, "lower the pinnace. You twelve get into it. The rest of you must take such chances as you can."

The men hesitated.

"Come on now," said Roger. "What are you waiting for?"

The men still hesitated. There were the supplies, they said, the muskets, the ammunition, and the cargo they had brought to trade with.

Roger smiled.

"If you can save yourselves you may consider yourselves lucky. Get busy and away with you."

Then turning to the rest.

"It's every man for himself now," he said.

The crew made no reply. Quickly and neatly the pinnace was lowered into the angry waters. No attempt was made by any of those who had been left behind to force a place for themselves. The moment the pinnace had been lowered they turned to the preparation of a raft, breaking up chests, destroying doors, pulling planks up in the deck.

From the bridge Roger watched their efforts. For nine months now these men and he had faced and shared the various hardships and recompenses of the sea. Now in as many minutes these bonds were to be broken. Already the pinnace was plunging its way towards the shore. The sea was angry, the current strong, the harbor was set with rocks, there were sharks as likely as not in the lagoon; the betting was against their reaching the palm-fringed stretch of beach. The other sailors with their raft were on the whole the likelier to get there. With a shrug of the shoulders he turned back towards the bridge. The captain, his chin rested on his hands, was leaning forward, looking out at the struggling pinnace.

Side by side they stood there watching the small boat pitch and toss in the trough of the short angry waves; at times buried beneath a wall of water, then rising on the high crest of foam, plunging like a frightened horse. For half a league it struggled. Then as a gray-green wall of water sank, there rose on the crested foam not the narrow boat but a medley of oars threshing feebly in a wake of white.

The other sailors, minute by minute, as the settling ship listed over, lowered themselves over the side in groups and couples, trusting to hastily strung rafts and spars. The sea was soon full of dark objects tossing on the mounting waves. In a little while the ship was empty, save for the two upon the bridge.

Roger turned towards the captain.

"Well?" he said.

"Well?"

"Are you going to stay here?"

"The captain goes down with his ship."

The emotion that, an hour earlier, had lit that hard, lined face had vanished. Impassive and indifferent, he leaned forward, his chin rested on his hands.

"Two can play that game," thought Roger. He was not going to be outdone in composure by the man he had deposed. And so they stood side by side together, while the waves beat against the high, red-painted poop, and the ship settled deeper, till the water had risen over the lower deck, lapping against the quarter-deck from whose stairway Roger had addressed the crew.

"We'll be down in a minute or two now," the captain said.

Already the level of the water had begun to mount the bridge; the slant had become so great that it was scarcely possible to stand upright.

"She'll go down in a rush, when she does," the captain said. "We'll be sucked right under."

He spoke in the detached informative manner of a schoolmaster instructing a class.

"We'll be sucked down, then thrown up wide. The great thing is to hold your breath."

Roger listened calmly. Of certain things he was afraid, of being made to look ridiculous, of being unable to look any man between the eyes. Of those things he was afraid. Those were of the things that shamed a man, that diminished a man's stature. But death could be a gallant episode. Unmoved he stood there, with the wind cold and spasmodic on his cheeks and the sun warm upon his neck, waiting for the sudden lurch that should spill him into that gray-green coldness.

It came, as the captain had told him that it would, without warning. A lurch, and the water from the lower deck had risen, and the great carved mermaid upon the poop had curved above him and down, down, down he was plunging into the gray water, with his ears singing and his eyes a mist, with a stinging pain in his wrist and a numb throbbing at his knee; with his lungs strained, and only the captain's warning to stay him from the gasp for breath that would have sent him down, down and beyond recall into the gray forest.

Down, down, down, with the pain in his wrist and knees increasing; with the throbbing growing intenser in his ears; with his eyeballs stinging, and the strain on his lungs intolerable. Down, down, down. And even when the interminable descent was ended, when slowly foot by foot he began his slow rise to the surface, even then he could scarcely believe that his limbs would have the power to carry him to the blue-shot grayness above his head. Up, up, up, with scarlet lights flickering before his eyes, with strange sounds beating upon his temples, with his lungs taut like a strained silk that must surely snap. Up, up, up, and when at last he had come to the surface with daylight before his streaming eyes, when his lungs could let loose their burden of stale air, and inhale the fresh, sun-baked air, even then it was only a second later to be hit sideways by a gigantic wave that stunned, choked, smothered him so that he staggered up blind and spitting water.

"I've got to be careful, very careful," he thought, "if I'm to come through this."

Close to him was a piece of driftwood, the lid of an oak chest; desperately he swam to it, caught it, and held it close. Then he looked round.

Thirty yards away the *Bordelais*, its keel, foul-barnacled and lifted above the water, was lying on its side. The proud swan that had withstood so many tempests was submerged already. The mermaids, whose shapely breasts had inspired so many ribald pleasantries, were no longer supporting but diving head foremost from the bridge. Its captain, who had stood for so many hours rooted there, was in the water a few yards from them. His head was held high above the water, but he seemed to be making no effort either to conserve his life or to end it. He gave the impression of being content to swim till his strength failed him.

"He's a man," thought Roger. "Nothing worries him."

And gathering into his voice all the strength of which his lungs were capable, he shouted through the gale.

"There's room for two here," he yelled. "Swim over if you can. There's just a chance for us."

The captain made no reply, but with slow, unhurried strokes he paddled his way across to Roger. Then hooked his arms over the wooden plank. Neither he nor Roger spoke a word. They knew, both of them, that the betting was against their reaching land. But there was in their hearts the resolve to reach it and the knowledge that their two lives, for worse or better, were now one. They struck out towards the shore.

Five hours later, cold, bruised, and hungry, they lay at the edge of the palm-fringed beach.

Showing through the stems of the trees was the outline of an occasional hut. The Spanish raids were recent and many. Cayona had not yet become the dissolute and prosperous town that the lessening of Spanish power was to make it. Nobody lived upon the beach except the few old traders who were too old to fight or hunt, who kept stores where rum and clothing and ammunition were for sale, and with whom foreigners bargained for the wild bull-skins whose stripping and dressing was the chief peaceful occupation of the buccaneers.

§

It was to a strange group that Roger and the captain were to ally themselves.

From many countries, from many stocks, from many ways of life they had come, these derelicts of seven nations, to achieve in their exile an indistinguishable similarity of appearance. They wore a common uniform, a little close-fitting cap, a jacket of cloth with breeches that came half-way to their knees. One had to look carefully to tell whether this garment was of cloth, so stained was it with blood. They wore a belt, set with a bayonet and four knives. Few of them were taller than their musket. On their feet, like the Indians, they wore moccasins, made out of ox-hide or pigskin. As soon as the animal was dead they would cut away the skin that had covered the beast. Setting the big toe where the knee had been, they would bind it with a sinew. The rest of it was taken a few inches above the heel and tied there till the skin had dried when, having taken the impress of the man's foot, it would keep in shape.

They had neither family nor children. There was scarcely a woman on the island. Each was constrained to take one of his fellows to himself, to help him in the ordinary business of life, to tend him when he was sick. They lived together sharing their possessions; he who lived the longer inheriting them. They shared their work. The one would hunt while the other would protect the hut and cook.

Food was plentiful in Tortuga. There was a profusion of fruit, of yams, pineapples, and bananas, and on the mainland there were herds of wild boar, and flocks of pigeons which in certain seasons of the year were admirable, but after the season, because they fed on a bitter seed, were as rough as gall upon the palate. They ate uncouthly; turning their pigs on a spit above an open fire, which they called a *boucan* and which later was to lead to their nickname *boucaniers*, which the English were to mis-pronounce buccaneers; in the same way that the French were to miscall the English freebooters, filibusters.

Dark-skinned, with long beards and bristled hair, they lived in amity for the most part, breaking out only occasionally and under the influence of drink into wild tempers that would end in duels; content to have found a place where they could conduct life as they pleased, living quietly when they chose, till restlessness or a longing for adventure spurred them to the high seas, to plunder.

It was to this rude society that Roger and the captain found themselves admitted.

Membership for the resolute was easy. They built themselves a hut. In exchange for their work they earned the knives and muskets on which sustenance depended. In the same spirit that they had brought the ship from Magellan over the Equator, so now in silence did they set themselves about the construction of their new life. They rarely spoke to each other. They exchanged no confidences. They never referred to the mutiny; to their homes; to their ambitions; to their dreams. They never wondered how chance had dealt with their shipmates. No two men could have known less of one another, divided as they were by thirty years of life and a long cycle of experience. But they drew comfort, a deep strong comfort from each other. They were happy, as they sat silent over their pipes after a day of hunting; with the air cool after the long day's heat; the moon silvering softly the metallic palm fronds; and in their ears the murmur of the savannahs. They drew peace from each other's presence. They were fretful in each other's absence, as though they were incomplete, as though a part of themselves was not there.

Sometimes they would go down to the beach, when they had skins to sell and the need for raw liquor was upon them. There would, usually, be another *boucanier* or two down there. For a day or two days, sometimes a week, they would stay drinking till the last remnants of their six weeks' work were squandered. Sometimes when they were drunk they would grow quarrelsome, but never with each other. For the most part they were content to idle in a warm content; watching with faculties made sharp by alcohol, the changing lights and shadows on the blue-gray water; dozing now and again; waking with replenished thirst; breaking periodically into song. Occasionally, when the gathering was large, there would be recited earlier adventures; raids upon the Spanish mainland; expeditions as far as Carthagena. Sometimes there would be talk of the countries their youth had known.

"Tell me," would ask one of them, "what is England like?"

A dark-skinned, rough, bearded figure would shake his head.

"It's so long ago," he would say. "I left when I was a boy. It was a gentle country as I remember it. With the sun not too hot; and faint mists covering it; with rain so soft that you scarcely knew it was rain. Then there were hills, with the grass so smooth that you would think it velvet, hills that as children we used to slide down. At the top of the hills there were round ponds where the sheep would drink."

At which some fellow would sway drunkenly to his feet, maintaining that he was English, too, and that England was not in the least like that; that England was a cold country; with a fine

cold air that set the blood racing through your veins; that it was
bleak with gray skies and hills and narrow gorges up which you
saw the great clouds riding; and the rain dashed into your face,
stung you, and made you feel a man; and if anyone said England
was not that, then he was no Englishman and he would fight him.
And knives would be jerked out from the ox-hide belts, and only
the superior force of their companions would keep blood unshed.

But for the most part, the reunions at Cayona were pacific.
And it would be with empty pockets, glad hearts, and heavy heads
that Roger and the captain would retire to their cabins and their
log fires, and gorgings of roasted pig; to the days of hunting and
the evening meal; to the long silences under tropic stars; to the
tropic rain with its steady drum-beat upon the hard surface of the
plantain, to the swish of the palm frond in the wind; to the bi-
monthly visit to the coast; the heavy drinking there; the bargaining with traders; the quarrels hastily made and hastily patched up;
with now and again restlessness and the love of danger sending
them to meet danger across blue seas.

And so the days went and the weeks and months; and the years
along with them. They lost count of years, and they lost count of
time. They judged the hour of the day by the sun's height and
the sun's heat. They spoke of wet seasons and of dry. Sometimes
the old captain would feel pain and stiffness in his limbs, but it
was many years since either of them had looked into a mirror.
There were no women whose grace and suppleness could remind
them of youth's ebbing; whose fading beauty could speak to them
of the transitoriness of things. They knew nothing of what was
happening outside their rock-girt island. No rumor reached them
of Cromwell's attempt to capture San Domingo for the Commonwealth. When they went roistering across the windward
passage, the sound of English voices and the sight of English uniforms in Port Royal did not tell them that to a great future a great
bulwark had been set. The fact that it was less often Spanish and
Portuguese than Dutch, French, and English vessels that they
plundered held no clue for them to the decline of Spanish glory.
They had no means of knowing that the New World that had
made Spain's greatness had at the same time overthrown it; that
the fabulous riches of the Caribbean had made Madrid confuse
wealth with bullion; that the wars for free thought had set Eu-

78

LOVE AND THE CARIBBEAN

rope at the throat of the Pope's attempt to divide the new world
between his chosen peoples; that the policy of Richelieu had prevailed; that the Sun King's glory had risen glamorously above
Versailles. They did not realize that soon at Utrecht piracy was
to be legitimized; that the spoil that had been wrung from Spain
was to be divided among her plunderers. They did not know that
the West Indies had become an organized source of wealth that
was to feed Europe for two centuries; that their island was the
last stronghold of outlawry in a sea that had been the home of
outlawry; that earnest letters were being addressed by colonial
governments to colonial secretaries, nor that three hundred years
later the students of colonial history would find state papers
riddled with references to their adventures. They believed the
world to be as ignorant of them as they were of the world.

If Roger had been told on the morning that he set out with
the Brethren of the Coast for the Spanish mainland that the
month was May and the year 1665, the information might as
well have been given him in Chinese.

It was a raid, very like the dozen others in which from time to
time Roger and the captain had taken part.

In spite of their lawlessness, the Brethren of the Coast showed
in regard to one another a very precise observance of the law.
Their motto was "no prey, no pay." The articles of their code
established the principle of equality. Each brother was entitled to
a vote on matters of policy and to an equal share of the plunder.
An exact scale of penalties was agreed upon. Death was the punishment for the brother who brought a woman in disguise on
board. Whoever stole from a comrade had his ears and his nose
slit and was disembarked on the handiest strip of beach with no
other provision than a fusee, some shot, a bottle of gunpowder,
and a bottle of water.

In the same spirit were indemnities agreed upon. For the loss
of a right arm a brother was recompensed with six hundred
piastres or six slaves. A left arm or a right leg was valued at five
hunderd piastres. A finger or a toe was worth one slave. The
hauling down of the flag on a hostile ship was rewarded with
fifty piastres, and there were such innumerable minor bounties
as the five-piastre reward for the throwing of a hand-grenade over
the walls of a besieged fort.

There was little variety in the general strategy of a raid. There was a privateer to be boarded; a town to be descended on; a garrison put to the sword; churches to be plundered; cellars emptied; girls ravished; old men tortured till they divulged the hiding places of their neighbors' gold; a final ransom to be levied; with the holds full, a sailing back to the taverns of Port Royal. In retrospect one raid seemed very like another.

This one, too, would have, had not the corpses left behind on the swampland of Maracaibo numbered the shrivelled frame of the old captain.

With a heavy heart for all the plunder he had brought back with him, Roger set his face towards Tortuga. He had no stomach for the riots in Port Royal with which his companions would swill and wanton away the rewards of courage. While they caroused there with dark wenches in the wine shops he remained on the ship alone, abrood upon his past. He wondered how he would maintain life now that his old friend was gone. He would have to make some new friend, he supposed. But he felt old and opposed to change. The captain and he were used to one another. They knew each other's ways. It would be hard to begin afresh. When he returned to Tortuga he handed his share of the booty to the trader with whom he transacted the majority of his bargains.

"You can credit me with that," he said. "I'll be coming down to drink it away in a day or two."

He was too tired and too heartsore to take any interest in the local gossip that they brought him. A new governor had been appointed to Tortuga, they informed him, a man called D'Ogeron. Roger shrugged his shoulders. What was D'Ogeron to him?

He could not have been expected to see in D'Ogeron's appointment the first serious attempt of the French Government to regulate and regularize West Indian trade. The appointment had been made in much the same spirit as Elizabeth's appointment of Kildare three-quarters of a century earlier to the governorship of Ireland. D'Ogeron for twenty years had been a *boucanier* in the Caribbean. Since all Tortuga could not have ruled him, there was a chance that he might rule all Tortuga. When the trade with the French Antilles was handed over by Colbert to the Occidental Company, D'Ogeron was its choice. It was a sound choice. D'Ogeron was practical, hard and middle-aged. He knew the material with which he had to deal. The *boucaniers* as far as they trusted anyone, were prepared to trust him. Roger, as their spokesman, explained the situation. They were French, nine-tenths of them. They were ready to admit the suzerainty of the King of France. But they had fought for Tortuga before anyone in Paris had realized that it existed. They had made favorable trading treaties with the Dutch. They proposed to keep in force those treaties, Paris or no Paris. If France chose to protect them, they would acknowledge the suzerainty of Louis. More than that Paris could not expect.

The gist of this, in more diplomatic language, D'Ogeron set out in a despatch to Colbert. Colbert, reading it in his large study three thousand miles away, shrugged his brocaded shoulders. Provincials and Colonials, they were all the same, he thought. They just would not realize that the King was France; that Paris was the King's home; that the departments and the colonies existed so that the glory of the Sun King should shed its gathering radiance over Europe. Colonies existed as aids to the royal debts.

Colbert did not think it necessary to explain this to D'Ogeron. D'Ogeron would learn that soon enough on his own account. D'Ogeron did.

The *boucaniers* were not forbidden to trade with Holland; but as any Dutch vessel visiting them was considered contraband by the French Marine, their freedom to trade with Holland profited them little. Still, as long as enough ships came into the rock-girt harbor, they did not mind what flag they flew. They explained as much to D'Ogeron. He thanked them for the explanation.

D'Ogeron was ill at ease. "The matter about this place," he thought. Then paused. There were so many things that were the matter with it. From the beginning it had been a mess. The Spaniards had been too thorough.

The Indians had been, D'Ogeron was ready to concede, a hopeless people. What could you do with a race that had been trained through centuries to believe in happiness and freedom? They were well out of the way, no doubt. His task was simpler now that, what with suicides and *autos-da-fé* and deaths from weariness in the mines, there remained scarcely a trace of the two million original inhabitants of the island. The Africans who had been brought from the Guinea Coast to exchange the freedom they had enjoyed in their native land for the Christian gospel of personal salvation were a far more satisfactory race. At the same time, D'Ogeron insisted, the Spaniards need not have been quite so thorough. The Indians, for instance, who had escaped from the mines and taken refuge in the hills, might surely have been left to starve. It had really been rather unnecessary to import blood-hounds to chase them down. The hounds had certainly done their work. But the result of their efficiency was that a century and a half later the savannahs of San Domingo were populated with a vast progeny of wild dogs with a fancy for human flesh. After dark one's life simply was not safe.

"Suppose," D'Ogeron suggested to his second-in-command, "that we were to kill a number of horses, fill their carcasses with poison, leave them about and let the dogs eat of them and die."

The second-in-command nodded his head. A number of horses were slain and their intestines poisoned. The savannahs were thick with stiff and groaning hounds. But even though one horse might account for a hundred dogs, the process was too slow. The dogs bred faster than they died.

"The only way to get rid of them," said D'Ogeron, "is to culti-vate the entire island until there is nowhere for them to hide. This place is underpopulated."

"We want women," said D'Ogeron, "white women."

He explained this in his next despatch to Paris.

It was not an impossible request.

At the time black slaves were not the only human cargo shipped to the sugar islands. White men in return for a free passage signed on as *engagés* for three years. Their treatment when they arrived was in some circumstances considerably worse than that meted out to slaves. The employer knew that he only possessed the *engagé's* services for three years. He was uninterested in his subse-quent future. He made the most of his three years. A number of the *boucaniers* were escaped *engagés*. If men could be persuaded to come out, surely, thought D'Ogeron, women could. It was most necessary that the island should be populated. Women from Europe might domesticate certain of the *boucaniers*. "I will fetch chains from France for the fettering of these rascals," was the way he put it. He did not ask that the women should be beautiful, virtuous, or well-bred. He merely asked that they should be capa-ble of childbearing and unscathed of pox.

D'Ogeron got his women; fifty of them; shipped with a cargo

of claret from Bordeaux. When he saw them his heart sank. They were the gleanings of the sorriest stock in Paris. They had been little enough to look at when they started. Now, after six weeks on a two-hundred-ton trader, for the first fortnight of which they had been profoundly sick; during the last month of which they had itched with scurvy; during the last fortnight of which they had been sunburned, so that the skin on their cheeks and noses had begun to peel; during no period of which they had attended to their personal cleanliness; after six weeks of discomfort, of dirt, of unwholesome food they looked in their tawdry, draggled finery infinitely less appetizing than the erect, firm-breasted Negro women who had gathered on the quay to watch the unloading of this unusual cargo. They were women and they were white. But that was the most that could be said for them. D'Ogeron was not the man to make the worst of a bad job, however. He did his best to cleanse and decorate his cargo; then sent messages to Tortuga.

Five hundred or so of the *boucaniers* came over. In a mute, suspicious group they stood glaring at the nervous, simpering but hard-eyed, hard-mouthed group that had gathered on the veranda of the Governor's house.

"My friends," said D'Ogeron, "with great courage and with the cherishing kindness that distinguishes their sex from ours, these gracious ladies having heard in their country, which is your country, too, of your hard and lonely lot, were moved with compassion and have come across these many miles to share and make sweet that loneliness for you. As you see there are fifty here. Each has consented to take unto her from among your number a husband whom she will obey and honor. It is fitting that the choice should be made not by her, but for her, and by you. So, as there are more of you than there are of them we have agreed that those of you who wish shall draw lots among yourselves as to the right and precedence of choice. I am confident, as a consolation for those who will be disappointed in the fall of the lots, that the example of these brave ladies will not be overlooked in France and that in a few months others will have come to follow them."

And he looked blandly and encouragingly at the half-circle of surly, bearded faces.

Roger in the center of the group, as the group's spokesman, made no comment. He did not know that the idea particularly pleased him. Still, if wives were going, he had better have one.

When D'Ogeron had finished, he moved his glance along the row of women who flanked the Governor. Slowly his eye travelled along the line. The woman on whom his glance settled finally was by no means the youngest of the group. Long ago such beauty as she may ever have had had left her. Her body was plump and loose. Her cheeks were flabby, and her mouth was lax. But there was a friendliness in the straight, level look of her hazel eyes. Roger had a feeling as his eyes met hers that they talked the same language, he and she; that each knew what the other was about; that similar streams had brought them to this fair island. By no means the best favored, she looked the likeliest to suit him. With a clatter he brought the butt of his musket on to the gravelled path.

"The others can draw lots or not draw lots as they may choose," he said, "but that's my woman there."

He pointed proprietorially at the smiling, limp-lipped woman.

D'Ogeron had expected and was prepared for some such outburst.

"If the lot falls to you to choose first," he said, "this lady will certainly be yours to choose. But in the meantime we had better draw the lots."

"The lots," said Roger, "may go to hell. That is my woman."

"It is possible," said D'Ogeron, "that one of your friends may have contracted a similar predilection."

"Then if any one has they can contest her with me." And he swung round, a burly, strong-shouldered figure, with his head flung back and his eyes blazing out of his lined face. There was a murmur and a movement, but no protest among his fellows. He was their spokesman and, as far as they admitted one, their leader. He had the right to the first pick. There were forty-nine left anyhow for the rest of them.

"So that's that," said Roger. And on the veranda of D'Ogeron's bungalow, he swore the marriage oath of the Buccaneer; the oath that from history's dawn had been sworn by the outlaws, the Bohemians of life, to one another.

"I take thee," he cried, "without knowing or caring to know who thou art. If anybody from whence thou comest would have had thee, thou wouldst not have come in quest of me. But no matter. I do not desire thee to give me an account of thy past conduct, because I have no right to be offended at it at the time when thou wast at liberty to live either ill or well according to thine own pleasure, and because I shall have no reason to be ashamed of anything thou wast guilty of when thou didst not belong to me. Give me only thy word for the future. I acquit thee of the past." Then with a heavy clatter he smote the palm of his hand against the barrel of his musket, brandishing it above his head. "This will revenge me," he cried, "of thy breach of faith. If thou shouldst prove false this will surely be true to my aim."

§

It turned out better than D'Ogeron, when he had looked at his motley cargo, had dared to hope.

To those who were prepared to undertake the duties of a plantation the Compagnie Occidentale was prepared to make certain loans, to be paid back out of the plantation's revenue. Roger was persuaded by his woman that this was a sound proposal. With the proceeds of the raid on Maracaibo that he had deposited with the Tortuga trader, a supply of slaves was bought. In the flat plains behind Port de Paix, he set himself to the task of creating a plantation.

The first, the Homeric period of the Buccaneers was over.

From Tortuga during the next decades would set forth the expeditions of which two and a half centuries hence, wide-eyed European schoolchildren would be reading. Thence would Morgan set out to Carthagena and to Panama. The great era of piracy was yet to dawn. But Roger, who had been the forefather of that era, who had endured the difficult and cruel days, was to hear vaguely in his bungalow in the Plain du Nord, the rumors of those engagements. The white fetters from France were about his neck. He was to beget children; to gather wealth; to see the founding of a name that was to be famous through a famous island.

He did not pride himself on the achievement. It was wealth that was easy come by. He happened to be in the lift when it was going up. Such credit as there was, was due far less to his efforts than to those of the hazel-eyed woman for whose sake he had beaten the palm of his hand against his musket.

She was the most, or to be more exact, the first efficient person he had ever met. She had a passion for organizing expenditure. To Roger money as a thing in itself had never been real. You acquired it, masses of it, on a raid. You anchored off Port Royal. You drank and wenched and most of it got taken from you. Then you went back to your savannahs; you roasted pigs; you shot bulls; you dried their skins. On the beach of Cayona they made some calculations on a sheet of paper; they handed you some rum and some ammunition. You supposed it was all right. That was how Roger had seen money. He could not understand these rows of figures that impassioned his wife so fiercely.

For hours she would sit calculating the price of slaves, the food of slaves, the clothes of slaves, and the number of francs they gave you for rum and sugar in Port de Paix. It meant nothing to him.

"Then in that case you can leave everything to me," she said. "Otherwise you'll never become the rich man you're going to be."

She explained to him at great length the extent and nature of his future riches. She was always explaining things to him. He had no idea that anyone could be so voluble. He never done much talking. During his years on Tortuga, he had averaged ten sentences a day. Sometimes he would talk a little more. Usually he would talk considerably less. He could not understand why people should want to talk except when they had something definite to say. Animals didn't. They could neigh if they were frightened or cold or amorous or hungry. Otherwise they kept quiet. He couldn't think why human beings should not as well. If there were no other sounds; no wind in the banana plants; no ripple of water on the beach; no drum beat of rain upon the palm fronds; no sound of crickets in the fields; then it might be companionable to hear the sound of human voices, occasionally. But when there were so many other things to listen to, he did not see why human beings should add their noises to the universal orchestra.

As the years passed, he often found himself regretting the still evenings when he and the captain had sat side by side on the doorstep of their cabin silent for hours upon end. He was philosophical about it. Men solaced you mentally; women physically. You couldn't have a thing both ways. And at least his wife left him to himself. She was content enough that he should spend the days riding round the plantation, supervising the work desultorily. He was happy doing that. He loved riding slowly with the sun hot upon his back, through the long fields of sugar-cane, to the cocoa-covered hills where the red flowers of the immortelle protected the young shoots. He loved to watch the Negroes move along through the lines of cane, cutting at the green spears with their long, rounded knives; and the women, with their skirts tucked up above their knees, treading the cocoa seeds, polishing them with their hard-soled feet.

His happiness was at its height during the season of the sugar crop. It was a happy time. Even the most meager of the Negroes looked healthy when once the mills were set, not for that but for the thick, drained juice that Negroes sweated in the fields and boiling houses; the thick and golden juice that time would mellow and ferment into that magic potion that could cure all griefs and heighten every happiness.

His love of wine was the sole issue that ever disturbed the harmony of his married life. His wife liked rum; unquestionably. She was in that respect appropriately companionable. But she was more interested in money than in rum. And as the price of sugar was considerably higher than the price of rum, she would persist in an attempt to improve and increase the output of sugar, even if it meant injuring the rum. She would, for instance, suggest that the skimmings should be sent back to the clarifiers instead of to the still-house; and when it was very pertinently explained that the rum crop would thereby be reduced by a third whatever the corresponding gain in sugar, she had the effrontery to suggest an increase of the amount of dunder which would doubtless affect the flavor of the rum but would restore the bulk.

On that point Roger was very firm.

"My rum shall not be interfered with."

"But it shan't," his wife explained. "Not yours, at any rate. That rum's for sale. None of it shall come into the house. We will have some especially good rum laid down for you."

But Roger shook his head.

"No," he asserted. "No. It's too great a risk. You never know where you'll end if you start monkeying with liquor. I'm not even sure that it isn't a mistake to use just skimmings. I'm not sure we shouldn't use the cane juice itself."

On that last point, Sara was able to dissuade him.

"It would be too sweet, very much too sweet," she explained. But as for the skimmings . . . well, if he insisted. Gracefully but reluctantly she yielded.

He patted her affectionately on the shoulder. Take it for all in all, she was an admirable wife.

His only real source of worry was his children. They were daughters which was in itself a disappointment. He would have liked a son. All the same they had been rather appealing when they were young. They were like puppies, affectionate, helpless things that needed you. It was a pity they could not have remained like that. So soon they became self-willed, self-important persons with ideas and ambitions of their own.

It was their ambitions that Roger found particularly galling. The elder of them, Claudine, had very grand ideas. She had had them from the moment she could speak. On her fifth birthday she demanded a slave for her private use. At seven she began to criticize her home.

"It's a pity we're so poor," she remarked one day.

Her mother bridled.

"We're not poor."

"Then why do you and father wear such shabby clothes?" She eyed her parents contemptuously.

"At Everard's home," she said, "they have silver knives and forks."

At the age of ten she became dissatisfied with the actual fabric of her home.

"You say we are not poor, and yet we live in a wooden house. All my friends have stone houses."

Her mother was, on this point, inclined to agree with Claudine. She examined her accounts and decided that a limestone house was within their means.

It was a decision that for a year added little to Roger's comfort. The wooden bungalow was consigned to a mulatto overseer. And a large stone house was built, with a courtyard and an imposing gateway. It was draughty in the wet season and very hot in August. The immense mahogany table that ran down the center of the dining-room was profuse with silver. At one end of it sat Sara, very fashionably and uncomfortably clothed after the manner of the French ladies of the court. Across the other end of it Roger reclined negligently in an open-necked shirt and sleeves rolled above his elbows. The long table was the one thing in the new house of which he thoroughly approved. It was so long that conversation was impossible.

For the most part he ignored his family. Their demands for a higher social standard he accepted in the same spirit that he accepted the irritating sallies of a mosquito. They could give their parties if they chose. But on the whole he was definitely relieved when Claudine announced that she was going to marry an officer in the French Marine and return with him to France.

The nuptials were amply celebrated. Sara wept copiously.

"We shall never, never see her again," she said.

"No," said Roger, "I don't suppose we shall."

He had hoped that life would be easier with Claudine away. It wasn't much.

His second daughter, Averil, had very similar ideas to her sister. There was the same talk of clothes, of parties, of the right thing, and the right people. Roger supposed that it amused them. He was content enough as long as they left him quiet.

One day Sara came to him in an agitated state.

"Averil," she announced, "is going to have a baby."

The announcement quite interested Roger.

"I wonder if it'll be a boy," he said.

It was rarely that Sara got annoyed with Roger. This was one of the occasions on which she did.

"That isn't the point."

"Isn't it?"

"Of course, it isn't. The point is that the young man's got to marry her."

"Who is the young man?"

"André Gastoneau."

Roger ruminated.

"Is that the weak-looking young fellow with too much money, who was sent out here because Paris had got too hot for him?"

"That's it."

"But she can't possibly want to spend the rest of her life with him."

"It's not a question of what she wants. She's got to marry him."

"I don't see why."

"Roger, don't be dense."

Roger shrugged his shoulders.

"Oh, very well then. Have the young fellow up for dinner."

It was a good dinner on which Roger concentrated in whole-hearted appreciative silence. He did not speak till the last dish was cleared away. Then he turned to his black butler.

"Have my pistols brought in here, and that priest."

To the astonished young man upon his left he explained that there was going to be a marriage ceremony. The young man was too astonished to protest.

"You can make your home here if you like," said Roger, when the service was at an end.

History proceeded to repeat itself. Roger's grandchildren were very like his children. They were boys, that was the only difference. The younger, Edouard, was well enough. He seemed happy, pottering round the plantation, talking to the Negroes and overseers, going down into Port de Paix to chatter with the sailors in the bars. But the elder, Louis, was a combination of his mother and his aunt. He had the same grand ideas.

§

To Roger life seemed little different from what it had been a generation back. Sara and himself were a quarter of a century older. There were two young boys instead of two young girls. Of his son-in-law the climate had taken speedy toll. There was, in Averil, an extra woman, but that was all. In just the same way that his aunt and mother had, Louis, seated half-way down the long table, looked with disgust at Roger's open shirt. He had persuaded his grandmother to dress reasonably. She had not, in fact, needed very much encouragement. He wondered how soon he would be qualified to take his grandfather in hand sartorially. "I must wait," he thought.

He waited till his eighteenth birthday. It was then through his grandmother that he approached him.

"Couldn't you do something about grandpa's clothes?" he asked.

There was to be a party on the occasion of his birthday. It was most important that his family should not be a discredit to him.

"He just can't sit down to dinner like that, can he, Granny? And he could be made to look quite presentable. He's not bad looking. Couldn't you persuade him?"

Sara was more frightened of her grandson than of her husband; reluctantly she set about her task.

"We're having a dinner party for Louis's birthday," she explained. "It will be rather an occasion. They will all be coming in elaborate clothes. We were afraid that if you came in those clothes, you would feel out of things. You would, now, wouldn't you?"

Roger fixed her with a slow, long glance.

"No," he said at length.

"But you'd be happier, surely, looking like everybody else."

"Why?"

A helpless expression came into her face.

"Please, darling, please," she said. "If only to please me."

He nodded his head. If she put it that way, all well and good. But if she imagined this decorating business was going to be any fun for him——

"Darling," she said, and kissed his forehead. "Now it would be best, wouldn't it, if we asked Louis what he thought about it."

It was the cue Louis had been waiting for. He was fecund with suggestions. He knew exactly the shade of green that his grandfather needed; the type of stocking; the pattern for the brocaded waistcoat; the buckled shoe.

Roger listened indulgently. Sara had let him have the kind of rum he wanted. She was entitled to make him wear the kind of clothes she wanted. He surrendered himself into her hands.

As a result of that surrender, he found himself a week later in a collar that was stiff and tight against his throat; in padded clothes that weighed upon his shoulders; in pointed leather shoes that pinched his toes; seated at the head of a long table with a comely, soft-scented, languid-eyed woman on either side of him; with Sara, extravagantly coiffed and extravagantly clothed, seated at the other end. In between them was a row of elegantly attired men and women. More glasses and more knives than a whole ship's company could need were set in front of him. Behind each chair stood a white-coated, bare-footed figure. His plate had been piled high with food. His wineglass sparkled. He drank two glasses hastily, but they left him in much the same condition that they had found him.

He tweaked the calf of the nearest servitor.

"Bring me some rum, quickly."

Warm, sweet, mellow on the tongue, it flowed reassuringly
along his veins. He felt better after that. First the lady on his
right, then the lady on his left addressed a series of remarks to
him. The remarks did not seem to call for any particular answer,
so he made none. The ladies turned away and began to talk to
the men on the other sides of them. There was a great volley of
talk, swelling, loudening and softening like the sea on a fair day.
As half a century back he had lolled in his cabin listening to the
sea, Roger sat now in his high armchair, savoring content.

Every few minutes the white-coated Negro at his side set some
fresh dish in front of him. He had never imagined there could be
so many varieties of food. They could do what they liked to his
plate as long as they replenished his glass at seemly intervals. He
would have been very happy had not the collar been so close
about his throat, nor the coat so heavy on his shoulders, nor the
shoes so tight about his toes. He was very hot. The sweat ran in
long streams down his cheeks. Most of the guests were in a
similar plight. The faces of the women were scarlet. Each man's
forehead was beaded heavily.

"I wonder if their feet hurt as much as mine do," he thought.
Had he been less stout he would have bent down and flicked
them off.

Interminably the meal ran its course. There was a scraping of
chairs. The women rose to their feet. Roger at the head of the
table remained seated. He always remained seated at the table.
He did not like drawing-rooms and padded chairs. He liked to
lean across the table on his elbows, a glass in front of him, a
decanter at his side, and sit there brooding till he fell asleep and
his servants carried him upstairs to bed. He always felt easier when
Sara had left the room.

"Take off my shoes, there's a good fellow, Jean," he said to
the Negro who was filling up his glass.

He felt happier when his feet were free. Then he broke the
clasp of his collar and eased his throat. It was only the heaviness
of the coat that irked him. The room was cooler now that the
women were away. He leaned forward on his elbows, the glass
clasped between his hands. From the end of the table came a
murmur of talk, like a tide ebbing. He dozed a little, to be aroused
by the tap of Louis's hand upon his shoulder.

"Grandpa, hadn't we better go into the other room?"

Roger blinked at him uncomprehendingly. To leave the table. What an extraordinary suggestion. Yet it was very clear that Louis was not joking. There was almost a critical expression on Louis's face.

"We should join the ladies."

"Why?"

"It's late."

"Is it?"

Roger could not understand what had occasioned the solemnity in his grandson's face. If Louis wanted to go, why shouldn't he. But there he was pleading fretfully for his grandfather to accompany him.

"We can't stay here for ever. And we can't go without you. You must see, surely."

Roger did not see. He grunted and leaned forward on his elbows. Louis left him. Presently the murmur of talk at the end of the table ceased. He leaned his head forward on his hands, and snored.

Next morning, Sara explained to him the enormity of his conduct.

"You shamed us all. It was Louis's birthday party. We had some very smart people here. People who've never been to the house before. Who'd come all the way from Dondon. Particular people, too, who know the way things should be done. And what do you do? Take no notice of the ladies you're sitting next; not address one remark to them the whole evening. And then, when we'd left the room, you sit there at the end of the table and get durnk; leave the men to come in by themselves and never say good-bye to a single guest. I felt so ashamed. Now, next time, to please me, you will, promise me you will, do better."

She explained in detail in what way she expected him to improve.

She repeated her explanation in greater detail a month later on the second experiment in entertainment.

It was an August day, hot and airless. Nightfall brought no breeze with it from the hills. Roger eyed with misgiving the clothes that had been set out for him. He lifted the coat. It was very heavy. He ran his finger meditatively round the collar. He held the waistcoat up against the window. There was a moon. But no light shone through the opaque fabric. He edged his foot into the pointed, buckled shoe. He had been riding all day. His feet were swollen.

"Oh, what the hell!" he thought. He had not lived all this while to wear clothes like that.

Quietly and breathing softly he tiptoed down the stairway; made his way round to the stable; mounted his unsaddled horse.

A tide of peace flowed about his heart as he saw the lights of Cap François twinkling round the bay. From the waterfront the guttered street ran straight and narrow to the hills. It wasn't much of a place. No one lived there whose job and income did not force him to. There were lawyers there and traders and officials; the houses were for the most part owned by half-castes and "poor whites." Still there were sailors and a number of taverns where the rum was good. With his arms bare, his shirt open at the throat, he sat, his legs thrust out in front of him, breathing slowly the warm, fragrant air.

A couple of sailors were lounging over an adjoining table. One of them was supporting in his lap the head of a comely mulatto girl. It was very like one of the taverns in Marseilles. However his life had gone, it would have finished up, he supposed, in some such place as this. With the half of his attention he listened to their talk of ships and seafaring. For an hour or so he sat there, brooding. Then a hand fell upon his shoulder.

"They were worried up there about you, Grandpa. I was sent to look for you."

It was Edouard, whose social equipment was not yet considered adequate for a large party. In his young, handsome, proud-held head there was a nervous look.

His feelings for his grandfather were of mingled respect and awe. They had seen extremely little of one another. Edouard was uncertain of his reception.

He need not have been. His grandfather signed to him to take a seat, had a glass brought up, and filled it half full of rum. For half an hour or so they sat in silence. Then Roger turned to Edouard with a smile.

"This is nice," he said. "We must come down here again."

Edouard's heart beat with pride. His grandfather was a hero to him. Already the *boucaniers* of Tortuga had taken their stand in history. The world was becoming too well policed for that earlier empery. The successors of Morgan were for the most part brutal and callous cut-throats hiding in whatsoever secluded bay they might chance upon. They had scattered, some of them to the Gulf of Darien; others to Terra Nova and the north; there were those who had gone east as far as Madagascar. Roger belonged to the Homeric days. His grandson honored him.

"You must have had an exciting time, Grandfather, in those old days," he said.

Roger pondered. Exciting? Well, he supposed it had been if you chose to look at it that way. But he had an idea that life in the end amounted to much the same. You had too much of a thing or too little of it. You were either on the Equator, with the sweat running down your face and the fo'castle too hot to sleep in; or you were soaked with Antarctic seas, shivering with cold, with your food sodden, and sleep only possible in uncertain snatches.

For days on end you would be cruising in the Caribbean, tacking to desultory July winds, bored, weary, listless. Then suddenly you'd sight a sail; you'd give chase to it. There'd be the noise of cannon and the clash of steel; the sockets of your arms would ache with fighting, so that you could cry with the pain of it.

For weeks on end you wouldn't see a woman; the thought of women would run maddeningly, inflamingly through your brain; then there'd be a sacked city; and suddenly half a dozen exquisite creatures would be yours for the taking, but with yourself so full of liquor that you could scarcely deal satisfactorily with one of them. Too much of a thing, or too little of a thing. Whatever the framework of your life, that was the way life went.

"You must have enjoyed life in those days, Grandfather," his grandson was repeating.

Roger shrugged his shoulders. Yes, perhaps he had. He had found life pretty good all through. But perhaps those days in Tortuga had been his best.

"They weren't bad," he said. "We wore a pretty comfortable kind of shoe."

The Black Republic

from HOT COUNTRIES

WRITTEN IN 1929

W<small>HEN I TOLD MY FRIENDS</small> that I was going to Haiti they raised their eyebrows. "Haiti," they said. "But that's the place where they kill their presidents and eat their babies. You'd better buy yourself a large-sized gun."

I did not buy myself a gun. It is those who go through the world unarmed who stand the best chance of passing unmolested. But it was certainly with the feeling that drama and adventure awaited me that I saw from the deck of the *Araguaya* the blue outline of the Haitian Hills. I was familiar with Haiti's story, a long and dark story—so long and dark that no historian can trace to its certain source the river of black merchandise that flowed during the early years of the eighteenth century to the slave factories of the Guinea Coast.

In large part it was composed, that merchandise, of weaker tribes that had been subjugated by their neighbors. There were, however, others of a different caste: proud princes of Dahomey taken in battle, in raids instigated by the slave traders—the conditions of slavery had made highly profitable the spoils of war— men of authority, used to the dignity and exercise of power; men of war, fearless and skilled in battle; the best that Africa could produce; fitted to match a colonial civilization that luxury and easily come-by wealth had weakened; men who were to write Haiti's history.

During the latter half of the eighteenth century and the early

95

years of the nineteenth, pamphlet after pamphlet, debate after parliamentary debate, expressed the horrors of "the middle passage." But the clearest picture of slave conditions that I have seen is to be found in a small handbook, published in 1811, on the treatment of Negro slaves. [*I very foolishly did not take a note of the publisher of this book and have not been able to trace it.*] It was written for the young planter, and was not unlike those tips for the newly joined subaltern that were issued in the war. It consisted of practical advice. The anonymous author regarded the Negro as so much machinery for the management of estates. His concern was the development of that machinery to the highest level of efficiency. One of the early chapters describes the treatment necessary for slaves on their arrival. He assumes as a matter of course that for days they will be unfit for work. They will be sick, weak, poisoned. He catalogues the diseases from which as a result of their journey they are likely to be suffering. They will need very careful treatment. He presents his facts without comment: he accepts the conditions as a matter of course. He intends no criticism; the criticism that is implicit in that acceptance is a more potent witness than the statistics of a thousand pamphleteers.

To those who are interested in the question of the slave trade that handbook is an invaluable informant. Its argument that the slaves are the most valuable part of a plantation is usually overlooked by those who dilate on the cruelty of plantation life. A Negro was worth between a hundred and a hundred and fifty pounds. One does not by wanton cruelty lessen the value of one's property. On the well-run estates the Negro was happy and well cared for. He had his own hut, his own garden, whose produce he could sell and from which he could make enough to purchase his freedom if he cared. His old age and his children were provided for. The Negro would show her babies proudly to her master. "Good nigger boy to work for Massa," she would say. There were a number of suicides, but that was due to the Negro's belief that when he died he would go back to Africa. In some plantations you would see cages containing severed hands and feet. This was not a warning of future punishment; it was a proof to the Negro that though the gods of Africa might be able to transport to Africa the bodies of the dead, they could not transport the limbs that the white man had cut off. "Do you want," said the planter, "to go home without hands and feet? Why not wait till you die of old age and can return there complete; for I shall certainly cut off the hands and feet of every one of you that kills himself."

There were punishments, and brutal punishments, but they were used in an age of punishment, when the flogging of sailors and soldiers was regarded as a necessary piece of discipline. Examples had to be made in a country where the white man was outnumbered by the black in the proportion of ten to one. The catalogue of punishment that Vassière has patiently amassed would make the Marquis de Sade envious. Such punishments, however, were exceptional. Bryan Edwards was of the opinion that the condition of the slave in the West Indies was no worse than that of the European peasant. Nor, though he suggests that the avariciousness of the French made them overwork their slaves, did he consider that the French planters were any less considerate to their slaves than the Spanish or English were.

Two facts, however, contributed to make San Domingo a more likely stage for disturbance than Barbados and Jamaica. The first that the French, though good colonists, are never really happy out of France. The second that the French system of the kept mistress led to a far more rapid growth of the mulatto class in San Domingo than in the English islands. The French never made their homes in the West Indies. They lived in large houses, in conditions of great luxury, attended by many slaves; but their halls were bare. They had no fine furniture, no pictures, no rich brocades. It was not worth the trouble, they said. They were there for so short a time. Their talk was of France; of their last visit there; of how soon they could return. Their one object was to live in Paris on the profits of their estates. And it was on the estate supervised, not by the owners but by overseers, that the atrocities were committed. It was the absentee system that was responsible for the barbarities of West Indian life. There were many such estates in San Domingo.

There were also the mulattoes. They were rich; they had been educated in Paris; they were numerous. By the end of the eighteenth century a tenth of the French part of the island was in their hands. They had a grievance. In spite of their numbers, their riches, their education, they were allowed no voice in the government of their island. They could occupy no official position. They could get no redress from justice when they were assaulted or insulted by the *petits blancs,* the clerks and adventurers, the registrars of estates, dissolute and incompetent, whom the mulattoes knew to be their inferiors, whose acquaintance they would have derided in France, but who here could order them and outrage them because of that quartering of savage blood.

Nowhere was the color line drawn more strictly than in Colonial France. Color precluded a man from every right of citizenship. Nowhere were the distinctions of color defined more exactly. Moreau St. Méry has catalogued the two hundred and fifty different combinations that interbreeding may produce. The man who was four-fifths white was incontestably superior to the man who was three-quarters white. But as long as there remained a drop of colored blood a man was debarred the rights of citizenship. The mulattoes were very conscious of their grievance. They were rich; they were educated; they were well-bred; they carried in their veins the blood of the oldest families of France, of the healthiest and handsomest of the imported Africans. The half-caste is usually despised because he is a mixture of bad blood, of bad black and of bad white. The mulattoes of San Domingo, however, combined the best of France with the best of Africa—a mixture to which most of what Haiti has achieved is due. Such men found intolerable the insults of the *petits blancs*. In Paris they were respected; why should they be despised in their own country?

Many were the complaints that they addressed to the French Government. But the French Government, blind though it was to the interests of its colonists at many points, supported them in this. "The color line," insisted the Whites, "must be maintained. We are outnumbered by the Blacks in the relation of ten to one. We must uphold our prestige. We are superior to the mulatto. And by refusing to countenance the claims of the mulatto we must keep this fact before the Blacks. Our prestige once lost, we should be powerless." The Government upheld its colonists.

It was, however, one of the few points in which it did. The Creole Whites had grievances. In the same way that the English Government had regarded its American colonies as nothing more than a profitable source of revenue to itself, so did the bureaucrats of Paris enforce harsh and tyrannical regulations on its colonial trade. Produce might only be carried in French ships and to French ports. Duties were levied at excessive rates. The planters grumbled. Everyone was grumbling. Everyone had a grievance of some sort.

Then came the revolution.

The story of those early months are too confused to be told in *précis*. To be understood they must be read in some such detailed study as Lothrop Stoddard's. In Paris there was a government that changed its mind only less often than it changed its leaders, that sent out commissions and recalled them, that imprisoned the colonial representatives as traitors, that one month passed an Act abolishing slavery and the next repealed it. There was a society called *Les Amis des Noirs*, very few of whose members had ever seen a Negro, demanding the cancelling, with every distinction of class, of Moreau St. Méry's two hundred and fifty carefully compiled distinctions. There were the absent French owners, suspect as aristocrats, asserting that only on the old color basis could the allegiance of the colonies be maintained, and Robespierre thundering back that it was better to lose a colony than a principle.

In San Domingo there were the planters, several of them aristocrats by birth, all of them aristocratic by sympathy, terrified at the thought that everything they had believed in was being taken from them: the constitution and the King of France, the tradition of colonial rule, the bar of color. There were the bureaucrats sent out from France, ignorant, prejudiced, distrustful of everyone who sympathized with the old *régime*. There were the *petits blancs*, a worthless and crafty lot, knowing that there was nothing for them to lose, trusting that any commotion might be turned to their advantage. There were the mulattoes supporting the National Assembly, believing that at last they were to be recognized as their fathers' children. And there were the slaves, stupid and misinformed, vaguely aware that there was an idea about that they should knock off work.

A confused and hectic story, with the planters gradually losing faith in the French Government, deciding, with the example of the American colonies before them, on independence, appealing to the English to protect them; with Paris losing interest in its colonies; with the slaves rising and slaughtering their owners; with the mulattoes desperately appealing to the slaves to combine with them against the Whites; with English troops occupying Port au

Prince and the Môle St. Nicolas; and the Spanish pushing across from the west into the plain of the Gonaïves, and every man's hand against his neighbor's.

A confused and hectic story, from which emerges finally the figure of Toussaint l'Ouverture.

Few people have received more extravagant adulation. Certainly he was a remarkable man. A self-educated Negro, he was carried by circumstances on the crest of a mounting wave. From the leadership of a band of insurgent slaves, he was swept to the generalship of an army. He drove the English out of San Domingo, annexed the Spanish section of the island, defeated the mulattoes of the south who had risen under Rigaud, in protest against black domination, and declared himself dictator. Then, with peace established in two years, he restored the island to something of its former prosperity. He returned the Negroes to the plantations, and under the ruthless supervision of his generals restored a condition of industry unapproached during the days of the French planters. He was a remarkable man. But it is only the light of history falling upon him from a certain angle that has made him appear a hero.

Because he was self-educated, he has been called a genius. Because he spared the master who was kind to him he has been called human. Because he drove the English out of Haiti he has been called a patriot. Because he restored prosperity to the island he has been called a statesman. Napoleon's treatment of him has made him an object of pity. He was captured in a time of peace by treachery, shipped and left, the liberator and preserver of San Domingo, to die in a dark cell, without trial, in France.

That is one side of the picture. There is the other. Toussaint was the descendant of an African prince. He was born with the power to rule, with intelligence to develop his capacities. In time of revolution, for a man of force the stride is a short one from corporal to general. Toussaint was a good soldier, with the power to command. There are no signs in his character of any particular nobility. A great many Negroes saved their masters. The Negro is generous and remembers kindness. Toussaint was not trustworthy. He went where his interests led him. He was concerned with one thing only: the freedom of the Blacks. He began by fighting for the Spaniards. Then, on realizing that he would fare better with the French, he took his forces to the other side. During his long struggle with Rigaud he offered the island to the English in return for help. At the same time he was talking to the French of the *sotte crédulité* of the English. Neither side trusted him. After signing peace with Leclerc, he continued to plot against the French. He had to be got out of San Domingo; and Napoleon was practical. It was as well to let die in prison those who can do you no good and may do you harm.

Toussaint was a big man. But he appears important only because he was a forerunner; because Dessalines and Christophe followed him, in the same way that Marlowe's stature is increased by being the pedestal for Shakespeare. He did little more in San Domingo than Pélage did in Guadeloupe, and had Napoleon's expedition against San Domingo succeeded as rapidly as his other one against Guadeloupe, I believe that Toussaint would have seemed as inconsiderable an historical figure as Pélage.

Nor was it on account of Toussaint that the San Domingo expedition ranks as the chief failure of Napoleon's early career.

Fifteen years later at St. Helena Napoleon was to describe the San Domingo expedition as a great mistake. But at the time there were reasons enough for undertaking it. The Treaty of Amiens had been signed. He was at peace with Europe. He had sixty thousand troops that he would be glad to have out of France. San Domingo had been the richest island in the New World. He had need of money. The old proprietors in Paris were beseeching him to recover their possessions. The troops who had swept so easily across Europe and Egypt could surely cope with a brigand chief. There were reasons enough for believing that the expedition would succeed. And it might have done very easily.

As easily as did his other expedition to Guadeloupe. Side by side the two expeditions were sent across the Atlantic with similar instructions. The black leaders were to be cajoled, flattered, confirmed in their ranks; then when the French Army and French rule had been established the black leaders were to be returned to France; as prisoners if they had been obstinate, to serve in the French Army had they been obedient. To Guadeloupe he sent Richepanse; to San Domingo, his brother-in-law Leclerc, "a fellow almost damned in a fair wife."

Napoleon had planned the campaigns himself. In Guadeloupe

he was to succeed immediately. Richepanse landed, paraded the colored forces, complimented them on their courage, thanked them in the name of the Consul-General, explained that he wished them to board his ships so as to transport them further down the coast, marched them on board and into a hold, on which he closed the hatch. In a few hours Guadeloupe was his and Pélage on his way to France to serve in the French Army, to die in Spain, to pass out of history.

Things went less to plan in San Domingo.

And at St. Helena Napoleon was to blame himself. He was also to blame Leclerc. But the impartial historian can only reproach Leclerc with one real mistake, his attitude to Christophe, the general of the north. He might at one bold blow have taken Cap François, or he might by skilful diplomacy have overcome the black general. He delayed assault, however, and sent as an ambassador Lebrun, an ignorant, ill-bred popinjay who later, on a diplomatic visit to Jamaica, was so outrageously ill-mannered as to merit a reprimand from Nugent. It is hard to think how Leclerc could have chosen such a one as his aide-de-camp. Lebrun was handsome. Possibly he was Pauline's choice.

Christophe could have been won over. As it was, distrustful and offended by Lebrun's tactlessness, he burned Cap François and fled into the hills. By the time that he and the other generals had surrendered into the acceptance of commissions as French generals, Leclerc had lost half his men.

Even so, for the moment it looked as though the French had won. Toussaint had been shipped to France. Christophe and Dessalines were generals in the French Army; according to Napoleon's plan, they, too, should have been sent back. But fighting once started is hard to stop; the hills were filled with untamed brigands. Leclerc could not risk the loss of his troops in guerilla warfare. Bandits had to be set against bandits. Christophe and Dessalines were the only men that he could trust. He had to keep them on. "A little while," he thought, "a little longer. When the last brigand has been captured, then will I send Dessalines back to France."

But the dice were loaded against Leclerc. Long before the last brigand had been brought in, yellow fever, decimating his men, had broken out along the coast, and before the epidemic was at an end the news had come from Guadeloupe that slavery had been re-established there.

It was the news from Guadeloupe that decided the San Domingan expedition, decided by uniting with a common dread not only the black but the mulatto forces. Until then the black forces of San Domingo had consisted of three armies; the mulattoes of the south, the center under Dessalines, the north under Christophe. There had been no true combination. The generals had fought and acted independently of each other. Christophe had indeed made a separate peace with Leclerc. The news that slavery was re-established in Guadeloupe, with the certainty that it was the plan of the French to restore slavery in San Domingo, united the black forces. Christophe and Dessalines went back into the hills, and with them Pétion, the mulatto general who had been Dessalines' chief opponent in the early war.

For the next three years Dessalines' and San Domingo's become one story.

Today Dessalines is Haiti's hero. Streets and cigarettes are christened after him. His tomb is in the Champ de l'Indépendence. His statue faces the Chapel of Cap Haïtien. In Port au Prince it brandishes a sword in face of the green-roofed houses, the dim outline of Gonave. The visitor in Port au Prince will gaze wonderingly at that statue. He will scan the aristocratic, thin-lipped, straight-nosed face below the cockaded hat, and he will ask himself where in those bloodless features the signs of savagery are concealed. He may well ask himself. It was never for ungentle Dessalines that that mask was cut. It was ordered by a Central American president who was cast out of office before the statue could be delivered. His fall coincided with the arrival in Paris of a delegation from Haiti to commission a statue of Dessalines to celebrate the centenary of Haitian Independence. As there was a statue going cheap they took it. That was the way they did things in Haiti then. And, indeed, they might well have found a statue less symbolic of the tiger. As you sit at twilight on the veranda of the El Dorado, the outline of the cockaded hat and the thin curve of the brandished sword is dark and ominous against the scarlet sunset. They are the last things you see as the swift dusk settles on the Champ de Mars.

Today Dessalines' many brutalities are forgiven and forgotten.

There was much to forget and to forgive. In Haiti's blood-stained story he is the most ruthless figure. He was a great fighter and he loved fighting. As long as he was fighting he did not much mind whom he fought. As long as he was killing he did not much mind whom he killed. In the intervals there were women. But women were a side-show.

It is impossible to detect in his behavior a consistent policy. During the two years of Toussaint's pacific administration he drove his Negroes to work at the sword's point. During his war with Leclerc he butchered, because they were white, every Frenchman whose property lay across his line of retreat. As a general in Leclerc's army he was known as the butcher of the Negroes, and slaughtered with the liveliest ferocity a hundred blacks because a few French officers had been assaulted. The war he waged with the French when the news of French treachery in Guadeloupe was known is the bloodiest in history. Terrible things happened during those weeks when Leclerc, his body faint and his eyes bright with fever, wrote dispatch after dispatch to France, and Pauline dangled her pretty toes over the palace wall, her eye fixed broodingly on the green mangroves and the lilac outline of the hills, her ears avid for the caressing words of the young aide-de-camp beside her.

Darker things were to happen after Leclerc had sunk to death, after Pauline had sailed away to a less ill-starred marriage, and the fierce Rochambeau was left in charge of the French Army. On neither side was any quarter given; no refinement of torture was left unpractised. Rochambeau imported bloodhounds from Cuba. He prepared black dummies, their stomachs stuffed with food, with which he trained the bloodhounds to make always for the bellies of the blacks. The disembowelling of prisoners was the favorite Sunday afternoon amusement of the Creoles at Cap François. Lady Nugent's journal, in the intervals of deploring the moral lapses of the young Jamaicans, makes wistful references to the atrocities that were being staged four hundred miles away, while her husband was complacently informing Lord Hobart that the French would be unable to hold out—which was to the good, he thought. "We shall have nothing to fear from the blacks," he wrote, "provided we resume our former commercial intercourse, thereby preventing them from raising a marine. There are still chiefs of Toussaint's school. We should only have to play the same game as before between Toussaint and Rigaud to succeed as well in neutralizing the power of the brigands."

A few months later England and France were again at war. With the outbreak of war Rochambeau's last hope had gone. He could get no reinforcements. He could get no supplies. The Blacks were attacking him by land, the English were blockading him by sea. He made peace with Dessalines and, with the honors of war, delivered himself into English hands. [*It was at this point that Napoleon abandoned his plans for a colonial empire stretching up the Mississippi and arranged the Louisiana Purchase.*]

It is from this moment that Dessalines appears in his full stature. Over a distance of a hundred years one reads now with a brooding wonderment the story of the next two years. Say what you will of him, Dessalines was on the heroic scale. He was of the lineage of Tamburlaine. Though his speeches and proclamations were prepared doubtless by another hand, the voice of a conqueror rings through them. Each phrase is like the roll of musketry. There is the heroic gesture, a reckless arrogance of hate, in his tearing of the white from the tricolor and making the colors of his country red and blue; in his re-christening of San Domingo; in his wiping away of the last semblance of white rule in the new name, Haiti. He let Rochambeau go on Rochambeau's own terms. He signed the papers that they brought him. He promised immunity to the White Creoles. They could go or stay as it pleased them. They would be safe, he promised. Why should he not promise if it served his purpose? A good many promises had been made in the last twenty years. Had any of them been kept? With Rochambeau safely imprisoned in Jamaica, he would decide what it was best for him to do.

He decided quickly. The French had scarcely sailed before he was thundering out his hatred of those that stayed, before he had issued orders that none of those who remained should be allowed to leave. As the weeks passed his intention grew more clear. Edward Colbert, the English representative, was writing back to Nugent that he had little hope for their safety, and that Dessalines was counting his own departure as the signal for commencing the work of death. He had wanted to intercede for them with Dessalines, but "as their destruction," he wrote, "was not openly avowed by him, I was apprehensive that I might accelerate what I was anxious to avoid." He reports Dessalines' visit to the south.

"In his present progress through the southern and western parts of the island he is accompanied by between three and four hundred followers, the greatest part of whom have the appearance of being extremely well qualified for every species of rapine and mischief."

Colbert had prophesied correctly. Within a week of his return to Jamaica the process of slaughter had begun. Dessalines knew that as long as there was a Frenchman left in Haiti his position would be insecure. The total extermination of the French that he had planned was a task that he could entrust to no one else. From the south, through Jeremie and Aux Cayes, he marched north to Port au Prince.

"Dessalines arrived here on Friday afternoon," records a letter found among Nugent's correspondence. "Turned loose four hundred to five hundred bloodthirsty villains on the poor defenceless inhabitants. He gave a general order for a general massacre (strangers excepted)—in the original letter amusingly misspelled 'accepted.' I had five in my house. It gave me great pain to be unable to save a single one of them. They were all informed against by black wenches . . . the murderers are chosen by Dessalines. They accompany him from the south to the north. What havoc when they arrive at the Cape. The poor victims were slaughtered in the streets, in the square, on the seaside, stripped naked and carried out of the gates of Léogane and St. Joseph and thrown in heaps. A few days, I fear, will breed a pestilence. . . . Had you seen with what avidity these wretches flew at a white man you would have been astonished."

A few days later he was at the Cape. The massacre was carefully stage-managed. Guards were placed outside the house of every Englishman and American. It was the French only who were to be killed. For a day and a night the narrow, cobble-paved streets echoed with groans and cries. Then, suddenly, Dessalines grew weary. It was a waste of time breaking into houses, searching cupboards, dragging people from under beds. He announced that he would give safety to all Whites provided that they came into the square to testify their allegiance to him. One by one the terrified creatures crept from their lairs into the open. Dessalines waited patiently beside his soldiers till the square was full. Then he tapped upon his snuff-box. It was the signal for his men to shoot.

Next day he issued the challenge of his own defence:

"Quel est ce vil Haïtien si peu digne de sa régénération qui ne croit pas avoir accompli les décrets de l'Eternal en exterminant ces tigres altérés de sang: S'il en est un, qu'il s'éloigne de la nature, indignè de rependre de notre sein, qu'il aille cacher sa honte loin de ces lieux; l'air qu'on y respire n'est point fait pour ces organes grossiers, c'est l'air pure de la liberté auguste et triumphante. . . ."

In the constitution of Haiti was drafted the proud clause:

"Jamais aucun Colon ni Européen ne mettra le pied sur cette terre en titre de maître ou de propriétaire."

Four hundred miles away across the Windward Passage, Nugent, in the yellow-colored residence in Spanish Town, addressed Dessalines, whom he described to Hobart as the brigand chief, as "Your Excellency," and in the weary well-bred indifference of official English explained the terms on which Jamaica would be ready to trade with Haiti. Nugent had no doubt of what would happen. With a tired smile he listened to the accounts that came to him of Dessalines' extravagance, of the splendor and corruption of the court, of the troops encouraged to supplement by plunder a daily ration of a herring and half a loaf. Dessalines might declare himself an emperor. But the country was on the edge of bankruptcy. Dessalines might assert that Haiti, brown and black, consisted of one brotherhood. He might offer his sister to Pétion in marriage. But no declaration would convince the mulatto that he was not the superior of the Negro. No declaration would persuade the Negro to trust another Negro. The Negro could be ruled; on occasion he could rule. But he was incapable of co-operation, of rule by cabinet. When the news of Dessalines' murder was brought to Nugent—a murder, if not actually instigated, at least approved by Christophe—he was not surprised. He was not surprised six months later when history repeated itself; when the conflict of Rigaud and Toussaint, the conflict of brown and black that was to be the main issue in Haitian history for the next hundred years, had been resumed between Pétion and Christophe.

Christophe was Dessalines' second-in-command. With terror he had watched the gradual disintegration of the country under Dessalines, the disorganization of the troops, the emptying of the treasury, the abandoned plantations. What would happen, he

asked himself, when the French returned? Once the invaders had
been flung back. But Leclerc had advanced on a country prosperous and prepared by Toussaint's rule. What chance would a dis-
organized and impoverished country stand against Napoleon?
Haiti must be made powerful and rich, proud of itself, respected
by other nations. Dessalines stood in the way of Haiti.

Thus Christophe argued. He had no doubt of what was needed.
He had no doubt of his own power to realize those needs. When,
after Dessalines' death, representatives of the various departments
had met to draw up new constitutions, he was so sure that that
convention would place him with unlimited powers at its head
that he did not trouble to attend the meeting. He remained at
the Cape with the quick-brained little mulatto who was to be
raised to the dignity of rank under the title "Pompey Baron de
Vastey," planning the details of his campaign. He was the only
man in Haiti who could save Haiti; he knew that.

He had counted, however, without two things. One was his
own unpopularity; a year earlier Leclerc had written home that
Christophe was so hated by the Blacks that there was nothing to
be feared from him. On that he had not counted, nor on Pétion.

Pétion was one of the few with intellect in Haiti. He was the
son of a French artist and a mulatto girl. He was almost white; he
had spent much of his time in Paris. He had served in the French
Army and had studied in the military schools. He was mild and
sweet-natured, with a poetic mind. He brought with him to the
convention one firm resolution: that he had not driven out the
French tyranny to authorize another tyranny and a black tyranny
in its place.

Patiently, tactfully, diplomatically he argued clause by clause
the constitution that was to defend the Haitians' liberty and limit
the power of their ruler. It was no easy task. Sometimes, as he
looked round at that black semicircle of surly, stupid faces, a
feeling of discouragement came over him, a feeling of doubt.
"This is not really what I meant," he thought. It was something
quite other than this that he had planned. What was it that he
had planned? He had forgotten. It was so long ago. When one
was young one saw life in clear issues. Afterwards things grew confused. You fought for people with whom you were only three
parts in sympathy against people to whom with a quarter of your-

self you still belonged. You could never enter whole-heartedly
into any quarrel. There was always a part of you left outside. Just
as in life he had never anywhere been quite himself. Not here in
San Domingo, where his father had been ashamed of him; nor
in Paris, where they had pretended to ignore his coloring. Not
even in Paris among the young officers with whom he had joked
and drunk, with the woman he had loved. Always between himself and them there had been the veil of difference, this quartering
of savage blood. Never anywhere had he been quite himself. That
was the thing that he had dreamed of, that was the thing he had
fought for: a condition of society with which man could be in
tune, in which he could be himself. It was for that he was arguing
now in this hot room, to these ignorant savages. It was this he
dreamed of—a Utopia, where man could be off his guard.

Though even as he argued, his faith weakened in the thing he
argued for. They were not educated yet to democracy, these Negroes. Christophe would never accept these limitations to his
power. Later Christophe's indignant repudiation of the constitution came as no surprise to him. It was with no surprise that he
learned of Christophe's angry mustering of men, of his forced
march over the hills into the long, sun-parched, arid plain that
stretches from Ennery to St. Marc.

Without surprise, but wearily, Pétion heard the news. Wearily
and half-heartedly, he gathered together the remnants of the army,
marched out with it into the plain, to be flung back, wrecked and
scattered; himself escaping with his life and in the disguise of a
peasant woman, upon the outskirts of Port au Prince. A few hours
more and Christophe would be in the capital. Pétion, for one last
effort, gathered his strength together; with the hatred of the brown
for the black, with the hatred of brain for force, with the hatred
of breeding for unsponsored vigor, he mobilized his troops,
marched out with them into the plain and, employing fully for
the last time all that France and his father's blood had taught
him, he broke and dismembered Christophe's untutored powers;
broke them, scattered them; then let them go.

His generals turned to him with amazement. What, was he
about to let the tyrant free? Now, when he had him in his power,
when the whole of Haiti was his for the plundering! Pétion
shrugged his shoulders. That irresolution, that mulatto's doubting
of himself that stood always between him and real greatness,

mingled a little, possibly, with the poet's indifference, the poet's sense of the ultimate futility of all things, made him stay his hand.

Let Christophe, he said, go north beyond the mountains; the south was safe.

So Christophe went north to crown himself a king, and Pétion, in Port au Prince, drew up a constitution; a republican constitution with himself as president, and in Spanish Town, four hundred miles away, the Governor of Jamaica smiled.

It was less easy than Pétion had imagined. He needed money to strengthen his frontier against Christophe, to prepare his defence against the French. And Rigaud had come back from France. There was a year of civil war to empty the exchequer. An exchequer that it was impossible to fill unless the people worked. They would not work if they were not driven. He lacked the heart to drive them. In his way he loved them as they loved him; the simple people who laughed so readily, who would forgive you anything provided you could make them laugh. But to be loved was not enough when you were beset by enemies.

Pétion grew despondent. That doubting of himself—the mulatto's doubting of himself—and the mulatto's contempt and hatred of the Black, mingled with the mulatto's envy of the White, returned to him, making it easy for him to shrug his shoulders, to let things drift. Why worry? Why fight for a liberty that its possessors could not use? Let the Blacks go back to savagery. Why try to inoculate them with a sense of mission?

There was a sneer on his lips as he listened to the tales of Christophe that his spies brought to him. So Christophe was making a great man of himself up there! He had a splendid court and many palaces and counts and dukes and barons. He had a gold currency. And English admirals called on him. Professors came out from England to establish schools. The country was rich and that meant that the people of the country were enslaved. He smiled when they told him of the palace of Sans Souci. The Negro's love of vanity, he called it. They told him of the citadel above Milhot, of how the people of the plains struggled to carry bronze cannon up the slope. How when the slaves paused, panting at their load, Christophe would line them up, shoot every tenth man, with the remark: "You were too many. No doubt now you are fewer you will find it easier." Of how to prove his authority he would give his troops on the citadel the order to advance and watch file after file crash over the wall to death.

Pétion sneered at Christophe. What else could you expect from an illiterate Negro? How long did they imagine it would last? Tyranny had its own medicine.

He sneered, too, at the citadel. What was it, he asked, but an expression as was all else that Christophe staged up there, of the Negro's inordinate self-pride? What was the use of it, after all? It would be the easiest thing in the world to surround it, to starve it out. And as for all that gold stored there in its recesses, of what use would that be there? What could it buy but ransoms? Bullion was not wealth. One day he would take his troops up there to show what it was worth.

He never did.

Pétion was never to see the citadel. Never to see the sun strike yellow on its curved prow from the road to Milhot. But with the mind's clearer eye, the poet's eye, he saw it, and seeing it foresaw how that proud ship of stone would outlive the purpose it was built for, the imperial idea that it enthroned; would stand, derelict through the decades, to outlive ultimately even the quarrel so eternal-seeming of brown and black.

Today those pages of Vandercook's that describe all that Christophe achieved within his brief fourteen years of power read like a fairy tale. You cannot believe that *Black Majesty* is history, that one man, and at that a Negro, could in so short a time have done so much. You have to go to the Cape itself to realize that.

Milhot, from Cap Haïtien, is a half-hour's drive. It is a bad road through a green and lovely wilderness. You can scarcely believe that this bumpy track was once an even carriage drive, that these untended fields were orderly with care, that the crumbling stone gateways, half-buried in the hedge, opened on carefully-kept lawns, on verandaed houses, on aqueducts and sugar mills. Along the road passes an unending stream of women carrying, some of them on their heads, some of them on donkeys, bags of charcoal and sticks of sugar cane to market. They move slowly. The sun is hot. There is no hurry.

Milhot was once a pretty suburb of Cap François. It is now a collection of squat, white-plastered houses, the majority of them with cone-shaped, corrugated-iron roofs; looking down on them from the hills they seem like the bell-tents of a military encampment. Nothing remains of the old Milhot except the ruins of Christophe's palace. And of that, only the façade and the terraces are left. Goats and lizards drowse under the trees where the King delivered judgment. The underground passage to La Ferrière is blocked. The outhouse walls are creeper-covered.

At Milhot, at the police station, there will be mules or ponies waiting for you. Christophe's carriage drive to the citadel is little more than a mountain path. It is a hard two and a half hours' climb. You pass little along the way; a thatch-roofed hut or two from the doors of which natives will run out in the hope of selling you bananas; a gendarme returning from the citadel to duty; a Negro collecting coconuts. For a hundred years that road had been abandoned. The natives were frightened of the citadel. It was a symbol of tyranny. They could not be prevailed upon to go there. As the road mounts you have a feeling of Nature returning into possession of its own. The lizards are large and green that dart across the road, the butterflies brighter and more numerous, the birds that dip into a richer foliage are wider-winged. For ninety minutes you climb in silence. Then suddenly, at a bend of the road, you see high above you the citadel's red-rusted prow.

Words cannot describe the citadel. In photographs it would look like any other ruin. A motion picture camera, worked from a circling airplane, would give no more than an impression of it. To appreciate its meaning you have to come to it as they that built it came to it, with the hot sun upon you, with your back damp against your shirt, with the fatigue of riding in your knees, with the infinitely varied landscape before your eyes, with the innumerable jungle sounds in your ears, and in your nostrils the innumerable jungle scents. Then you can walk along the grass-grown courtyards, the galleries with their guns that will never fire, the battlements through the windows of which trees are sprouting; then you can realize the prodigious effort that the citadel's building cost; you realize that nothing that has been said of it has been an exaggeration, that it is the most remarkable monument in the modern world.

Pétion was envious. But Pétion was right. It could not last. As the months passed Christophe's tyrannies grew more barbaric. He trusted no one. He, in his time, had betrayed every one that

he had served. Toussaint, when he had made his truce separately
with Leclerc. Leclerc, when he had joined with Dessalines. Dessalines, whose murder he had plotted. What reason had he to believe that in just that way Marmelade and the rest were not
plotting against him in his turn. His cruelties increased with his
suspicions.

But the story of those last days has been already too well told
to need retelling here. Vandercook's *Black Majesty* tells all that
can be known of the tragic drama of those last hours, of the
trigger of the silver bullet pulled at length, of the mulattoes of
the south sweeping victoriously across the plain. There was to be
an end of tyranny. It was peace that had been fought for; it was
peace that was desired. If France wanted her six million pounds as
a compensation for taken property, as a guarantee of non-inter-
ference, as a recognition of Haiti independence, then let her
have them. Let Haiti be free and unfettered to rule itself.

Twenty years after the surrender of Rochambeau to the English,
peace was signed. For ninety years Hatiti was left to govern herself without white interference.

Bryan Edwards, writing of the Caribs in the Leeward Islands,
made this prophecy of San Domingo. "What they are now," he
wrote, "the freed Negroes of San Domingo will hereafter be: savages in the midst of society—without peace, security, agriculture,
or property; ignorant of the duties of life and unacquainted with
all the soft endearing relations which render it desirable; averse
to labor, though frequently perishing of want; suspicious of each
other and towards the rest of mankind: revengeful and faithless;
remorseless and bloody-minded; pretending to be free while groaning beneath the capricious despotism of their chiefs and feeling
all the miseries of sevitude without the benefit of subordination."

In 1830 Edwards was chastized severely by the *Quarterly Review*
for this prophecy. Forty years later, in part anyhow, it had been
fulfilled. Politically the story of Haiti is one of tyranny and mis-
management. Of the twenty-four presidents who held office, two
were murdered, one committed suicide, two died in office, two
only retired into civilian life; the remaining seventeen, with as
much of the national treasury as they could lay hands on, fled to
Jamaica. In 1907, when Kingston was badly mauled by an earth-
quake, the Haitians very generously dispatched a shipload of pro-

visions for the destitute, with a naïve letter saying how happy
they were to be able to do something for an island that had
shown so much hospitality to those of their own countrymen to
whom chance had been capricious.

The object of the majority of presidents—though there were
exceptions like Hippolyte—was to transfer as much of the national
revenue as they could to their pockets while the going was still
good. "Graft," an English Chargé d'Affaires wrote in his report
to the Colonial Office, "is the chief national pastime of the
country." In such circumstances, it is not surprising that the country slipped back into disorder. Houses and roads crumbled away.
God had spoiled the roads, said the Haitians; God would mend
them.

There was no organized industry. Nearly all the land was in
the hands of peasant proprietors. Coffee, which grew wild over
the hills, was the chief export. When the wind blew down the
pods the natives gathered them, put them on their heads or on
their donkeys, and carried them down to a middle-man, through
whom, by various stages of bribery, they reached the Customs
shed. No rich families needed to be supported from the land. All
that the land was required to do was to provide an export tax
high enough to support the expenses of government. That it was
perfectly capable of doing so has been proved during the American
occupation. It could not be expected to stand the strain of revolution, changing presidents, and corrupt officials.

Life in Haiti must, during those years, have been half comic
opera and half grim tragedy. During Spencer St. John's residence
as Chargé d'Affaires it had an army consisting of six thousand
generals, seven thousand regimental officers, and six thousand
other ranks. There was litle discipline. The sentries had chairs to
sit upon. Justice was casual. No prisoner had any right to be
considered innocent. The policeman's idea of arresting a man
was to hit him into unconsciousness with a *cocomacoque*, a large
iron-studded cane. Ordinarily the Negro, who has a great imita-
tive capacity and therefore a sense of precedent, makes an extremely good lawyer. But as judges were in Haiti appointed for
political purposes, instances would arise in court when, it being a
case of one witness's word against another's, the judge would turn
with a puzzled look towards the prisoner who was accused of theft
with no other testimony than the evidence of plaintiff: "But she

says she saw you steal her purse. You can't get away from that, you know." Inevitably, as the money destined for public works passed into private possession, the state of the towns grew fearful. There was no sanitation. It was maintained that the harbor of Port au Prince was half-choked with filth which could be smelled seven miles out at sea.

On the surface Bryan Edwards' prophecy was being proved correct. And the surface is about all that the majority of people who wrote of Haiti at the end of the nineteenth century ever saw of it. Like Froude, they read Spencer St. John's book, and landed in transit for a few hours in Jacmel or Port au Prince. Very often captains would not allow passengers to land. Haiti to the West Indian of that time was rather what the Russia of today is to the European. The Jamaicans were so desperately afraid that the Negroes of their island would follow the example of the Haitian that they leapt at any opportunity of exaggerating the condition of Port au Prince.

Very few of the visitors to Haiti stayed longer than their ship was anchored in the harbor. They never, that is to say, went into the country and saw the natives; nor did they in Port au Prince see anything of the Haitians themselves. Had they done so they would have learned two things. They would have learned that the peasant Negro under conditions of freedom is a far pleasanter person than he is in slavery; and the educated Negro, under conditions where he is not presented at every moment with the consciousness of his race inferiority, develops qualities for which you would look in vain among the rich Negroes of other islands. The Haitian peasant is a friendly and happy person, with no animosity to the Whites, with whom you can talk as freely as you would in Sussex with an English farmer. When it comes on to rain you can take shelter in his cabin and there will be no feeling of self-consciousness on either side, while in the towns there is a society of Haitians, the majority of whom have been educated in Paris, speak a pure French, are talented and cultured, with gracious manners and a gracious way of life. Haiti has produced its poets. I do not say that they are major poets, though Oswald Durand is unlikely to be forgotten, but the existence of poetry in a society is the proof of culture. I do not see how anyone who has been brought into touch with the Haitians on friendly terms can have failed to feel them to be superior to the Negroes of the other West Indian islands.

No one deplored more than the Haitians themselves the anarchy into which their country degenerated during the last twenty years of its independence. It was like a wheel going downhill: nothing could stop it. The country grew yearly nearer bankruptcy. Revolution followed revolution. No property was safe when the presidents were giving the order to their troops: *"Mes enfants, pillez en bon ordre."* The men in the country did not dare to come into the towns for fear of being conscripted into the army. The women who brought their produce into market were robbed by soldiers. The hills were infested by brigands. The public departments drew up schemes of development, but before these schemes could be carried out a new Government and a new set of officials were in control. As bankruptcy drew closer the certainty of white intervention grew more clear. Most of the securities of the country were pledged outside the country. America was only waiting for a convenient pretext. It came during the first year of the war when, with brigands' fires burning in the Champ de Mars, and after two hundred of the most influential Haitians had been slaughtered in jail without a trial, the body of the President was torn limb from limb by a maddened mob.

It is fourteen years since the American marines landed in Port au Prince, and during these years a good many writers have been to Haiti. Haiti has become news. There have been revelations about voodooism, and revelations about Congo dances, and it was, I suppose, in a mood of rather prurient curiosity that I sailed from Kingston on the *Araguaya*. I do not know quite what I had expected to find there: the primitive to the *n*th degree, I fancy, and I have little doubt that any one who took the trouble to make friends with the peasants could contrive to be initiated into some lively ritual. I am not sure that it was not with some such intention that I myself set out there. I had not been ashore five minutes before I had abandoned it. There is so much in Haiti that is more worthwhile.

I am not sure that I had not abandoned that intention before I had even landed. Port au Prince, as you approach it, is one of the loveliest towns in the New World that I have seen. It is white and green. The walls of houses and the twin spires of the cathedral gleam brightly through and above deep banks of foliage. The circling hills above them are many-shaded. It is through wide, clean streets, through the open park of the Champ de Mars, through a town that is half a garden, that you drive out towards the hills. It is a wild, untended garden. The houses that are set back from the road are wooden, two-storied, turretted, half-buried in the trees that shelter them. The roads linking the main streets are country lanes, rambling through shadowed hedges. You feel you are in an enchanted wilderness. There is nothing sinister. It is clean and fresh and green. It is everything that you expected it not to be.

There are slums in Port au Prince. Where are there not? Squalid successions of dust-covered cabins by the cockpits along the shore and on the road to Bizotin; shacks that can give you some idea of what the town must have been like before the American occupation. Once it was the dirtiest town in the Antilles; now it is one of the most attractive.

The Americans have done much for Haiti. They have cleared and laid out streets. They have made roads. They have built fine buildings. They have established hospitals. They have established order. They have wiped out the brigand forces. The men of the hills have no fear now when they come into the towns of being conscripted into revolutionary armies. The women know that they will receive in the market what their merchandise is worth. They will not have to pay toll to sentries along the way. Planters can breed cattle without the fear that they will be plundered by the *cacos*. And all this has been done with the surplus from the Haitian revenue, with the money that was before squandered in bribery. Haiti has become one of the most pleasant tropical places in the world. No island could be lovelier. Whether you are driving along the shore towards St. Marc or southwards to Aux Cayes, or whether you are climbing on horseback the hills beyond Pétionville and Kenscoff, whether you are looking across blue water to lilac-colored hills or looking down upon green valleys, you will be unable to find any parallel for that landscape. The climate is healthy; the healthiest in the Antilles, doctors say. There is plenty to do. There is reasonable bathing. There are horseback trips into the interior. There is the choice for the athlete of tennis, polo, cricket.

The atmosphere of Haiti is a combination of three things. There is the haphazard South Sea atmosphere of a simple, unex-

ploited peasantry living on its own land, working just so much as
it needs to support life; where there is no need to work hard if
your needs are simple. They are a happy and sweet-natured people.
You feel happiness as you ride past their villages, as you pass them
and are passed by them on the road. Where the streams run down
into the valleys you will find them in groups of six or seven seated
washing their clothes upon the stones; where the streams deepen
to a pool you will see them bathing, their black, naked bodies glistening in the sun. Every few miles or so along the road you will see
a woman with a tray and a few bottles, a wayside restaurant, where
the women will lower their loads from their heads or dismount
their mules and exchange the gossip of the hour. And always they
will smile friendlily at you as you pass.

There is a beauty in their little properties that you do not find
in the mathematically laid-out plantations. Stalks of sugar cane,
cocoa trees, and coffee shrubs trail side by side with mangoes and
bananas. You feel here the rich luxuriousness of tropic growth as
you will never feel it in Martinique. You feel that life is rich and
life is easy. That there is no need to worry much.

You will get the same feeling if you choose as your hotel the
wooden, two-storied house half-way up the hills to the American
Club that was the house, in earlier years, of a French admiral.
There is a long drive leading to the house, a drive that is grass-
grown now. Nor is there any fountain playing in the large stone
basin. Nor can you tell where lawn and hedge divide. But the
proportions of the house remain. The wide balconies, the spacious
courtyard, the cameoed picture through the trees of Port au Prince.
The rooms are cool and the cooking good. You never quite see
how things run themselves, for there never seem to be any servants.
And in the bar you will find the visitors at the hotel mixing their
drinks in such proportions as they choose; but things do run
themselves. Meals arrive, hot water arrives; in the end somebody
signs for drinks. At the end of the month a bunch of chits arrives,
and you have a pleasing sense of life crumbling round you like the
garden and house; but that it will last your time.

There is the South Sea atmosphere. There is also the French
atmosphere; a Parisian atmosphere of cafés and elegance and well-
dressed women. There is more grace of living, more culture in
Port au Prince than anywhere else in the Antilles. As you sit on
the veranda of the cafés in Port au Prince, or walk on the hills

in Pétionville, with its little green square in front of you, its church and *gendarmerie* and playing children, you feel that you might be in the heart of France.

Thirdly, there is America: the America of efficiency and wide streets and motor cars, and the feeling that always goes with them, that good though the past was, the best's ahead of us.

These three atmospheres are combined in Haiti, and when there is so much else to have, it seems a waste of time to set oneself the task of discovering the ritual of a religion that is based upon nothing but the superstitions of undeveloped minds.

At the moment Haiti is one of the world's pleasant places. No one can tell what the future holds for it. In 1936 the American treaty with Haiti will be reconsidered, and many assert that then the American occupation should end. (The American occupation terminated August 14, 1934; supervision of the customs ended in 1941.) In America, the same kind of person who in London asserts that the English should evacuate Egypt and hand back India to its princes, is claiming that America's interests in Haiti are an imperialistic violation of the Monroe Doctrine. While many Haitians contend that America has served its purpose: it has restored order, placed a balance in the Treasury; that it has started the machine, that the Haitians can now carry it on themselves. Having learned their lesson, they will be capable of administration; that if they are left with, at the most, a financial adviser they will be able to run their show.

They may be able to. It may be that they will be given the chance, that in six years' time there will be no khaki uniforms and broad-brimmed hats in Port au Prince. That once again a Negro people will be allowed to make the experiment of self-government.

And then . . . will history repeat itself? Will the *cacos* return to the hills? Will the road across the arid valley of Gonaïves crumble into a bridle path? Will the bridges justify the old complaint that it was safer to go round than over them? Will the peasant be afraid to come down into Port au Prince? Will the green lawns of the Champ de Mars straggle on to the puddled and untended roads? Will angry mobs shriek for vengeance outside the white palace of the President? Will the police with the *cocomacoque* batter the skulls of the suspected?

Sometimes one feels that Haiti is set surely now on the high road to prosperity. What else can you feel when you sit at twilight on the veranda of the Eldorado Café, looking on to the harbor, in which are anchored the ships whose presence there means riches, when Buicks and Pontiacs are sweeping with their broad beams the broad, smooth roads and the white buildings and the pretty women? Everything looks so secure, so confident, far too far down the road of civilization for anarchy. You think that then.

But you recall the hot and dusty mornings in the cockpit, where you have seen Negroes taking into their mouths the torn and bleeding heads of the dying cock, to suck and lick the wounds, in the desperate hope of restoring the will to battle to the beaten beast. You remember into what paroxysms of rapture and misery and wrath you have seen those black faces contorted as the chances of victory recede. You remember the hot-blooded passion of their dancing, their contorted bodies, their clutching fingers, the fierce luster in their eyes, and, remembering that, you wonder into what frenzies of savagery this people might not still be worked. You remember how, late at night, after the sounds of Port au Prince are still, you have heard in the hills the slow throbbing of the drums. It breaks the silence. It is slow, rhythmic, monotonous. It is like the beating of a heart, the beating of the black heart of Africa.

An Historical Synopsis

from THE SUGAR ISLANDS

When I first sailed for Martinique, I knew very little about the Caribbean. Before I had been there many days, I realized that it was impossible for me to understand its way of life until I had some knowledge of its history.

In 1947 the publishing house of Evans Brothers in England invited me to contribute to the Windows of the World *series of travel books, a book on the Caribbean. It was a short book, addressed to "the tourist, the intending tourist, and those who are forced for this and the other reason to travel in their memory and imagination. It is written for those who are interested in the West Indies, but possess no detailed or specialized knowledge of them. It is hoped that it will 'put them in the picture.'" In England it was called* The Sunlit Caribbean. *In America it was published as* The Sugar Islands. *Its second chapter was the following historical synopsis.*

WRITTEN IN 1947

THANKS TO THE GENEROSITY of the Carnegie Trust, most of the islands are supplied with excellent reference libraries, and it is easy for the inquisitive tourist to provide himself with a working knowledge of the history and present conditions of the group.

It is a long and tangled story; a story of courage and cruelty, of treachery and broken faith and high renown; so tangled and so long a story that no composite history of the Caribbean has been attempted. But, as the editors of fiction magazines know well, the most complicated narrative, the most intricate succession of inci-

121

dents and details can be resolved into a five-line synopsis, and the story of the West Indies is briefly this:

At the end of the fifteenth century Christopher Columbus, believing that the earth was round and in an attempt to find a western route to India, discovered a group of islands that, in the light of this belief, he christened the West Indies. In their attempt to exploit his discovery, subsequent European pioneers came into such conflict with the original inhabitants of the islands that within a very few years the Indians who had inhabited the northern islands and, a century or so later, the Caribs who had inhabited the eastern islands had been "liquidated." In the meantime, sugar cane had been introduced and, in order to supply cheap labor for the plantations, a slave trade with the Guinea Coast was organized. There followed a period of very great prosperity, when the phrase "rich as a Creole" was in daily use. Then "the conscience of mankind" was roused. The slave trade was abolished. The slaves were liberated. Cane sugar slumped. The islands, instead of being an asset, became a liability, a distressed area. [*A new phase has begun. Air travel has brought the Caribbean within easy reach of the winter vacationist and the Caribbean is enjoying an immense tourist boom.*]

That is the story in synopsis—a synopsis that may be amplified into four instalments.

There is the first period, roughly covering the sixteenth century, which is almost exclusively a Spanish period. During this period the Spaniards, having been granted by papal dispensation all the discoveries of the New World west of a certain line, colonized Hispaniola—the island which has since been divided into Haiti and San Domingo—Cuba, Puerto Rico, and Jamaica, exterminated the Indians, introduced sugar cane from the Canaries, and initiated the slave trade.

The second period, covering the seventeenth century, saw the gradual breaking-down of the Spanish monopoly. The French and English were in a position to challenge the Spanish Navy. The Spaniards, moreover, who had made the mistake as political economists of confusing bullion with wealth, lost interest in the islands on finding that there was no gold and silver there and moved farther west to Peru and Mexico. During this period the English captured Jamaica, the French captured the western and most fertile part of Hispaniola and called it Haiti, and the French and English occupied and disputed between themselves the chain of islands that stretches southwards between Florida and Demerara, exterminating in the process their Carib population. This period, which is the period also of the buccaneers, ended at the start of the eighteenth century with Spain's recognition of England's and France's conquests; the Treaty of Utrecht marking in 1713 the elimination of Spain as a monopolist on the Caribbean scene.

The third period, of the eighteenth century, saw the high-peak of West Indian prosperity. In its latter half there was much bitter fighting between the French and English. Some of the greatest and most decisive naval battles of all time were to be fought between Dominica and St. Lucia. Several of the islands were to change hands several times; cities were to be sacked and plantations burned. But war was not total in those days. War was the concern of the professionals, of the politicians and the chiefs of staff. Byron made the grand tour during the Napoleonic Wars; no one reading Jane Austen's novels would imagine that they were contemporaneous with Trafalgar and Waterloo, and, in spite of almost continuous war during the latter half of this period, there was no diminution in the general prosperity of the sugar islands. Actual statistics convey little; the value of sterling has changed so much; populations are so much greater. But the importance of these islands can be gauged adequately from the fact that, at the peace-making in 1763, England very nearly decided to retain Guadeloupe and return Canada to France as being of less account. It is indeed probable that during the Napoleonic Wars more British soldiers lost their lives in the West Indies than in Europe.

That third period ended or, rather, may be said to have begun to end with the French Revolution. By the time the Napoleonic Wars were over, the agitation against the slave trade had grown acute. The Spanish-American colonies were in revolt and the imperial policy both of France and England was turning southwards towards Africa and eastwards to the Levant and Orient. The red light was showing for the big plantations.

The liberation of the slaves ended the prosperity of the West Indies. The big landowners were compensated for the loss of their slaves, but most of the estates were mortgaged. The planters, instead of reinvesting their capital on the spot, returned to Europe, abandoning their estates to overseers who mismanaged them either through incompetence or on purpose so that they themselves might have an opportunity later of buying them at a bargain price. There were temporary recoveries and booms, but the descent was steady and grew sharper. Each time there was a slump, another group of estates was put upon the market, to be bought up by syndicates or split up among small proprietors. The large houses were left to crumble.

No new European colonists came out; one by one the colonists of purely European descent went home, and for those who remained the social line between those that were of pure European descent and those that had intermarried with Creoles of African extraction grew more and more difficult to draw. By the eighteen-forties the fourth period had begun; the period of decline, the period that has not yet ended.

The first and Spanish period is one of the least creditable in Europe's history. The aborigines of the northern islands, Hispaniola, Jamaica, Cuba, and Puerto Rico, bore as far as we can gather at this late day a strong resemblance to the Polynesians. They were of a clear brown complexion. They had straight black hair, broad faces, and flat noses; they altered the shape of their heads, depressing their scalps in childhood with a wooden frame, a procedure that so strengthened the skull that blows from a Spanish broadsword often broke the blade off at the hilt—a Spanish comment and complaint that provides a symptomatic testimony to Spanish treatment. By European standards they were not facially beautiful. But they had fine dark eyes and friendly smiles. They were tall, they moved gracefully, and every observer is agreed as to their attractiveness. Christopher Columbus wrote in his report to Ferdinand and Isabella: "So loveable, so tractable, so peaceable are these people that I swear to Your Majesties that there is not in the world a better nation nor a better land. They love their neighbors as themselves and their discourse is ever sweet and gentle and accompanied with a smile."

Something of their dignity may be gathered from the speech of welcome made to Columbus by one of the chiefs in Cuba:

"Whether you are divinities or mortal men, we know not. You have come into these countries with a force against which, were we inclined to resist it, resistance would be folly: we are all therefore at your mercy. But if you are men subject to mortality like ourselves, you cannot be unapprised that after this life there is another, wherein a very different portion is allotted to good and bad men. If therefore you expect to die and believe with us that everyone is to be rewarded in a future state according to his conduct in the present, you will do no hurt to those who do no hurt to you."

Everything that is to be read about these Indians reminds us of the Polynesians. They were unambitious, happy, and pleasure-loving. They supported themselves mainly upon maize. They had made no attempt to develop the resources of the soil, though they possessed some skill in the fashioning of domestic furniture, and made Columbus a present of some handsome ebony chairs. They would dance from dusk to dawn, often in large companies of many thousands. They amused themselves with a fiber football, which they kicked over their shoulders with the backs of their heels, maintaining it in the air for long periods. They welcomed the proud Spaniards as gods descended from the skies.

The Spaniards, however, suffered from the obtuseness of those who consider themselves a master race. They looked on the Indians as inferiors by whom they were owed, as a right, service and submission. They considered themselves, moreover, the subjects of a holy mission. They had crossed the ocean with great skill and courage, at considerable danger and discomfort, to spread the glory of Ferdinand and Isabella, to add to their Majesties' possessions, to acquire wealth, to preach the gospel, and to convert the heathen. Their first investigations convinced them mistakenly that the islands generally and Hispaniola in particular were rich in gold. It seemed to them only proper that the Indians should work for them in the mines; and their fury was limitless when the Indians failed to recognize their role of servitors, refusing to work, escaping into the hills, often committing suicide. Nor could the Indians be made to appreciate the application to themselves of the foreign creed which approved such practices and in which the Spaniards diligently and patiently endeavored to instruct them. When the Spaniards, in order to encourage the remainder to work and pray, roasted a few dozen over a slow fire, having gagged them first so that their screams should not disturb their officer's siesta, the survivors grew resentful, and whenever a bunch of them happened upon a solitary Spaniard, slaughtered him. The Spaniards thereupon ordered that for every European killed, a hundred Indians should be burned and disembowelled. It was all very much what was to happen in Europe four centuries later; only for the Indians there was no rescuing D-Day. But within twenty years the entire Indian population of Hispaniola had been wiped out.

How many Indians were liquidated during those early years it is impossible to assess. It has been said that there was originally in Hispaniola alone a population of two million. It is hard to believe that there were so many, and it is hard to see how this figure was arrived at, but there is much evidence to show that the islands were well-populated. Europe has often been criticized for the havoc that its traders wrought in the South Sea Islands, and there can be no question that the Polynesians, after receiving the benefits of Western civilization, deteriorated in health and morals. But everything that traders and missionaries did in the Pacific seems trivial in comparison with this extermination of an entire race. The only excuse that can be offered for the Spaniards is that, suffering under the delusion of being a master race, they did genuinely believe that salvation for the Indians could only lie through conversion to Christianity. It all happened, it must be remembered, in the days of the Inquisition. The medieval conscience was different from the twentieth-century conscience. One has to try to see historical events from the angle at which they appeared to contemporary observers.

A century later a similar fate was to befall, at the hands of the French and the English, the original Carib inhabitants of the Windward and Leeward Islands; but there the situation was somewhat different. In the first place, the islands were not nearly so densely populated. Barbados and Antigua are reported to have been uninhabited; and, secondly, the Caribs were a warlike race that was constantly raiding the northern islands and had possibly at an earlier period captured its own homesteads from the Indians. A few Carib settlements are still to be seen in Dominica. But the mild, dark-skinned, straight-haired creatures of today, who seem so out of place among the hardier Africans, are very different from the skilled warriors who resisted the foreign colonists. They were tall and brown, with shining, long black hair that they dressed daily with great care, and only cut short when they were in mourning. Like the Indians they altered the shape of their heads, but in an opposite manner—that is to say, by placing boards on the forehead and on the back of the head of the growing child, so that in adult life their heads had a box-like look. They scarred their cheeks with deep incisions, which they painted black. They also inscribed black and white circles round their eyes. They were beardless, removing all superfluous hair. Many of them perforated the dividing cartilage of their nostrils and inserted a fishbone or a piece of tortoiseshell. They made bangles for their arms and ankles out of the teeth of their dead enemies. Their children were taught the use of the bow and arrow by having their food suspended from trees out of reach, and having to go hungry till they could shoot it down. A boy before he was admitted to the rites of manhood underwent a cruel initiation ceremony. The Caribs were zenophobic and loved fighting. It was a long and bitter battle that they fought from their strongholds in the hills against the English and the French. In St. Vincent they were unsubdued at the time of the French Revolution.

This second period of West Indian history, during which the French and British divided the Windward and Leeward group, is in many ways the most romantic period of the four. It is this period that provides the material for all those serial stories of buried treasure and galleons stranded in the Sargasso Sea with which our boyhoods were entranced. To every young Englishman of spirit, the Spanish Main was a "finger beckoning to adventure." There was glamor there and danger and high reward. The Spaniards had made the usual "Whitehall error" of imagining that the lives of colonists living three thousand miles away and in the tropics can be ordered by minutes and memoranda drafted in city offices in a temperate climate. The bureaucrats of Cadiz insisted that their colonies should only trade with the mother country, and regarded as privateers the ships of all other nations. The colonists, on the other hand, were eager to welcome the Dutch, French, and English merchants who brought the goods on which their comforts and often their existences depended. It was in fact a "free for all." Every Englishman, Frenchman, and Dutchman was likely, if he were captured by the Spaniards, to be tortured and put to death. The Spanish Main was not only filled with pirates, waiting to pounce upon Spanish convoys, but with honest merchantmen trading from Bristol and Brest and Amsterdam, as well as with peaceful emigrants seeking "the land of opportunity." The *Mayflower*, for instance, had it been intercepted by the Spaniards, might have been regarded as a privateer. No Englishman knew what support he would receive from his own Government. He did not know if he would be treated as a patriot or a pirate. His position was that of an agent in the Secret Service, who is recompensed when he succeeds and unacknowledged when he fails. Drake was knighted. Raleigh was beheaded.

Nor had England, distracted as she was by civil war, any settled colonial policy. Vincent T. Harlow's book on Christopher Codrington gives a significant picture of the difficulties that a serious English administrator had to face during the French Wars at the end of the seventeenth century, when the soldiers' pay was six years in arrears and "colonial governors were required to enforce unpalatable laws while drawing inadequate salaries." It is remarkable that under such conditions the foundations of the British Empire were laid, that Jamaica was captured from the Spaniards, and that Barbados, Antigua, Nevis, Montserrat, and half of St. Kitts were colonized. As Harlow has said, however, "a defective machine works tolerably well in the hands of skilful mechanics," and in the Elizabethan and post-Elizabethan era many of the finest Englishmen in the country's history were seeking their fortune across the seas.

Vast fortunes were to be made during the next hundred years. It was only recently that Europeans had had an opportunity of enjoying warm, sweet drinks—until the seventeenth century they had subsisted on beer and wine—and there was an unlimited demand for sugar, for coffee, and for cocoa. The big landowners lived in state, attended by many slaves, entertaining in a Trimalchian manner.

The foundation of their prosperity was the slave trade. By the beginning of the eighteenth century, twenty thousand slaves a year were being transported to the British colonies in America and in the Caribbean. Bryan Edwards states that shortly before the American War of Independence the cities of Liverpool, London, Lancaster, and Bristol were operating in this trade alone a fleet of nearly two hundred vessels, with accommodation for fifty thousand slaves. Other countries were engaged as well, and British ships did not by any means trade only with British colonies. Forty factories, as they were called, were maintained on the coasts of Africa, of which seventeen were owned by the British and fifteen by the Dutch. It was estimated that seventy-four thousand slaves were shipped annually across the Atlantic. And it is important to remember the populations at that time were everywhere much smaller than they are today, the population of England and Wales being, in 1750, about six million!

Judged by contemporary standards, the slave trade cannot be regarded as anything but one of the most criminal enterprises that Europe ever undertook. It must be remembered, however, that no one at the time felt that it was wrong. Africans were apparently not considered altogether human, and in 1517 Las Casas, the Bishop of Chiapa, who was greatly shocked at the treatment the Indians were receiving in Hispaniola, proposed as a solution of the problem that each Spanish resident should be allowed to import a dozen Negro slaves. Later he was to regret this suggestion. But the fact that such a proposal was made by a good and holy man is an indication of the ideas prevalent at the time. African Negroes were looked upon as animal machinery; when there was a shortage of labor it was only good business to transport supplies of it.

The average man today is appalled by such brutally elementary logic. But it is well for us to remember that we cannot tell how posterity is going to judge our present actions. To very many people, at this moment of writing, the dropping of the atomic bomb on Hiroshima is ethically justified because it shortened the war and saved the million or so American and British lives that would have been lost in the invasion of the Japanese mainland. It is possible that different opinions will be held in two hundred years' time. And it is very necessary in considering the slave trade, of which present conditions in the West Indies are the direct consequence, to keep in mind the scope of the eighteenth-century conscience.

It is also necessary to remember that practically every account we have of the actual working of the slave trade is based either on the propaganda organized by the abolitionists or the defence put forward by the planters. The abolitionists argued their strong case well. Diagrams were produced showing how Negroes were packed close in holds, three feet high, without light or air or sanitation, their ankles manacled by chains that, as the ship rolled, cut into their flesh. Laid on their right sides to make easier the action of the heart, they were arranged in the fashion of spoons, the bent knees of one fitting into the hamstrings of the next. These gruesome diagrams were accompanied by telling descriptions of how the Negroes were nourished on rotten rice and tainted water; of how, though they were taken on deck each morning and soused with water while the holds were scrubbed, the stench grew so overpowering that "a slaver" could be smelt a mile away. Pamphlet after pamphlet has described the horrors of the "middle passage," maintaining that fifteen per cent of the cargo died on the journey over.

But when we read these pamphlets today and when we read the accounts of "the middle passage" that have been based upon these pamphlets, we should remember not only that these pamphlets were written with a propaganda purpose, but that the conditions in which the sailors of the Royal Navy then lived would today fill with disgust the sorriest slum brat. We should also remember—and this is a far more important point—that it was in the commercial interest of the captain and of the company which employed the captain to see that the cargo was delivered in sound condition. Real money had been paid for it at the factories. Unless real money were received for it at Cap François and Port Royal, the voyage would show a loss. The captain who did not earn a good profit for his owners would not be commissioned twice. It was in the captain's interest to keep his cargo healthy. It might, of course, be more profitable to ship two hundred slaves under conditions that killed off fifty than to deliver one hundred slaves in good condition, provided that the price on delivery was sufficiently higher than the factory price to justify a writing-off of twenty-five per cent as damaged stock. But the condition of the cargo was always of primary concern.

"The horrors of the middle passage" constitute far less of a crime against humanity than all that was involved by the factories on the Guinea Coast. There they were, those forty forts whose job it was to provide cargo for the slaver. Their presence on the edge of the bush was a constant incitement to crime, an encouragement and intensification of all that was most barbarous in the African. In their greed for Western commodities, the chiefs not only raided hostile tribes but even their own villagers. The companies that owned the forts did everything in their power to foment tribal wars. The factories along the Guinea Coast were far and away the worst feature of the slave trade.

We may assume that when abolition came, many slaves of the

first generation considered they had been better off when they were the direct responsibility of their masters.

Indeed, it is doubtful whether the poorer types of West Indian laborers are very much better off today than they were a hundred and fifty years ago. Harold Stannard wrote in *The Times* in 1938: "For most inhabitants of the West Indies life means work for a white boss at the subsistence level and has never meant anything else since the first Africans were brought over some four hundred years ago." In an earlier article he had written of the agricultural worker of Jamaica: "The first time I saw one of their hovels I could hardly believe that it was intended for human occupation. Strands of dried bamboo are woven round a framework of stakes and 'the room' thus formed is covered with palm thatch. There is no furniture except sacking on the earth and some sort of table to hold the oil stove. . . ."

"Urban conditions are," he continued, "if anything, worse. In a region of Kingston now marked down for slum clearance are shacks put together anyhow out of the sides of packing cases and sheets of corrugated iron."

In the same year a commission appointed to make an economic survey of Grenada wrote of the conditions there: "The housing of the agricultural laborer is disgraceful. It is impossible to use any other word to describe it. Houses little larger than small bicycle sheds are made of beaten-out Kerosene tins or old packing-cases. Others are made of pitch-pine specially purchased, but since there is seldom money to buy paint or some other preservative for the wood, it soon rots. Perhaps a better type of house is made of wattle and daub. They are said to be damp, but if they have board floors they are probably superior to the ordinary wooden house. . . . In this rickety structure miscalled a house the laborer and his family have to live. Sometimes the house is divided into rooms by a partition and old newspapers are eagerly sought after to stick on the walls. Very often there is only one room and in this room the laborer, his wife, and children, are crowded pell-mell. There is no privacy; baths and proper sanitation are absent. Usually there is only one bed (or what passes as such) and the children sleep huddled together on the floor. So far as possible every crack in the floor is stopped at night to prevent the ingress of mosquitoes, draughts, and 'evil spirits.' "

If one considers how the housing and general living conditions of the European laborer have risen during the last century and a half, it is very clear that there has been no proportionate rise in the standards of the West Indian laborer. I would recommend anyone who is interested in the subject to read some of the abolitionist tracts and speeches, to read "Monk" Lewis's *Journal of a West Indian Proprietor* and Bryan Edwards' *History of the British West Indies*, recognizing that both Lewis and Edwards were apologists; then to examine the conditions under which the poorer types of West Indian live today, assessing from that examination the progress that has been made since emancipation. He should then be able to form an opinion as to the extent to which the old plantation system was, in terms of the slaves themselves, practical and paternal and to what extent it was tyrannical, brutal, and corrupt.

I have dealt at this length with the plantation system and the slave trade because that system and that trade are the foundations on which present West Indian life is built. In that system and in that trade are inherent all the problems of today. Apart from Cuba, which has a population of four and a quarter million, the present population of the West Indies is about ten million. That population is increasing fast. Jamaica's rose by fifty per cent between the wars. The vast majority of these inhabitants, not only of the laborers and longshoremen, but of the planters and legislators, are partly at least of African origin—are the descendants, that is to say, of slaves. Emancipation took place little over a hundred years ago: the slave trade was started over four hundred years ago. It would be surprising if there remained no traces of a slave mentality, if those years of servitude had not left a legacy of suspicion and resentment; a legacy that explains the sullenness of expression that I had noticed on the faces in Martinique.

Nor is it surprising that I should have been conscious of the vast difference between the villagers of Martinique and of Tahiti. Tahiti was the home, had always been the home of a freeborn, liberty-loving people. The Tahitians have never been uprooted; they can still draw sustenance from the immemorial traditions of their race. The West Indians, on the other hand, are a mingling of a hundred tribes, a dozen races. The forty factories were scattered down the length of the Guinea Coast. The eighteenth-century planters recognized and appreciated the immense difference between one tribe and another. The men of one tribe would fetch higher prices than the men of others. The young planter was issued with manuals explaining how he could distinguish between one tribe and another and instructing him how to deal with each particular type. As far as possible, the planters tried to separate the different tribes on their estates. They were afraid that they might combine together and rebel. The planters did everything to break their links with Africa, to teach them a new language and a new faith. Old differences of tribe are now obliterated; a new language has been evolved by the natives out of their original African and the English, French, and Spanish that they have heard spoken round them. They think of themselves now as Barbadians, Haitians, or Jamaicans. But the difference of their origins is still marked upon their features. They are still a transplanted, an uprooted people.

There are other legacies as well of that original plantation system; two main legacies, I think, the first and the more important one being the inherent, hereditary laziness of the West Indian laborer. In quite considerable part, the decline of West Indian prosperity in the middle of the nineteenth century was due to the inability of the planters to induce the liberated slaves to work. For three hundred years the sugar estates had been run on a system of the laborer working under compulsion, with his old age protected and with private enterprise limited to the cultivation of his own small allotment. It is not surprising that the laborer of today, nurtured in that tradition, should be idle and improvident, and that consequently his standard of living should be so low and the profits on the estates so small.

That is the first legacy of the plantation system: that the laborer has not yet grasped the idea of working for a wage or planning for a future. The second is the color question which today through the whole group of islands is no less acute because it is nowhere honestly and frankly faced.

Color from the start has been a problem in the islands. Before the eighteenth century was far advanced, the rise of a mixed population had become a very serious consideration. For if the white overlord was the superior of the black man, through the mere fact of being white, then it must follow that a man who was half white was superior to the pure African. It also followed that the man who was half white was the superior of the man who was quarter white and the inferior of the one who was three-quarter white. Elaborate systems of protocol were devised and no one was more insistent than the members of the mulatto class themselves that these distinctions should be recognized and regarded. It is said today that the French do not draw a color line, but before the Revolution the French were even more "nice" than the English and the Spanish.

A people that has been brought up in such an atmosphere cannot suddenly lose their sense of color because some advanced thinkers in Bloomsbury and Greenwich Village have decided that racial discrimination is "all my eye."

I met during the First World War a man who had been born in the West Indies. A few years older than myself, he was tall and thin and handsome, and dark only in the way that certain Mediterranean types are dark, with an olive complexion and with straight black hair. He was a cricketer, and later, after the war, in London I was to meet him a number of times at Lord's and in club matches. We became quite good friends; then, as one does, lost touch. A few years later I was to find him on the quay when my ship docked at Bridgetown. He had seen my name on the passenger list and had come down to meet me. I was not breaking my journey in Barbados. I had made no plans for myself. "That's fine," he said. "In that case, I'll consider you my guest."

He was now, he told me, in the Colonial Service. Meeting him in England, it had not occurred to me—it had not occurred to any of us—that he had colored blood. Meeting him now in the atmosphere of the West Indies, I recognized the fact at once. There was a sixth to an eighth part, I should imagine. His father had a plantation on the windward coast, and we drove across to it for lunch. It was a modern house with a prosperous appearance. His father was dignified, well-educated, with a somewhat patrician manner. But there was not the slightest doubt that one at least of his grandparents had been very nearly black. There was a girl to make a fourth, very young and very pretty, with a pleasantly modulated, sing-song West Indian voice. She did not talk a great deal. But she was an interested listener. She watched my friend all the time.

My friend asked me about her that night when we dined alone in town.

"What did you think of her?" he said.

"Charming, naturally. And very lovely."

"Would you say that it was quite obvious that she had colored blood?"

I hesitated. It is the kind of question that one does not like to have asked one in the West Indies. One is uncertain as to the kind of answer that is expected. Usually I tend to prevaricate. But she was so very obviously colored, rather more than quarter caste, and I knew the man pretty well. "Well, I suppose it is," I said, "a little."

He laughed rather ruefully. "I was afraid you would say that. Yes, it is obvious. And I'm in the Government service. I'm ambitious. As you know I did well at Oxford. I got a 'mention' in the war. There's no reason why I shouldn't go quite a long way. Of course, I'm a West Indian myself. You may not have noticed, but I am. It isn't very obvious. I don't think anyone in England was aware of it. It wouldn't do me any harm in my career—particularly if I were to marry someone who was a hundred per cent white. But if I were to marry Cecile—no, it would never do. I should never get anywhere. I should be offered minor, insignificant appointments all my life. And the damnable thing is that I don't suppose I shall ever care for anyone in the way that I do for her."

I have not seen him since. But I have followed his career. He is in West Africa, relatively high up in the service. He is married to an Englishwoman, and is the father of two children. The second war brought him a C.B.E. He is in the middle fifties and will be retiring soon. He has a reasonable chance of being knighted. He has been successful. But I wonder if he has been happy.

This happened, or rather this choice was presented to him, twenty years ago, and the issue of color as the issue of class is, it must be remembered, a different one today. Lines are not so strictly drawn. He was a Barbadian, too, and as such would be more conscious of this particular issue than a Jamaican or a Trinidadian. Moreover, it is possible that my friend was exaggerating the effect on his career of marriage to a girl of obviously African ancestry. But the fact that he was conscious of those dangers, that those dangers should have constituted so actual a problem for him, is symptomatic of West Indian life. Everywhere under the surface that problem lies. For over four hundred years there has been interbreeding between black and white, and brown and quarter-white. Every shade of color is to be found. And the man with a greater degree of white considers himself the superior of the man with a lesser degree of white, and the man with the lesser degree resents it. It is a problem that affects business, local politics, and all social relations.

For the visitor it is a tricky and a tiresome situation. It is tricky because he does not know who is considered colored and who is not. Except in Barbados and in Antigua there are few local families without some African ancestry. Yet these slightly colored families rigidly exclude from their clubs those with obviously dark skins. British governors and administrators refuse to recognize these distinctions and invite impartially to Government House dinners and tennis parties the white, the near-white, the colored, and the coal black. The various groups meet amicably there at the cocktail bar and the bridge table. Then they scatter to their separate cliques. In every island except Grenada there are two camps and the visitor has to make his choice.

In the cool of the evening he will stroll up from his hotel to the savannah. He will pass a succession of small shacks and shops, with radios playing and bright interiors and children tumbling over one another in the gutter. He will reach an open space. A couple of tennis courts flank a long, wide bungalow. He will pause and watch the play. The young and the middle-aged are meeting on equal terms; the standard of play is high; the bungalow is brightly lighted; a man in shirtsleeves is leaning forward across a billiard table; a boy in white uniform is carrying a tray of drinks to a quiet corner of the veranda where a bridge four is in progress; a dozen or so persons of mixed sexes are at the bar; there are others, sitting out in deck chairs on the veranda, watching the play. It is all very cosy and congenial, a friendly mixing of sexes and age groups. But this is not the club towards which the visitor is on his way. The faces of the members are dark, or fairly dark.

He will go on a little farther. He will pass another succession of shacks and shops. Then once again he will reach an open space. A couple of tennis courts flank a long, wide bungalow. He will pause to watch the tennis. The standard of the play is high; the

young and the middle-aged are mixing on equal terms; the bungalow is brightly lighted; a man in shirtsleeves is leaning forward
across a billiard table; a boy in white uniform is carrying a tray of
drinks to a quiet corner of the veranda where a bridge four is in
progress; a dozen or so persons of mixed sexes are at the bar; there
are others, sitting out in deck chairs on the veranda watching the
play. It is all very cosy and congenial, a friendly mixing of sexes
and of age groups. It is the club of which the British Administrator is the patron. Its membership consists of British officials
and the families of those planters, agents, and store-owners whose
skin is either white or nearly enough white to pass as white. This
is the club for which the visitor is bound, and unless he is very
bigoted, he can hardly fail to feel that it is ridiculous that these
two social camps should exist side by side, identical but alien, in
a small island whose fortunes and future depend on a pooling of
effort and resources. Nor can he fail to find tiresome the inevitable
corollary to this situation, the persistence with which the near-
whites stress the failing and deficiencies of their darker cousins.
"Do they really believe," he asks himself, "that they are, as they
claim to be, the direct unclouded descendants of English noble-
men and French aristocrats fleeing from the Terror?" He will find
it hard to believe in the complete mental honesty of those whose
whole life is the perpetual maintenance of a façade.

The situation is moreover made even more tricky for the visitor
by the fact that the color bar is fixed in a slightly different way in
each separate island. In Grenada it barely exists; in Barbados it is
rigidly maintained. Between these two extremes there are varying
degrees of strictness—degrees that have been determined by the
varying fortunes and histories of each separate island and in particular by the extent to which each island was brought within the
influence of the French Revolution.

The French Revolution is indeed, since the landing of Columbus, the most important single event in West Indian history—a
contention of whose truth the best evidence is provided by an
examination of the three original French islands: Haiti, Martinique, and Guadeloupe.

In 1789 no three islands could have had more in common.
There they were French and prosperous, sharing the same traditions, owing the same allegiances, the product of the same period

and culture. A quarter of a century later they had scarcely a trait
in common.

The Haitian story has been told in an earlier chapter [*In the
original version in* The Sugar Islands, *the story was told in part in
this synopsis. It has been cut here to avoid a repetition.*] and that
of Guadeloupe in part. At the beginning of hostilities, the British
who had been beaten off at Haiti, captured Martinique and
Guadeloupe. For the moment the position in these two islands
was the same. Within a few weeks, however, Guadeloupe was
recaptured by a French expedition under Victor Hugues who
freed and armed the slaves, proclaimed the revolution, set up the
guillotine, executed the rebels, and instituted a four years' terror.
But Hugues did not recapture Martinique.

Until 1801 Martinique was to remain in British hands. It felt
none of the effects of the Terror. Its slaves were never freed. There
were no massacres, no plunderings. The old colonial traditions
were maintained, and though Martinique was returned to France
at the Peace of Amiens, it was recaptured early in the Napoleonic
Wars, to remain a British island until 1814. Napoleon re-established white rule and slavery in Guadeloupe, but by then the old
colonial traditions had been destroyed.

No three islands could have been more alike in 1789; no three
islands could have been less alike in 1815. Haiti was an independent black republic. The tricolor flew over Guadeloupe. The old
landowners were dead or scattered. Few had the heart, courage,
or inclination to return. The land was split up among peasant
proprietors, owned by limited companies in Paris. Guadeloupe
was to recover under the new régime a very real measure of prosperity, but it was no longer a sister island to Martinique, which
was to return to its French allegiance in the manner of a Rip van
Winkle. For nearly twenty years its planter aristocrats had been
cut off from France, and the France to which it was now possible
for them to return was their home no longer. France had become
a country for which they had little use. Those of their friends who
were still alive were unprivileged and dispossessed. They could
no longer feel at ease in Paris. Different ideas were in the air.
They felt happier, more themselves in their own green island.
They no longer thought of that island as a place where they could

amass money to spend in France: Martinique had become their home. They put their money back into the soil; the rich way of life that is typified by the ruins of St. Pierre was spread through the entire island. At a time when the British islands were being drained and impoverished by absenteeism, Martinique, through a reversal of that process, was growing rich.

The different fates of those three islands during that fateful quarter of a century are typical of that essential characteristic of West Indian life—the dependence of each island upon the caprice of history.

No British island—or island that became British during the Napoleonic period—was affected by the French Revolution to anything like the same degree. But every island was affected to some extent—some to a very great extent.

Most of the Lesser Antilles had come under French rule at one time or another and were susceptible to the mental atmosphere of French events. The Paris Convention offered the assistance of its arms to all peoples ready to fight for freedom. Victor Hugues in Guadeloupe frantically urged the slaves of the British islands to revolt against their masters. There were risings in Grenada, St. Lucia, and St. Vincent. Each rising was accompanied by a firing of estates and a slaughtering of planters, on each occasion in the name of the Revolution, with the watchword of "Liberty, Equality, Fraternity." What happened on a large scale in Guadeloupe happened elsewhere on a smaller scale.

By a natural inevitable process, by the logic as opposed to the caprice of history, the West Indian islands are returning now to the conditions of rule and ownership that existed there before the arrival of the Spaniards, to the rule and ownership, that is to say, of a dark-skinned people. In islands where the colonial traditions of the eighteenth century were broken, if only for a brief time, by the revolt of slaves and the massacres of planters, that process was accelerated. Each island has a different history; the life of each island is in consequence in its own way unique, the product of special circumstances. The visitor to the West Indies needs to know something of the history of each island that he visits if he is to understand completely what he is seeing there.

CHARACTERS: The Judge

Obeah

A Beachcomber

A Creole Crooner

In the spring of 1937 I spent a week in Cuba.

In the autumn of 1938 I went again to the West Indies, this time to the Windward Islands, making long stays at Grenada, St. Lucia, St. Vincent. On the way out I paused at Antigua and Barbados. On the way back I sailed northwards for Boston by one of the Canadian Lady boats; stopping at Dominica, Antigua, Montserrat, St. Kitts. I also spent three days in Martinique. By the time I reached Boston I had seen, with this trip and my previous one, most of the islands in the Caribbean area.

In February 1948 I revisited St. Lucia, Grenada, Dominica, Trinidad, Montserrat, Antigua. From then on I went down nearly every year. I visited the American Virgin Islands, Puerto Rico, Saba, Anguilla, St. Martin, Curaçao. A warm friendship grew up between me and Hugh Burrowes, the Administrator of St. Kitts, and his wife Margaret. I spent many happy days in their G. H. guest room. In the autumn of 1952 I rented for three months a bungalow in Nevis. I never went back to Jamaica or Barbados, but I went several times to Trinidad and in 1956 I was for two months the guest of the Shell Oil Company in their camp at Point Fortin. All the time I was gradually absorbing the atmosphere of the smaller islands and obtaining the material that I used later in ISLAND IN THE SUN.

It is hard for me to say which is my favorite island. When Darryl Zanuck had to decide where he would film Island in the Sun *he sent down photographers to all the islands. When he saw their stills he said, "Grenada is the place." He shot a few scenes in Barbados. All the photographs of the plantation house "Belfontaine" were taken there, but it was Grenada that I recognized nearly all the time. I did not, however, have Grenada particularly in mind when I wrote the novel. Santa Marta, the scene of the story, is a composite picture based on all the smaller islands. I also used the Seychelles.*

In 1951 I published a travel book, Where the Clocks Strike Twice, *published in England in 1952 and titled,* Where the Clocks Chime Twice, *that contained a West Indian section. I wrote a number of articles on the West Indies for magazines and newspapers. I have divided these pieces under three headings: character sketches, snapshots, and pictures of the individual islands.*

In the character sketches I have altered circumstances once or twice, so as to avoid an identification that might cause distress.

The Judge

from HOT COUNTRIES

WRITTEN IN 1929

Before Eldred Curwen and I were five days out of Bordeaux we had heard about him. He was one of those figures round whom legends grow. "What, going to Dominica? Well, then, you must be sure to go and see the judge. He's the most original thing the islands have produced."

"In what way original?" we asked.

And heads would be nodded and anecdotes retailed, and gradually from this person and that the facts of his life took shape. He was an Englishman, the son of a West Country solicitor, who as a young boy had been sent to Antigua for convalescence after a long illness. He stayed a year, and when the time came for him to go he was so silent that his friends looked inquiringly at him.

"Are you as sad as all that to say good-bye?" they asked.

"I'm not saying good-bye," he answered. "I'm coming back."

They laughed at that. So many people had said they were coming back. So few had. "In England you'll forget us quickly enough," they said.

He didn't, though. During his three years at Oxford, where he rowed in his college boat, and in London afterwards, where he was studying for the Bar, his resolve to return strengthened. He was homesick for the Antilles, for the sunlit skies, for the green spears of the young cane, for the yellow sands, and the sea turquoise and green above them. But it was not only for the obvious beauties that he was homesick, for sunlit and moonlit skies, for

143

warm seas and heavy scents. In London, where the rain beats
round windy corners he listened vainly for the sound of wind and
rain, for the drum-beat of rain upon the palm frond and the corrugated-iron roofs, for the wail of wind upon the jagged leaves of
the banana. It was not only the sunlight that he was longing for.
"I must hear rain again," he said. At the age of twenty-seven he
sailed for the countries of the typhoon.

He has never left them. Today, forty years later, an old man,
his life's work over, he lives on the windward coast of Dominica,
on an estate that just pays its way, with a retired Army captain
who came out to him as a pupil and stayed on. He has been there
for eight years and he will never leave it. Roseau is seven hours
away; seven hours of rough and hilly riding; a journey that he
would be too heavy now, even if he had the wish, which he has
not, to make. "I shall never leave here," he says.

Round such a figure inevitably legends grow. And during his
young and middle years he gave ample opportunity for the spreading of many legends. He was a just judge and a fine lawyer. No
one has ever questioned that. But he was a fighter. He bore fools
ill. He stood no nonsense from officialdom. When people irritated
him, he let them know it. They were his intellectual inferiors.
His rapier was the sharper. He made enemies. He made friends.
He had the belligerence of a man who knows his mind. The
generosity of a man who is unafraid. "He's on a big scale," they
told me.

It was in a mixed mood that we set out to see him, as the result
of some vague telephonic talk. We were curious to see him, but a
little nervous as to the reception that awaited us.

"At any rate," said Eldred, "we'll see something of the country."

Dominica has been called the loveliest of the Antilles. In a
way it is. It is very mountainous. It is very green. It has not the
parched barbaric thrill of Guatemala nor the terrifying austerity
of the Blue Mountains of New South Wales. But, of their kind,
its succession of deep gorges is as good as anything I have seen. It
is rather like a reading of *Endymion*: like *Endymion* it is lush and
featureless; like *Endymion* it becomes monotonous. Hour after
hour it is the same. You descend hills and you mount them. At
the foot of each valley, wherever a stream is running into the sea,
you will find a group of native girls washing their clothes. In
Dominica the Negro type is purified by a Carib strain; the hair

is straight and black, the features finer, the hands and feet less squat. As you pass they wave their hands and shout you friendly greetings in Creole *patois*. Occasionally you will pass a village: a collection of fishing huts beside the sea. You will pass no big houses, no sign of extensive cultivation. Here and there you will come across the ruined masonry of wall and house, relics of the prosperous days before disease had ruined the coffee crops. Occasionally you will meet some local industry, some Heath Robinson contraption of bamboos and pipes and braziers by which the bay rum is extracted from the bay leaf. But that is all. Dominica is a poor country, though its soil is fertile; the heavy rain makes the upkeep of roads impossible. There is no way of marketing profitably the fruits that grow in profusion in the interior. It is a long, monotonous journey.

We had been travelling for seven hours. We were very sore; riding in cotton slacks when one has not ridden for many months is arduous; when, at a sudden turn of a mounting road, we saw, many feet below us, the Atlantic beating on the windward coast; half-way down the slope the red roof of a bungalow, the green flatness of a lawn, the stately dignity of the royal palm.

We were tired and we were sore and more than a little nervous as we rode up to the timbered bunglalow. On the lawn there were peacocks, white and blue, spreading their vast tails. From a flagstaff the Union Jack was flying. On the veranda, in a deck chair, our host was waiting. His appearance had been described to us many times. And as he rose to welcome us he looked very much as I had expected him to look. He was tall, broad-shouldered, and immensely fat. He wore a shirt that was slightly soiled, and open at the neck. The belt that held his trousers had slipped, so that his shirt protruded, revealing an inch or two of skin. He wore slippers; his ankles, as he shuffled towards us, gave the impression of being swollen. He looked as I had expected him to look. A typical colonial planter. But what I had not expected was the voice with which he welcomed us. It was the courtly voice of the old-world English gentleman, with generations of breeding at the back of it.

"You have had a long journey," he said. "It is very good of you to come all this way to see an old man. He appreciates it. You must be very tired. We will have a glass of our *vin du pays* before your bath."

The dining-room was almost entirely filled with a long table. At the head of it were laid four places. "Captain Armstrong sits upon my right. Will the elder of you sit upon my left?"

I took the place beside him. In front of each of us he set a decanter. We filled our glasses. He bowed towards each of us in turn. Then in one long sip finished the admirably mellowed rum. "And now," he said, "I will show you to your rooms."

It was a large rambling house; a bachelor's house. Its walls were lined with bookshelves and the odd assortment of pictures that bachelors at various periods of taste annex. There were hunting prints and college groups, and nudities from *La Vie Parisienne*, war-time caricatures of "Big and Little Willie." Over the washstand of each room was a printed text: "Work is the ruin of the drinking classes"; "If water rots the soles of your boots, think what it must do to your inside." A library is an autobiography. I looked carefully along his shelves. There were a certain number of novels, bought casually, a complete set of *Wisden's Cricketer's Almanac* since 1884, some legal books, the publications of the Rationalist Press, Darwin and the mid-Victorian agnostics, a few classics, a Horace and a Catullus, Thackeray and Dickens.

Dinner was ready by the time that we were. A planter's dinner. A Creole soup, a roast chicken served with Creole vegetables, boiled yam, fried plantains, sweet potatoes. But I could not believe that we were sitting at a bare deal table, in cotton and tieless suits, eating Creole food from earthenware, served by a shambling-footed Negro. I felt, so completely did our host's personality dominate the atmosphere, that we were in some old English house; that the table was of polished walnut, reflecting the gleam of candles and old silver; that saddle of mutton was being served us by a silent and venerable butler; that it was Burgundy, not rum, that we were drinking.

The conversation was of the kind for which you would look in such an atmosphere. The judge did most of the talking. He was an admirable raconteur. His anecdotes were scattered with reflections. He was a staunch Tory, with little use for the philosophy and the sociology of the day. What did they want to start educating the working classes for? Education meant discontent. The working classes thought so much of themselves nowadays that they couldn't make good servants.

"And what else are they any good for?" he asked. "They're no happier now. They're less happy."

We discussed religion. He was the practical late Victorian rationalist. A Huxley, but the grandfather of Aldous, was his god.

"All this talk about heaven, as though life were a Sunday School, with prizes for the best boy. When you're dead you are dead."

The *National Review* was the only magazine he read. The old Imperial flame burned bright in him. Let the Americans build Dreadnoughts if they wanted to; it could only mean the more for us to sink. It was thus that they talked, the English of his class, thirty years back, before the war had broken finally the power and prestige of the feudal system. He typified an England that has passed.

We did not leave the table after dinner. The plates were cleared away and we sat there over our rum. The judge was a heavy drinker; every quarter of an hour or so he filled his glass, looked round the table, gave a little whistle, lifted his glass and drained it. He was a heavy drinker, but he was too well bred to put any pressure on us to drink with him. We had each our decanter at our side: we could take as much or as little as we chose. They say that wine mellows man. But I have hardly ever met a man of over forty whom wine in large quantities improves. Young people it does quite often. It removes their self-consciousness, releasing their natural gaiety and high spirits. But with older people it is more often grievances that are released. By the time one has come to seventy one has accumulated a good many unsettled scores. Now and again a peeved look came into the judge's face.

"One has to suffer for being patriotic," he said, and began to tell us some story, the details of which I could not clearly catch, of a naturalized German whom he had insulted in the Roseau Club. "Once a German always a German. I told him so. If I had been a younger man I should have flung him into the street. But I was fifty. They've never forgiven me down there. They all took the fellow's side."

For a moment a hard, harsh look came into his face. In an instant it had gone, replaced by the suave, courteous look of hospitality. But I could understand how that reputation for violence had grown up in Roseau. I could picture the evenings when boredom and indigestion and the tiresome company of people

who would argue and contradict him would goad him, who had
never borne fools lightly, into one of those outbursts that would
make even his most true admirer a little frightened of him. They
were few who had not felt at some time the sting of that pointed
rapier.

It was after eleven when we left the table. It had been one of
the best evenings that we had had since our farewell dinner to
Europe in Bordeaux at the Chapeau Rouge. But it was, never-
theless, in a puzzled, almost embarrassed way that we turned to
each other the moment we were alone.

"Do you realize," said Eldred, "that he's no idea we're going
away tomorrow?"

I nodded my head. Our invitation had been arranged over the
telephone. Telephones in Dominica are notoriously inadequate.
And during the evening several such remarks as "Captain Armstrong will take you and show you over there in a day or two" had
made it very clear that we were expected to stay at least a week.

"I wish to heaven we could," I said.

Wished it both for our sake and his. There was no doubt that
we should have had a delightful time there, and it was clear that
he would enjoy our visit. He loved company and saw little company. It had been many months since he had seen travellers from
England.

"I suppose we can't, though," said Eldred.

For a while we debated the problem. The boat on which we
were booked to sail left within three days. There would not be
another for a fortnight. We had arrangements to make in Martinique. We had written to friends in Barbados announcing the
date of our arrival. We did not see how those plans were to be
cancelled.

"It's not going to be easy telling him," I said.

It wasn't. I have enjoyed few things less than I did the next
morning the making of that first inquiry to the judge about the
time at which we ought to start.

"Start," he said; "but where?"

"To Rosalie. I was wondering how long it would take to get
there."

"But Rosalie? I do not understand."

We had exchanged half a dozen sentences before he understood.

"What!" he cried. "You are going to leave me?"

It was said on such a note of pathetic, almost child-like disappointment that I almost then and there cancelled all our Barbados plans.

"I had not realized," he said. "I thought. . . ."

I began to explain. Our ship was sailing in three days. There were connections waiting. He scarcely listened. "You are going to leave me?" he repeated.

For a moment he was completely overcome by disappointment, but only for a moment. He was too good a host not to realize that a guest must not be embarrassed by a host's personal feelings.

"I am sorry," he said. "I am very sorry. But since your boat is sailing it cannot be helped. We must see about preparing you a lunch."

Immediately he had begun to make preparations for our journey. A bottle of rum was to be packed, with cheese and a loaf of bread, cold meat and fruit and pickles. He abused roundly in patois the servant who made up the packet; but the servant laughed; his master might abuse him; but his master liked him. A Negro will do anything for you provided that he knows that.

"I'll write you a letter to the overseer at my sister's property," he said. "He'll put you up for the night. He'll make you comfortable."

And he talked cheerfully as we talked of the island and the island's history, its personalities and peculiarities. But there was a wistful look on his face as he said good-bye to us.

"Come back one day," he said, "and make it soon. I won't be here much longer."

We promised that we would. We believed we would.

"Within eighteen months we'll be back," we said.

When we turned at the corner of the road we saw him standing on his parapet waving his arms to us.

For quite a while we rode on in silence, picturing that long bungalow and the old man returning to his chair, his hands hanging limply over the sides, his mind abroad; thinking of what during those long hours, when the sun was too hot and he too tired to leave the cool shade of the veranda? Did his mind turn backwards to the past, to the thatched cottages of the Wiltshire where he was born, to the gray stone and green lawns of Oxford, to the mullioned windows of Lincoln's Inn? Did he relive the ardors and optimisms of youth, the tumult and the feuds of middle life, the successes and disappointments, the friendships and the enmities, the loves that went awry? Or did he, who had no faith in any immaterial heaven, look forward, adoze there in his chair, to a day imperfectly discerned when the veranda on which he sat would be a bank of rubble, when the grass would run raggedly between the palms, when one more plantation had been reclaimed by the jungle from which it sprang, with he himself mingled with the roots of the tall mangoes under which by moonlight the brown people that he loved would dance?

Obeah

from THE SUGAR ISLANDS

WRITTEN IN 1939

I SPOKE OF THE WEST INDIANS as an uprooted people. They have lost their country, their language, and their faith. They have brought with them and retained, however, many of their superstitions. Much has been written in recent years, particularly since it has become possible for white men to visit Haiti, about Obeah men and voodoo rites, and there can be little doubt that in the last analysis most West Indians have more faith in their own witch-doctors than in the priests whom their education has approved for them. Until recently there was a clause in the Haitian Code forbidding the use of Zombies, the raising of dead men to work as laborers in the fields. Seabrook's *Magic Island* has dealt at length with this question.

The authority of the "Obeah men" is little questioned. Most residents in the West Indies have had personal experiences of "the spirits." A planter in Grenada wrote me the following account of one of his:

"Two of my laborers had not been at work for some time when I met one of them and asked him why? He said, 'Boss, the spirits troubling us too much. We never get any sleep at night.'

"I questioned him and he said for the past twenty days things had been thrown about in the house and that anyone who went near the house after dark got beaten with sticks and had stones thrown at them.

151

"I laughed at him and told him I would come myself to see what was going on.

"Two afternoons later I went to where he was living. He took me through a nutmeg grove and on up a grass-covered hill to a small laborer's house built of mud and wattle. He told me this was the house where things first began to happen, and they had left the house and were living in their grandmother's house down below in the nutmeg grove, but that the spirits still attacked them.

"I sat and talked to the two young men aged about twenty, a wife of one of them, and two children till it began to get dusk, when I said we would go to the lower house.

"There was a worn path down the grass slope and no trees or bushes anywhere near. I sent the woman and children in front; then I came, and then the two young men. A few yards down the path the two men tried to run past me, shouting, 'Oh, God! They're getting us.'

"I thought they were trying to frighten the woman, and so I made them walk in front of me. After a few yards I felt gravel and dust being thrown at my head, and they started to cry out again. I pretended nothing had happened, although I had dust and fine earth over my neck and shoulders.

"We reached the lower house, and while it was light I examined it. There was a ladder of four steps to reach the door. On the left a half-partition, behind which was the bedroom. I looked under the bed and saw a basin with a corn cob in it, used for washing clothes. Sitting on the floor in the other room was the grandmother, leaning against the partition holding a baby. Opposite her was a bench along the side of the house and under the bench some baskets full of nutmegs. Facing the door was a table with a lamp on it and a pickle bottle. I saw all the windows shut and barred, and stood in the doorway facing into the house. The occupants sat on the bench—two men, two women, and the two children. I tried to persuade them that it was someone playing tricks on them and throwing stones, et cetera, on the roof, but they said 'Wait, Boss. You will see things.'

"It was then dark. After some time there was a crash on the roof and a few minutes later a lump of earth *inside* the house came from the ceiling and fell on the floor at my feet. The people started singing hymns, then suddenly the corn cob out of the basin in the next room flew over the partition and a few minutes later a shower of nutmegs out of the basket under the bench flew into the air and fell all round us. My hair felt like standing on end and when a few minutes later the bottle jumped off the table, hit the roof and fell at my feet, I thought it time to go; so, making some feeble remark about being late for dinner, I beat a retreat.

"These people next day had the Anglican parson to come and say prayers and when that had no effect they got the Roman Catholic priest to do ditto. The spirits took no notice and so they decided to call in the African Shango Dancers.

"They had to pay these people five pounds. They built a roof over a flat piece of ground about twenty feet square cut out of the hill above the top house. They started dancing—an old woman, a girl of about seventeen and a man to beat the tomtom—at 7 a.m. on Friday morning. On Saturday afternoon myself and a fellow planter went up to see it. They beat the same monotonous beat on the tomtom and the old woman and girl made the same motions, dancing all the time. You could see they were self-hypnotized. The old woman fell on the ground from exhaustion and her limbs still continued to jerk in time to the drum. She then started to roll, and rolled over and over out of the shed down the hill and, to our amazement, when past the empty house, she rolled along the side of the house and then *rolled up the hill* into the shed again. It was a very steep hill—quite as steep as the hill from the Hospital in St. George's past the St. James's Hotel. It looked impossible and the whole thing was so inhuman and beastly that we left. I told the occupants to send away the young girl aged twelve, as I had read of poltergeists and felt sure she was the cause of the trouble. I don't know if they did so, but the manifestations stopped, as the Africans had said they would."

Such occurrences, my friend wrote me, are very frequent. In more than one respect the traditions and the faith of Africa made the middle passage from the Guinea Coast.

II

from MOST WOMEN

WRITTEN IN 1939

No ONE DOUBTS the power of the evil eye. If a laborer who is unhappy can go into a decline, turning his face to the wall and dying in the course of a few days without any visible complaint, there is no reason why the same powers of will and concentration should not work harm upon an enemy.

During my first days in Martinique, before I had moved into the bungalow, Eldred Curwen and I stayed in a small hotel in Fort de France. As they only charged us forty francs a day and as that included, in addition to our food, as much red wine as we could manage, we did not expect a high standard of comfort. We did expect, though, something rather better in the way of service than the slatternly half-caste who clattered the plates like muskets, upset sardine oil on my trousers, and brought no potatoes till we had finished our *entrée*. It was not even as though she had made up for her inefficiency, as do so many Negroes, by an amiable readiness to smile. She was sour and ill-favored. Without being old, she looked as though she had never been young. Her features were set in a sulky scowl. Her long, red print frock was soiled and shapeless. There was no pretty handkerchief knotted in her hair. She was, we decided, just too much of a good thing.

"We'll change our table this evening," Eldred said.

We did not expect to meet with any difficulty. A boat was sailing for St. Thomas that afternoon, and the dining-room when we came down to it for dinner was comparatively empty. The *maître d'hôtel* became flustered, however, when we asked to be placed at another table.

"I have put you at Floria's table," he said.

"I know," we answered. "But we want to be moved from it. There are several tables vacant, aren't there?"

He nodded his head. Yes, certainly there were tables vacant. At the same time. . . .

He was still hesitating when Floria shuffled across the room on her bare feet.

"That's your table, there," she said.

"We are arranging to change tables," Eldred told her.

The sullen look on her face darkened. "That's your table," she repeated, "there."

But by this time I had begun to grow impatient. "We can't wait here the whole evening," I said to the *maître d'hôtel*. "Please find us another table. That one over there is empty, isn't it?"

I had begun to move across to it, when Floria pushed in front of me.

"Why?" she asked.

Her manner was so offensive that my impatience conquered my self-control. "Because I don't want to have all my trousers covered with sardine oil."

I spoke angrily. And as she heard me, the sulky expression of her features deepened into a stare of fierce malevolence. Her eyes followed us as we crossed the room.

At the table next to ours was a French Creole who had come out on the same boat with us.

"That was a black look she gave us," I remarked.

He nodded his head. "It certainly was," he answered, pausing significantly, as though there were more that he would say. He shrugged his shoulders casually, however. "Ah, well," he said. "It may mean nothing."

That night I could not sleep. I was weary with the exhaustion of a long sea voyage, of packing, of early rising, of the excitement of arriving at a new place; but I could not sleep; all night I tossed restlessly under the mosquito-net. I felt limp and lifeless as I came up from my shower bath to the wide veranda on which my morning coffee and fruit were awaiting me, to find that Eldred Curwen, usually a late riser, was already down. There were red rims under his eyes.

"How did you sleep?" I asked.

"Twice, for three consecutive minutes."

"That's more than I managed."

At the other end of the veranda the French Creole who had travelled out with us was dipping a crust of bread into his coffee. He laughed at our admission.

"I was wondering about that," he said. "If I were you, I should go back to Floria's table."

We stared at him in surprise.

"What are we to take that to mean?" we asked.

"Only that black magic does exist."

We laughed at that. "Are you trying to tell us that Floria's put a spell on us?"

"More or less."

"And are you expecting us to believe that?"

He shrugged his shoulders. "You can believe it or not believe it, as you chose, but do you fancy the people who run this hotel would keep a woman like that if they weren't afraid of her? Anyhow, wait and see how you sleep tonight. It may be that last night you were too excited."

Throughout that day I thought of nothing except sleep. As I strolled through the narrow, colored streets of Fort de France, as I sat on the balcony of the Club sipping a rum punch, looking out over the green savannah to the white statue of Josephine, as I drove in the afternoon through green fields of cane to the palm groves of La Fontaine and Carbet, my eyelids ached and throbbed. I counted the moments till the sun should have sunk into the Caribbean.

It was only a few minutes after eight that I went to bed, feeling that not for another second could I keep awake, but once again I was to toss, hot and restless and exhausted, through the interminable hours of a tropic night, and once again, when at last dawn came, I found a fractious and red-eyed Eldred awaiting me on the veranda.

"Really," he said, "this is too much of a good thing. I haven't had two minutes' sleep."

The Frenchman laughed knowingly over his coffee. "I should change your table in the dining-room if I were you," he said.

We were less sceptical now than we had been on the previous evening.

"Has she been poisoning us?" we asked.

He shook his head. "She doesn't need poison—not material poison, anyhow. She's got beyond that. You wouldn't be surprised at the hotel keeping her on here if you knew her story." He paused; then, seeing that we were listening, went on.

She was sixteen, he told us, at the time, and in the Martinique fashion she was lovely. She was straight and tall and supple. She wore a long, flowing, green silk robe, a yellow *madras* about her neck, and a green-and-yellow handkerchief for her hair. There were rings swinging from her ears; the gift of a sailor brother. And she was proud, as are the women of Martinique who know their beauty to be famous through the length of the Antilles.

It is of such a one that he spoke to us, and of an evening twenty years before when her dark eyes had smiled softly through a moon-silvered dusk at the young Frenchman at her feet.

"So you were afraid to speak to me. Silly one, there was no need to be," she whispered.

Her voice was soft, and her French had that unslurred purity of accent which is for those only to whom it comes as a taught language.

From the adjacent flank of the veranda came the sound of voices, of a phonograph, of ice rattled against glass. Below, many feet below, the gentle waters of the Caribbean were breaking upon the beach. From the encircling hills the murmur of innumerable crickets ebbed and throbbed. But for the two young people crouched on the long flight of steps there existed beneath that velvet sky no sound but their own voices, no being but themselves.

"And all this time," she went on, "you've been missing me, really and truly missing me?"

"From that first instant, beautiful. Do you remember?"

She nodded her head slowly. "How should I forget?"

That first instant. It had been within an hour of his arrival at Martinique to take up a post there as a minor Government official. He was frightened and he was excited. He had never seen the tropics before. He had never left home even. He had never had any responsibility. He was only twenty-one. He was frightened and he was homesick. It was so new, so strange. And yet it was so lovely, the green square with its palm trees and its statue, its flanking of blue sea and shuttered houses. And it was so friendly. He had been welcomed enthusiastically, he had been taken to the Club, had been stood rum punches. He had sat looking down over the balcony when suddenly in the street below. . . .

"There you were," he said, "in that mauve-colored frock of yours. And you looked up at me. And oh, my dear, for six months I've not been thinking of anything but that."

"Why didn't you tell me, silly?"

"How was I to? I didn't know even who you were."

He had been shy of asking: shy with the inexperience of twenty-one and with the exaggerated sense of dignity that he felt was due to his position. Even when he had discovered who she was, the daughter of a Frenchman and a native, killed, both of them, in the disaster of St. Pierre, living with cousins in Fort de France, supporting herself with her needle, he had felt no nearer to meeting her. She went out little. He knew none of her friends. There was no link between them. "It's ridiculous," he told himself as the months went by. "You won't meet her. You'd far better stop thinking about her."

He had not been able to. He could not believe that that look, that had seemed on her side as on his an utter admission of surrender, could be an end as well as a beginning. For six months the memory of that look had held him back when the moment and the mood had flung in his way the opportunities that inevitably come to a young man, handsome and well-placed.

"No, no," he had thought. "I must keep free. One day I'll be meeting her again. One day all of a sudden it'll happen."

As it had happened. Never had he felt further from meeting her than he had that afternoon as he walked down from his office to the Club. Five o'clock, he had thought. For an hour I'll play bridge or billiards, make or lose some three or four hundred sous, then it'll be sundown and I'll be sitting on the big veranda looking out over the savannah. There'll be five or six of us. And we'll discuss the things one does discuss in a place like Fort de France: the price of rum, the price of sugar, the rival merits of various kinds of car. And we'll go on talking there till seven or half-past; till it's time to go back to dinner. And I'll be at the hotel, at my table, by myself, with the exhilaration of the punch subsiding, and I'll be sleepy and a little lonely, and I'll feel that it should be all different, that there should be some other use to make of the early twenties. I'll be thinking how different *she* could make it for me.

That was how he felt as he had walked down the Rue Perinnon towards the Club. And then, just as he had turned to the right at the street's foot, a voice from a car had hailed him.

"What are you doing? Nothing? Well, come out with us to swim at Founigaut. Yes, of course you can. There are three carloads of us. Just room for you in this. Jump in."

It was from a man he did not know well, a mulatto of no particular account who directed a small photographic establishment, that the invitation had come. Ordinarily he would have refused it. No sooner, indeed, had he accepted it than he began to wish he hadn't. In no French colony is the color line drawn strictly. But there were many people in Fort de France whom he felt it would be better for him, as an official, not to know. "What am I doing here?" he thought as the car, with its load of shrieking, laughing half-castes, rattled round the sharp corners of the uneven, mounting road; as he stood, nervous and silent, trying not to look superior, on the fringe of the chattering crowd that was splashing about the water's edge. He felt embarrassed, self-conscious, out of place. "What am I doing here," he thought, "among these people?"

And then suddenly he saw her. And instantly he was unconscious of the silly, noisy crowd. The slim, erect figure, the black eyes, the sleek skin whose dark coloring betrayed its origin. "You," he whispered. And the dark eyes smiled and she stretched out her hand to him. "Let's swim," she said. They ran into the water, to swim side by side with slow, even strokes as the sun, red and largening, sank into the Caribbean, and the first stars in the violet sky behind the hills began to glimmer. They said nothing: there was no need for words. Not yet. It was enough, after these months, to be together. In silence they swam back to shore, followed the rest of the party to the bungalow, where on the veranda a phonograph was playing. In silence at the head of the long flight of steps they turned into each other's arms to dance. And it was as though all their lives they had danced together. It was an utter harmony, so that afterwards, with the record finished, when they walked away to sit side by side on the veranda steps, it seemed the most natural thing in the world that he who was so nervous, should without nervousness speak to her of all the things he had thought and felt during those dividing months.

"All these weeks I've been longing for you," he said. "I can't really believe that we've met at last."

"And now that you have?"

"It's more of a dream than ever I dreamed it could be."

Slowly the short, thin fingers that work had roughened stroked his hair.

"And for how long will you think that? For how long, my very dear one? For a month, for two months, for a year: for longer than a year? For two years, longer than that even? For how long, then? For ever? Because that's what it must be: for ever, or for nothing. No, no. Don't interrupt me. Listen. That is what it has got to be. That is the only way that I can love you—that way or not at all. We can love, the women of my race, lightly, many times. But to love really, that comes once only to us, and when it comes it is for the ages. Are you ready for it to be like that?"

The short fingers were vibrant in his hair; the dark face was very close to his. The dark eyes through the dusk were very bright. Seated there at her feet, with the awning of the eternal sky above him, "for ever" seemed a very little word. She would not let him pronounce it, though.

"No, no," she cried, "not yet. Think well. You have only to say the word 'Come' and I will follow. But if I do come it will be for ever. My love will be a chain about you: a chain between you and me: a chain that will hold you fast, hold you for ever to this little island. That is what the word 'Come' will mean. Have you the courage, my very sweet, to say it?"

She spoke slowly; her voice, whose French had the precision of an earlier age, gave to her words the feeling and volume of Biblical utterance: it was like some prophecy, some warning out of the Old Testament.

It was with a sense of awe rather than of triumph that he whispered, "Come."

Past Schoelcher on the road to Case Navire there was a bungalow; not a large bungalow. You do not need in the tropics more than two rooms with a veranda round them. And it was a wide veranda with the red of the hibiscus and the purple of the bougainvillea strung in profusion about its porches. It was through flowered shrubbery that the steps ran steep from the veranda to the beach. And all day long as he worked at his office, as he played billiards in the Club, as he lunched at his solitary table in the Pension Galliat, the young French official counted the minutes till five o'clock should come, till he should be free to drive out to that bungalow along the mounting, curving road. All day his thoughts would wander from his task and papers, picturing the moment when he could climb the veranda steps, when from a long rattan chair a slim, erect figure would leap to greet him, when dark arms would be flung round his neck, when a face like a dark flower would be pressed to his. And "What have you been doing all day?" she'd ask. "Counting the minutes till I could see you again," he'd answer. And they'd laugh and run down to the beach to swim side by side through the sunset-reddened water; and afterwards while he sipped slowly at his rum punch she would sit curled beside him, his hand held against her cheek; and she would sing to him in a low voice. For half an hour they would sit there, savoring, after the heat of the long day, the unutterable peace of dusk. Then she would jump to her feet. "Supper-time," she would say. And she would scamper to the kitchen, to reappear a few minutes later with some simple but exquisitely flavored dish of eggs and fish and vegetables. After supper they would bring the phonograph out to the veranda, and dance to it. As they danced, they kissed.

It was an idyll too perfect to be compact of details. They never quarrelled. She was never moody, never difficult, never jealous. At times he would surprise on her face a strange and brooding look, as though she were looking at things—dark things that were many miles, many centuries away. But he had only to touch her on the shoulder, and she would turn round with a shiver and a start, blink quickly, and with a laugh become once again the merry, the adorable companion who asked no more of life than to be in love and loved.

They lived very much to themselves. Though everyone in Fort de France was well aware of the bungalow on the road past Schoelcher, its existence was tacitly ignored. Officially he was still living at the Pension Galliat, where he lunched and, for the sake of appearances and the occasions when his duties forced him to remain in town, he kept on a room. No French family would visit him in the country, and though he would have been himself received and welcomed everywhere he wished to go, he had no wish to go where he could not take her with him. Their only visitors were in consequence her cousins and an occasional man friend of his who would drop in on Saturday or Sunday for a rum punch on his way back to town. For the most part they were alone and were content to be.

"You're very wise," said to him the only man, a middle-aged doctor, who had lived all his life in Martinique, with whom he had cared to discuss the situation more than casually. "You're very wise. Make the best of it while you've got it. It won't come twice. And it couldn't last. It's lucky for you that you're going. It'll be an exquisite memory for you. You're young enough to get over it, both of you."

He looked quickly and intently at the doctor.

"You're sure of that? It's true, is it, what they say about having one's place taken within a week of sailing?"

"Ninety-nine times in a hundred. It's a country of quick forgettings."

"But the hundredth time?"

"I shouldn't worry about that hundredth time, if I were you."

He could not help worrying, however. The time for his leave was drawing close: the leave during which his parents would insist almost certainly on his applying for a transfer. He did not know how he was to break the news to her. He did not know how she would take the news. Were the Martiniquaises really as casual-hearted as the Frenchman would have him think? It was only with a half of himself that he hoped they were. He knew how long it would take him to forget the little bungalow at Schoelcher. And he would have in France so many things to help him to forget: his career, his friends, his interest in the stir of life; whereas she, what medicine would she have whose life was absorbed so utterly in his? How was he to break the news to her?

The letter from Paris authorizing his leave arrived. For the first time in three years he walked slowly up the long, steep flight of steps, and for the first time in three years the slim, erect figure did not leap from the long rattan chair to greet him.

For the first time the low voice did not ask, "What have you been doing with yourself all day?" Instead, the dark eyes met his not angrily, not suspiciously, not self-pityingly, but thoughtfully, as though it were from vast distance of wisdom that that slow look came. "She knows," he thought. "She knows already." And, walking across to her, he put his hand upon her shoulder.

"Pretty one, I've heard from Paris. I'm going on leave in March."

She nodded her head, slowly.

"How long will your leave last?"

"Nine months."

"And you will come back here after it?"

He hesitated. It would have been easy to have promised her, as would the majority of men in his position, that he would. But to her he could not lie; not completely lie, at least. He shrugged his shoulders.

"Darling, how can I tell?" he said. "If it were my own choice I would. You don't need telling that. I shall try to; try my hardest. But my parents—you know what parents are, they have ambition —they'll want me to apply for a transfer, to go somewhere where there's more scope. I don't know. I can't tell what'll happen. Perhaps"—again he hesitated—"perhaps it would be better for us to act as though I weren't going to return."

"How do you mean?"

"Well, there are certain arrangements to be made."

"Arrangements? What arrangements? I don't understand you."

"I can't leave you unprovided for."

She looked thoughtfully at him.

"Is it money that you're trying to talk to me about? Because if it is, you needn't. There'll be no need to worry about that. Let's go and swim."

For the first time in three years they did not speak as they walked down the steps to the little beach, as they swam side by side together. And afterwards it was not at his feet but on the arm of his chair that she sat as he sipped at his rum punch. And it was not his hand that she held against her cheek, but his hair that her fingers stroked as she sang to him in the tongue that he had never learned. Tonight there was a new temper to her singing: it was less crooning, more barbaric, almost terrifying.

"What are you singing?" he asked abruptly. "What are those things?"

"They are the songs of my people. They are very old."

Next morning she was once again the laughing, light-hearted comrade that she had been to him through their three shared years. They danced and bathed and swam and kissed just as they always had, and just as though every night were not bringing them nearer to the hour when his steamer sailed. Sometimes he looked wonderingly at her: for all that they had shared, did he know her any better now than he had on that first evening so many moons ago? What was she thinking? What was she feeling? Had she as so many maintained the child's mind that could see no further than tomorrow, that could not picture to itself in advance the actuality of separation? Would she at the last moment break down into a fever of tears and passion? He did not know. But increasingly as the days passed he dreaded what that last night might hold.

When it came, however, it was very different from what he had expected. There was not the angry, hysterical outburst that he had dreaded. Instead, it was with an almost maternally protecting tenderness that she drew down his head upon her shoulder to repeat against his ear the low words he would never hear again: a tenderness more painful than any torrent of anger would have been.

"Tomorrow," he thought. "I don't know how I shall have the courage to see it through."

But when the morrow came it brought with it the merciful medicine of haste; there were bags to be packed, trunks to be labelled, good-byes to be said. There was a farewell lunch party for him at the Hotel de France. It was not till he was seated on the balcony of the Club over a last liqueur that he had time to realize what was happening. Then suddenly it flashed on him. This balcony on which he had sat on that first morning three and a half years back, from which he had seen for the first time the green square of the savannah, from which he had met that dark glance looking up at him. Never again would he sit on it, looking out on to the calm white statue. Never again would he drive out from it at the day's end along the curving, mounting road. Never again would that slim, erect figure leap with dark, shining eyes out of a rattan chair to welcome him. Never again. Clear in front of him his future stretched—the future of the average competent young official. There would be a couple more colonial posts: North Africa, perhaps, or Indo-China. Then in the early thirties influence would secure him a post in Paris; and with Paris would begin the process of settling down: marriage, a prudent marriage, children and the safeguarding of the future. That was what lay ahead: cares, responsibilities, the end of the unknown. While at the back of him was youth and freedom and romance. What could life hold for him sweeter than that bungalow at Schoelcher, that love so true and careless, so uncomplicated by the maladies of vanity and profit? What had life to offer in compensation for his loss?

His heart was heavy. And suddenly as he sat looking out over the square there was a pain across his eyes, a pain so excruciating that he screamed out loud.

"Good heavens!" said someone. "What's the matter?"

"I don't know. I'm ill. I'm going to die, I think."

In an instant a little crowd had gathered round him.

"This is what often happens after a farewell lunch," laughed someone.

But a second glance was sufficient to prove that that was not what was wrong with him. Wine could not have brought that livid pallor to the cheeks, that drawn misery across the eyes.

"He's ill. Get a doctor quickly."

The middle-aged doctor who had lived all his life in Martinique looked thoughtfully for a moment at his young friend, lifted an eyelid, felt the heart, then scribbled some words on a piece of paper. "Take that round to the chemist. It may do some good."

In frightened silence, the group waited round the moaning figure.

"Will that medicine never come?" said someone.

It came, but it was powerless. The moaning did not cease.

"Take me home. I'm ill. I think I'm dying. Get me home. I can't stay here."

There was an exchange of glances.

"How can we? You're going to France. The steamer's sailing in an hour."

"Steamer. France. Good heavens, do you think I can go on a journey when I feel like this? Get me home, I tell you. Get me home."

There was another exchange of glances. The doctor nodded his head.

"Yes. Best get him home."

All the way out along the curving, mounting road he groaned and shivered.

They had to carry him up the long steep flight of steps. From a long rattan chair on the veranda an erect, slim figure rose to meet them. They began to explain to her, but she waved aside their explanation.

"Bring him in here," she said.

The bed was already open, the sheets turned back. At its head was a carafe of iced water. She stood quietly by while they laid him down, then seated herself at the bed's foot. The men who had brought him hovered indeterminately in the doorway. Was there anything to be done? they asked. No, there was nothing for

them to do, the doctor said. They could go back to town. Himself,
he'd stay there.

The slim, erect figure at the foot said nothing. She was looking
out over the sea. There was on her face a strange, rapt brooding
look, as though she were looking at things—dark things that were
many miles and centuries away. From Fort de France, five miles
off, came the steamer's siren. She rose out of her chair, walked
over to the moaning figure, placed her hand softly on his forehead
and with gentle, caressing fingers stroked his hair, murmuring to
him words that to the doctor who had lived in Martinique all his
life were strange. And as she stroked the pallor went out of the
lined cheeks, the moaning ceased, the taut misery vanished from
behind the eyes. With a start and a blink of the eyes, he sat up
in bed.

"What's the matter?" he said. "I've felt like death. What's
happened?"

"Nothing," she said. "It's over. It's all right."

His knees were weak as he tottered on to the veranda to lean
against the balcony, to see, steaming slowly on its way to Guadeloupe, the liner that should have taken him back to France. His
knees were weak, but her hand was pressing on his shoulder. He
felt her strength flow to him.

"It's all right, Doctor," he said. "You needn't worry."

It was with a white and frightened face, however, that five
weeks later he broke into the doctor's consulting-room.

"Doctor," he said. "What's the matter with me? It's happened
again. You've heard?"

"I've heard."

"It's inexplicable. I don't know what it is. It was just like that
other time. On the morning that the boat was sailing I woke with
that same blinding pain. I couldn't stir. I couldn't think. I was
conscious of nothing except that pain. I just lay there moaning;
right through the day; right on till evening. And then suddenly
just as that other time, it went. I walked out on to the balcony,
and I might never have been ill at all. What's wrong with me?
What's the matter? Do you know, Doctor, what it is?"

"I think I do."

"Then what is it? What's to be done about it?"

"If it's what I think it is, there's nothing that can be done about
it. You will think I am romancing: but I have lived all my life

among these people. They have secrets that are dark to us. When
they want to commit suicide they do not shoot themselves or cut
their throats. They lie upon their beds and die. They can will
mischief or death upon their enemies. They have philters that will
win them the love of the stubborn-hearted. It would be no hard
task for them to make one who wishes to leave them incapable of
movement."

"My good Doctor, but that's ridiculous."

"That is what I knew you would say. But consider this: there is
nothing wrong with you. You can take my word for that. You are
as fit as any man in Martinique. Yet each time that you have tried
to leave the island, you have been so ill that you could not move;
and each time, at the moment when the ship's last siren went, the
illness passed."

"It's ridiculous! Ridiculous!"

But though he spoke truculently, even to himself his outburst
carried no conviction. What were those warning words that three
years back on the moon-drenched balcony those soft lips had ut-
tered? "My love will be a chain about you, a chain that will hold
you fast—hold you for ever to this little island." It was ridiculous,
ridiculous, and yet . . .

Impatiently, he walked over to the window. In the street below,
the familiar, commonplace life of every day was pursuing its comfortable course. Motor cars were honking cheerfully, tourists with
cameras and sun helmets were boisterously calling each other's
attention to the handcart announcing a cinema performance that
was being pushed by a couple of minute black infants. Across the
harbor a four-masted schooner was picturesquely drifting. The
sheltered tables in front of the café on the savannah were filled
with laughing, chattering groups. It was impossible to believe that
contiguous with this merry, familiar, sunlit world existed the dark
mysteries of Obeah. Impossible to believe, and yet, and yet. . . .

With a frightened face, he spun round to face the doctor.

"You believe it, Doctor? Really and truly, that's what you believe?"

"Yes."

"Then what's going to happen to me? What'll be the end of
˄ Do you mean that it'll go on like this, that every time I try to
ˉsland I shall be ill? That I never shall be able to get
⌐ here? Is that what you believe?"

The doctor nodded.

"But I can't. No, I can't," the young man persisted. "To stay here for ever, to grow old here, to watch one's career going; never to see France again. To have one's juniors coming out here, and three years later going back, as oneself one should have, to promotion. To lose interest in oneself; to lose faith in oneself; to lose one's self-respect. You can't really believe that that's what's got to happen to me?"

"Till the spell is broken, yes."

"And how is it to be broken?"

The doctor shrugged his shoulders. It was an expressive shrug. And, looking him in the eyes, the young man read his meaning. "I can't," he thought. "I can't." Though even as he thought it he knew that, were that calamity to be averted, there was no other course. Sorcery and the sorceress were one. Even sorcery could not outlive the snapping of the thin thread of life that bound it to its origin. It was his life or hers. As long as she lived, he was her slave. As long as that . . . but for no longer. "I can't," he thought. "I can't." But there was no other course.

Slowly, with a tread that dragged, he climbed that evening the steep flight of steps to the veranda. And for the second time in their many months together the slim, erect figure did not leap to greet him. From the long rattan chair she lay and looked at him, not angrily, not suspiciously, but thoughtfully, as though it were from vast distances of wisdom that that slow look came.

She beckoned to him.

"Here, at my side, just gently, for a moment."

On the ground beside her chair she dropped a cushion. As he knelt on it she drew his head upon her breast.

"It's so lovely here. All day long I've been lying, looking out, wishing you were here to share it with me. Have you ever seen anything lovelier?"

It was very lovely. The hour before sundown when the air after the long day's heat is cool; when the lights grow gentle after the long day's glare; when the shadows lie level along road and beach; when the blue of the sea grows softer, and the bright greens of the hill grow fresh as though dew were falling on them.

"Have you ever seen anything lovelier?" she said. "Do you think that anywhere in the world there is to be found anything lovelier

than this? Do you not think that the man is foolish who would
run away from it?"

Her voice was low and musical. But there was purpose behind
her words. And he felt weak and irresolute; in the presence of
something old and dark and very powerful. And he felt tired:
grateful in his tiredness for the softness of her breasts, content to
lie there, savoring the peace of evening, watching across the
bay in front of them the little steamer paddling from St. Pierre to
Fort de France.

"Let's go and swim," she said.

Side by side, they swam through the sunset-reddened water, and
afterwards, as he sat sipping at his rum punch, she crouched beside
him, his hand held against her cheek, while she sang softly to him
the love songs of her people. For half an hour she sang to him.
Then she jumped to her feet. "Supper-time," she cried. It was his
favorite dish that she had prepared for him: lobster spiced with
coconut, served upon fried bread. Afterwards they brought the
phonograph out upon the veranda. As they danced, they kissed.

That was the story as the Frenchman told it us.

"And that's fifteen years ago," he said; "and the man she did
it for's been dead for five; they keep her on here because they just
daren't not."

We listened in silence. Below us in the street motor cars were
honking noisily. Out of a clear blue sky a heavy December sun
was pouring its amber light across the green savannah onto the
white statue. In the harbor were the funnels and the masts of
liners. It was hard in such a moment at such a place to believe in
the black magic of Africa.

And yet, and yet. . . .

"I think," said Eldred, "we'll have our table changed tonight."

Floria's face showed no pleasure or satisfaction when we told
her of our decision. Her scowl was as surly as ever. Her incompetence was as marked. She spilled the soup over the tablecloth,
clattered the plates, brought us our fish cold, and butter when we
had ceased to need it. We had a thoroughly uncomfortable meal.

But that night we slept.

A Beachcomber

from THE SUGAR ISLANDS

WRITTEN IN 1938

I WAS MET on the landing-stage by the kind of chauffeur—scrubby, unshaven, swarthy—to whom several months of West Indian travel had accustomed me. He might have been an octoroon, he might have been a quarter-caste, or he might have been simply sunburned. He wore sandals, blue cotton trousers, and a short-sleeved shirt. A rough-rimmed straw hat was pulled low over his eyes. His step was shuffling and his manner surly.

"You Mr. Wilding's guest?"

I nodded.

"His car's over there, by the Customs shed."

Long and low, a glittering stream of color in the morning sunlight, a six-cylinder Chrysler presented a reassuringly opulent contrast to its driver.

My host's rich, I thought.

I corrected myself a quarter of an hour later as we swung into a long avenue lined with royal palms at whose far extremity was a white, two-storied, many-windowed house. He was more than rich: he was very rich.

From a rattan chair on a wide, flower-flanked veranda a tall figure rose to greet me. He was a man of about sixty. He had an open, smiling face. I made an addition to my estimate. He was more than very rich. He was nice as well: a final estimate that confirmed me in a mood of contented anticipation.

170

I had good reason to be in such a mood. I had long wanted to pay a second visit to Dominica.

Dominica may not be a tourist's island. It has no smart hotels, no bathing beaches, no casino. Its climate is damp and sultry. The sky is more often gray than blue. In a sense it is a melancholy island: with its cloud-hung mountains and its long story of ill-luck; one crop and then another—cocoa first, then limes—ruined by disease. It is not an obvious island: not at all. But it has the power to attract eccentrics. It has "character." Square pegs, after long efforts to fit themselves into round holes, have made their homes there and been happy. It is the background of Elmer Napier's novel, *Duet in Discord*. The lovely and unusual talent of Jean Rhys has its roots in Portsmouth. Its society is stimulatingly heterogeneous. On my return to England, I had found myself thinking more often of Dominica than of any other of the West Indian islands that I had visited. I found myself wishing that I had stayed there longer, that I had done more and different things, that I had thrown a wider net. I was more than grateful when, through the kind offices of a friend, an exchange of cables brought me, on a later visit to the Caribbean, an invitation to Wilding's bungalow.

I settled myself comfortably beside him.

"I've so many things to ask you . . ." I began.

So many things that the hour of the morning swizzle had arrived before he had had time to say, "I wonder, by the way, if you ever came across the man who had this place before me? He was in your line. Weston."

"Max Weston?"

"You knew him, then?"

"I should say I did!"

I spoke decisively. Though I had not met him half a dozen times, the impression he had made upon my memory was ineffaceable. I have met no one who was more completely allergic to me.

I had met him, fifteen years before. Little and dapper, in the early forties, he was slightly bald, with a high forehead and very prominent, staring, pale blue eyes; but his distinctive feature was the texture of his skin. There are some men who at no matter what hour of the day you meet them look as though they had not shaved for thirty hours. You wonder when they actually do shave, since they are never either more nor less unshaven. Weston, on the other hand, always looked as though he had at that moment left the barber's chair, where not only had he been shaved with exhaustive patience, but where the kind of varnish with which women anoint their finger nails had been smeared over his face from chin to cheekbone. The effect of that glazed and glistening surface was singularly repellent, yet at the same time singularly magnetic. He exuded electricity. I do not suppose that he ever made a friend; but he fascinated a great many people—young women in particular. He was purposeful in conversation. He had confidence. He was a lavish and effective host. He had, moreover, a background of achievement—of very definite achievement. At a time when professional English authorship was dominated by the American market, he was one of the chief New York lecture agents.

He specialized in English authors. During the nineteen-twenties he came over to London every autumn to interview novelists, agents, publishers. I should imagine that during those years he not only knew but had entertained everybody of any consequence in the literary racket. My most vivid memory of him is a lunch that he gave at the Savoy for a dozen or so of the younger writers. As a lunch it was one of the best that I have ever sat before. But none of us enjoyed it, really. When I hear Englishmen who have never been to America describe Americans as purse-proud, money-conscious, reducing all values to a dollar basis, my answer is, "Well, I have known *one* American like that."

At the end of the meal he leaned across the table.

"Now listen. You're promising. Every one of you," he said. "That's why you're here. You've got it in you to turn yourselves into the kind of successes I can use. But you're on the wrong track. You're all too literary, too clever-clever. I want life, real people, real problems, real backgrounds. That's what I can put across. The moment you start writing real books, I'm the man to sell you. Till you do, we're wasting each other's time. But when you do start . . . well, I reckon I don't need to introduce myself."

The knowledge that, as regards his powers, he spoke the truth was the most infuriating part of the whole performance. He might boast, but he could call his bluffs. I left that table praying that

circumstance should never force me to owe him a debt of gratitude.

That was in 1925. And much had happened since: in the literary
racket, as elsewhere; New York was not in 1937 the happy hunting
ground that it had been. Publishers on Murray Hill had ceased to
advance on the delivery of each new manuscript a sum three times
as great as its predecessor had earned in royalties. Editors in Phila-
delphia no longer commissioned serials that they "might find a use
for some day." Even Hollywood had consulted balance sheets.
But it was the lecture market that had taken the biggest toss.
Through the nineteen-twenties any English novelist of standing
could, by signing an American lecture contract, liquidate at the
cost of a few weeks' casual conversation the accumulated liabilities
of as many years. All that was over. Through the English authors'
own fault, mainly. Those casual conversations had been a bit too
casual. Long before Wall Street broke, American audiences had
grown as weary of listening to ninety minutes of trailing impromptu autobiographical reflections as they were of reading a few
weeks later the articles in which on their return to England those
same lecturers lampooned the absurdities of the American Wom-
en's clubs that had financed them. By the end of the nineteen-
twenties the lecturing English novelist was the most generally
disliked commodity throughout the Union. And the climax was
reached in the spring of 1931 when. . . . But perhaps that is a story
that at this late day it is more charitable to forget. Let it suffice to
state that it was a very long time since I had heard a brother novelist remark: "My arrears of income tax are ceasing to be a joke. I
shall have to run across and pick up a few easy dollars."

So completely indeed was the lecture racket finished for the
English novelist that I do not suppose that I had heard Weston
mentioned five times in as many years.

That he of all people should have come to Dominica!

"Why on earth did he come?" I asked.

"To die."

"What!"

"He had a breakdown: you know the way he drank, last thing
at night, first thing in the morning. One day he collapsed across
a table. His doctors gave him a year to live."

I started; stared and started. A year to live! Is there anyone who has not imagined himself faced with such a fate; who has not wondered how in such a predicament he would himself behave? How had Max Weston faced it?

Not that I need have wondered. The story of that year, as Wilding told it me, was in every detail consistent with the conduct and previous spirit of his life: a mixture of pettiness, spite, swagger, vanity.

Spite came first. There was one person in his life that he had hated—his wife. I had never seen her. No one in England had. But everybody in New York knew that he owed his success to her: that her money had carried him through his early years. She was older than he was, considerably: she was neither clever nor smart nor handsome. But people liked her; had done things for Max because of her; had let him know it. He never forgave her that. He wanted to believe that he had done it all himself. When the chance for revenge came he took it.

It was the summer of '29. He sold his contracts and goodwill— at a typical boom figure. He handed his wife a tenth. For fifteen years, he told her, she had made life a hell for him. He had only stayed with her because a scandal would have done him harm. Now he did not care. He was going to clear right out. She could send detectives after him if he liked, but the law worked slowly. By the time she had got the machinery of the law in motion, he would not be in the world to worry.

Spite had its innings first, then vanity. Most of us have one point on which our vanity is raw. Max could not forget his personal obscurity. However successful he might be, no one outside his immediate circle could ever hear of him. He was the middleman pocketing his commission. His name meant nothing, never could mean anything across any column, in any paper. He had no news value. It was a fact that never ceased to rankle.

If most of us have one point on which our vanity is raw, most of us also have one person we are jealous of. Max had two: George Doran, the publisher, and Ray Long, the editor. Year after year through the nineteen-twenties they crossed to London to "contact" authors. They held the field. English authors owed more to those two men than to any twenty others in "the racket." It was not their success but their prominence that Max resented. There was no bookshelf in the world on which the name Doran could not be read among its covers. The name Ray Long stood big on every copy of the two million copies of *Cosmopolitan* that month after month were scattered across the world. Everyone knew who Long and Doran were; nobody knew who Weston was. All three, in their separate ways, were doing the same thing, introducing and establishing English authorship into and in America. All three successfully. But while two were "figures," one was not. When the doctors gave Weston his year to live, he saw his chance, not only of getting even with his wife, but of making himself a "figure."

He saw that chance, as one should have known he would, in terms of swagger. He had a year to live. He would make a legend of that year. Every dollar he could command would be spent on it. His plan had the simplicity that is said to be the half of genius. Fortnight after fortnight he staged in the house that now was Wilding's a succession of house parties. He knew practically everyone on Broadway. His guests' fares were paid. On such a basis, it was not difficult to make the pattern of those parties read like a Cholly Knickerbocker column. And on each party he invited one first-class journalist. As each fortnight passed, he read in his imagination the obituaries that would be starring the New York Press within a year. No journalist, wearily looking for fresh copy, could fail to make Weston's last months in Dominica the subject of his column. Weston's eyes glittered as he looked ahead. His "year to live" would become a legend. He himself would become a legend. Whenever the literary background of the nineteen-twenties was discussed or written of, his name would be linked with Doran's and Ray Long's.

I smiled to myself as I listened to Wilding's account of that year of parties. I looked forward to hearing other accounts from other residents. Max was a cad. But he was in character. I could not help admiring anyone who could carry through an act so thoroughly.

"And then . . . ?" I asked.

Wilding smiled, then shrugged.

"Doctors aren't always right."

He chuckled as he said that. I stared, not understanding for a moment. He laughed as the truth came to me.

"That's it. You've got it. He got well again. They thought he had an organic ailment. But he hadn't. It was simply drink. And drugs. When he was down here, in a decent climate, with no money left to buy a drink with, he was as fit as he'd ever been within a fortnight."

"But . . ." I paused, visualizing the incredibly impossible position in which Max had found himself. His money gone, his boats burned. The depression in full flood. No business, no chance of starting one. Hated by his wife's friends; discredited. A laughing-stock because a doctor'd fooled him. He could not go back to New York. There was nothing he could do in London. There was no opening for him, anywhere.

"What on earth did he do?" I asked.

"The only thing he could do: stayed on here."

"Here?"

"He looks after the electric plant. I kept him on because you can't trust a native with machinery: too ticklish for them. He does his job quite well. As a matter of fact, you've seen him. He met you on the wharf this morning. It's the kind of thing," he added, "that would happen in Dominica."

A Creole Crooner

from THE SUGAR ISLANDS

WRITTEN IN 1939

I MET HIM FIRST in London in the spring of 1927. Though he did not know it, he was then at the peak of his success. The bright-young-people period was at its flood, and the bright young people "had a thing" about colored artists. Florence Mills and Robeson were in London. Layton and Johnston were at the Café. In Grafton Street "Hutch" was singing his nursery rhymes series at Chez Victor. The Black Birds were playing to packed houses. *Nigger Heaven* was heading the best-seller lists. The Black Crow records had just arrived. It was not only an artistic but a social craze. No party was a party without its Black Birds. A lift was going up: any number of people contrived to climb on it. Louis was one of the first ones in.

He was young, tallish, supple; with bright, bold eyes, very white teeth, and a voice that was amply adequate at a time when that kind of voice was essential, not only to every *restaurateur's*, but to every hostess's success. He was a bare twenty-three. Two years back he had been an obscure singer in Montmartre. It turned his head, inevitably. His swagger became a challenge, his bold eyes grew insolent. At Henri's he would sing his songs directly at some girl in the audience in such a way that his singing appeared a courtship. On the least appropriate occasions he would display an initialled cigarette case. "Mary gave me this: charming of her, don't you think? You know her, of course: Lady Mary Rocheford. A most agreeable lady." And his eyelids would lower; not a wink,

177

no: but as though he had withdrawn into an intimate, recollective trance. Even those who were least restrained in their enthusiasm for Black Birds admitted that Louis was nearly too much of a good thing.

At the time of our first meeting, I had just returned from the South Seas. My host had asked me a question about Tahiti. Louis listened for a minute or two with a show of interest, then interrupted.

"Tahiti, yes. It's well enough. But you should see my island. You should see Saint Lucia."

I had not then been to the West Indies, and I asked him where St. Lucia was. He laughed, patronizingly. St. Lucia, he explained, was the northernmost of the Windward Islands, within sight of Martinique. In the days of the great admirals, Rodney, Nelson, Hood, it had been the key to naval power. It was high and green. "It must be lovelier, far lovelier than your Tahiti," he insisted. "In Tahiti, so you tell us, there is only that one road round the island. The interior is so overgrown that you can follow the streams a bare mile or so. But my island is cut by valleys. Every inch of valley is planted thick with sugar cane. It is so green; you cannot imagine how green it is. And there are coconut palms along the beaches: just as you described them in Tahiti. Tahiti cannot have anything we have not too. And then our fishing villages: little clumps of huts where the streams run out into the bays. And it's all so French. They still speak patois. I don't know how many times the island didn't change hands before it became English finally. The fishermen have French names for their boats: such funny little boats too, with square sails."

His voice began to glow. It is impossible to reproduce the quality of a West Indian vocie: it is not a question of words, of phrases, of the turning of a sentence. It is a question of tone, of a lift and pitch of voice: a sing-song quality peculiar, not only to the West Indies, but to each separate West Indian island; so that the Creole can always tell after a few minutes from which island the voice comes.

"They call Saint Lucia the pearl of the West Indies. But very few people ever see it," he went on. "Many ships may call there. But only for an hour or two. The tourist drives up into the hills: the *Morne* we call it. He'll bathe at Vigie, lunch or dine at the Saint Antoine. They'll serve him Creole dishes; there is a fine view of the harbor from the terrace; and as likely as not he'll say, as his ship sails eastward to Barbados, 'Yes, I certainly would like to come and stay here.' He may say that. But he'll never have seen Saint Lucia."

Louis paused, shrugged, went on. "The beach at Vigie, yes, that's well enough. But it's always crowded. And that row of bathing huts. No one would go to Vigie who's seen Réduit. That's the perfect beach: a great curve of yellow sand; not a hut along it, a mountain at the back of you; and to the right at the end of the curve, Gros Ilet, the model fishing village. In front there's Pidgeon Island, where Rodney waited for the French fleet before the Battle of the Saints; and across the forty miles of water there's Martinique. You'll search the world and never find a beach like Réduit. And Castries. It's all right when you're looking down on it; but when you're actually down there, it's hot and noisy and there's the smell of gasoline. And as for those Creole dishes at the Saint Antoine, they're good enough. But you should eat Creole cooking in a Creole household. While, as for that view of the harbor from the *Morne*—it's wonderful, I'm not denying that; but it's too domestic. To see the real Saint Lucia you should go where there aren't wharves and houses. You should go where the country's wild. You should go to my part of the island, to the south, to Soufrière."

Not only his voice was glowing, but his eyes. He reminded me of Josephine Baker: "*J' ai deux amours: mon pays et Paris.*"

"No tourist ever goes there," he continued. "It's under the Pitons; you must have read of them. Those two great cone-shaped mountains that rise sheer out of the sea. It's half a village—a fishing village, with its small boats and its nets hanging out to dry. But it's a town as well, with a cobbled square by the jetty, with a great banyan tree to shade it; and there's a church at the end of the main street. And it's all very clean and neat. That's where I was born: Soufrière. We had a house on the waterfront. We had a clock handed down by my great-grandfather: it had a little soldier in red uniform who came out and struck the hours on a drum. The square was always crowded with fishermen, with peasants coming down from the hills to ship their fruit. I had an accordion. In the evenings I would sing; the boys would join in the choruses. The women worked on the men's nets. The girls would dance: they'd be wearing their native costume, the French *madras.* The sun would be setting and the air'd be cool. That is the real Saint Lucia."

He paused; his voice had taken on a deeper, richer tone—a tone that explained not only his success, but the nature of his success. I could understand how at certain moments to certain people he could be irresistible. He was not only a satyr; he was Pan as well.

"Sometimes, when I'm singing at my restaurant"—and I smiled, wondering how Henri would like to hear Louis talking of "my restaurant"—"sometimes, when it's late, and the air's hot and smoky, I close my eyes, I think myself back again on to my doorstep, in the cool of the evening, with the fishermen and the peasant girls: I think myself back among them. My heart *is* in my singing then."

He had actually closed his eyes while he was speaking. I too closed mine. Behind the darkness of their lids I relived a Tahitian evening; at Taravoa; a Chrysler parked beside a Chinese store. The strumming on a banjo. The wash of water on a reef. The glint of moonlight on the palm fronds. The soft Polynesian voices. The sweet, heavy scent of the tiare. From my knowledge of other islands, I could picture his. One day I'm going to St. Lucia, I told myself.

But it was twelve years before I did.

Eighteen months later, as I have already told, I was to take a longish trip to the West Indies. In Martinique, from the beach below my bungalow, I was to see morning after morning the outline of the Pitons faint and misty across the water. But inter-island communication is not easy. In the end I was to find myself doing what Louis had assured me every tourist did—spending a mere four hours there on my way between Dominica and Barbados.

They were, I am gratefully ready to concede, four very pleasant hours. Charles Doorly was Administrator then. A car was waiting for me at the wharf. On the high terrace of Government House, we sat, he and his wife and pretty daughters, talking of his schemes, his many schemes to restore to the island the prosperity that it had known before the opening of the Panama Canal had ruined its coaling trade. We sat, looking out over the harbor till the network of lights spangled the long, straight streets, till the siren of the *Lady Hawkins* sounded in the harbor: till the time came for me to leave St. Lucia, as ninety-nine tourists in a hundred leave it, with a vivid, superficial memory. It was twelve years before I was to carry my suitcase through the Customs. And in those twelve years much had happened.

From that immediately pre-war world of 1938, with its revolution, its civil wars and threats of war, its pogroms and concentration camps, its swastikas and sickles—from that shadowed, overcast world of the late nineteen-thirties, the bright-young-people period of the 'twenties seemed centuries remote. But even before that period had closed, torpedoed by the Wall Street crash, the craze for colored singers had been superseded by other crazes; by the craze for eccentric parties—parties in swimming baths, parties in anchored yachts, by the whole *Vile Bodies* period. Long before that dark October of 1929, the boom as far as Louis was concerned had ended.

I would sometimes wonder what had happened to him.

What had happened in general I knew. That which does invariably happen in a "craze." For a while certain artists of true merit are valued above their worth: then through the exposure of their imitators they are written down. There is an interval, a readjustment, a pause, and merit finds its level. Layton, Johnston, Leslie Hutchinson—they had all got back where they belonged. Real merit was re-established. But for the others, those who like Loius had done no more than clamber on to a lift when it was going up, what had happened to them? I wondered.

I made inquiries, but no one knew. Shoulders were shrugged. He was working in some cabaret. He was back in Paris. He was in New York. He had gone off terribly. He was fat and gross. He was ignored by that part of London that for a dozen months had made an idol of him. He had been sold short like the small fry in New York who had imagined themselves millionaires during that one wild summer. No one knew where he was. And no one cared.

It was by the merest chance that I came across him a few days before I sailed for the West Indies, in a Soho night club called the Alcove. It was a place of which I had not heard, to which I was taken by a taxi-driver; the kind of place that you could only find in a city such as London, where drink regulations make it impossible for any reputable restaurant to stay open after two o'clock;

the kind of place to which the average Londoner would never think of going more than once a year; of which he will say next morning, with a heavy head, "I can't think why on earth I went."

The Alcove was like all those places: a single long room on a basement floor; some twenty tables drawn along a wall; a small square of polished boarding; a piano at one end; no band; the air thick with smoke; a few tinselly decorations; at the head of the stairs a military-looking man in a tail coat proffering a form to the effect that you had been invited by Captain Ferguson to a bottle party and had contributed five shillings to its cost. Whisky was on sale at two pounds a quart, to be purchased by the bottle. A drab and dreary spot.

Louis was its chief attraction. He had "gone off" all right. He had not probably in actual weight put on more than a dozen pounds, but he had lost his lean, panther look. And there is a camel-hair's difference between ugliness and beauty: a milligram less, a millimeter more. He was Pan no longer. He was a satyr, gross and heavy-footed. He could not have faced the hard spot-lights of a restaurant. Only in such a place as this, ill-lit and smoky, could he retain his glamor. Even his voice seemed throaty.

I had met him a bare half-dozen times. I half hoped that he would not remember me. It would embarrass him, I felt, to be reminded by the presence of an old acquaintance, of his days of prominence. But it was with a brazen grin displaying his fine row of teeth that he came across. He grasped me by the hand. He brought his left hand heavily upon my shoulder.

"This is swell. This certainly is swell. Why haven't we seen you here before? Everyone comes here now. It's nice, isn't it? Intimate? Not like those big, noisy places. You must bring your friends along. We always have good fun here. To-night . . ." He paused, looked round him, shook his head. "No, there's not much here to-night. But sometimes, you should see . . ." He half-closed his eyes, in that way of his.

Across the smoky room, he caught a summoning glance: a female glance. With the old arrogance, he took his leave of me. With the old insolence, he swaggered across the room. I watched him as he leaned across the table, his neck creased in a heavy roll above his collar. As I foresaw the inevitable stages by which he must drop from one shoddy platform to another, I could not but remember the old Greek theme of retribution, of those who invite the gods' wrath by likening themselves to gods.

Six weeks later, on an afternoon of blinding rain, the *Nerissa* docked at Castries.

During the next fortnight I was to realize what Louis had meant about the half-day tourist never seeing the real St. Lucia.

Destroyed in large part by a recent fire, Castries has little architectural beauty. Vigie, though an easy ten minutes' row across the harbor, cannot compare with Réduit which is a full forty minutes' drive. And though the view from the Morne is certainly melodramatic—the bay a figure of eight; Castries below you in the hollow; across the water the outline of Martinique with Diamond Rock silvered in the sunlight; the Cul de Sac Valley, a brilliant emerald, at your back—I can understand why Louis argued that that panorama, terrific though it may be, gives you no insight into the island's life, its agriculture, its fishing, its small peasant properties. To get any real idea of one of the world's most charming islands, the tourist *does* need to stay over between boats.

But in a week he can see a lot. And that week can be a most, most pleasant one. The St. Antoine is one of the best hotels in the West Indies. It is cool, the rooms are large, and though Louis had assured me that to appreciate Creole cooking you should sample it in Creole households, I cannot suppose that he had ever entered the hotel by its front entrance. He might change his opinion if he did. The tourist arriving in St. Lucia with letters of introduction will within a few hours find himself caught up into and made a part of a varied and gracious social life. St. Lucia is not one of the richer islands. But money in the tropics is a luxury. By the European standards of that day, the Creole families of St. Lucia would have been considered poor. But there is no less entertainment and entertaining on that account. The traditions of West Indian hospitality were maintained there amply in an atmosphere of picnics, bathing, sailing, riding; most evenings at one house or another there were rum punches and savory *canapés*. My fortnight passed so quickly and so enjoyably that I do not think I should have deserted Castries had it not been for my curiosity to see Louis's home.

Yet the journey was not a hard one. Soufrière is only some fifteen miles along the coast. A small motor launch, the *Jewel*, made the round trip daily. She left, or was supposed to leave, at half-past two. From one o'clock onwards that section of the wharf was chaos. The narrow first-class section was jammed with packages, suitcases, baskets, sacks. The roof was very low. The steerage passengers were packed as close as their African ancestors in the Guinea slavers. Livestock was carried aft. When it rained—and the rainless day is as rare as is the sunless day in the West Indies—waterproof flaps were lowered from the roof. The fumes of the engine were just, but only just, the predominant factor in the general atmosphere.

It was rough on the day that I went down. Only for brief intervals could the waterproof flaps be lifted to reveal high, scrub-covered hills, broken here and there by valleys, with sugar factories or fishing villages at their foot. On the bench beside me a young colored girl was using the shoulder of an adjacent Indian as a writing-desk. Professional curiosity overcame my manners. It was a love-letter, headed like any trans-Atlantic passenger's "On Board." It was a grammatical but impersonal little note: devoted in the main to the headache that the atmosphere of the launch was causing her. When she folded away the note before she had reached the signature, I was afraid that she was about to follow the example of the child two places off and vomit. But clearly she was a serial correspondent. Leaning her elbows on the Indian's shoulders, she scoured his scalp for white hairs which she then proceeded to extract.

I was glad when the ninety minutes of the trip were over, but as the launch swung round at last I could understand Louis's nostalgia. Set in the wide semicircle of a bay, with towering mountains at its back, with the guardian Pitons on the right, Soufrière in a catalogued description might sound a melancholy, overshadowed place. It is not, though. It is friendly, cosy, intimate; with its grove of coconuts, its fishing nets, its sports ground fringed with casuarinas, its banyan tree on the right of the jetty to shade the cobbled square, its church at the end of its center street to give it an air of Switzerland.

As the launch drew level with the jetty, a number of urchins, bare-footed, with ragged shirts and shapeless hats, rushed forward, clamorous for our bags. Twenty years earlier Louis must have looked like that, must have run forward just like that, touching his hat. "Your bag, sah. Douglas Fairbanks, sah, that's me." Run-

ning my eye along the row of chattering faces, I wondered whether
for any of them a fate so romantic waited; to travel so far, to
reach so high, to fall so fast. Here Louis had been born: here his
family had lived—in what circumstances I did not need to ask.
The setting changes, but the story of the child of humble origin
who touches fame is universal. It is del Sarto's story:

> "They were born poor, lived poor and poor they died . . .
> And I have labored somewhat in my time
> And not been paid profusely. Some good son
> Paint my two hundred pictures—let him try."

I foresaw what I should find.

I found it, more or less.

His mother, I was told, had died; but there was an aunt left,
living with a cousin in her sister's house. It was in a side street;
not, as Louis had told me, on the square. It had two rooms, cur-
tains, and some furniture. It was not actually dirty. A visiting
member of the Royal Commission might indeed have considered
it with approval. "The home, I presume, of the rather better kind
of fisherman." It was only when I remembered that flashing of an
engraved cigarette case that in contrast it seemed squalid.

The aunt was very old, very infirm, her body shrunken with
age, so that her head appeared top-heavy—she was suffering probably from some kind of dropsy. She was a macabre object, sitting
in a high-backed rocking chair, in a shawl, with a long skirt falling
over the hems of innumerable petticoats round swollen ankles.

She shook her head sadly when I spoke of Louis.

No, he never wrote. When his mother had died, yes, he had
been kind then. He had sent some money. They had put up a nice
gravestone for her. I should go and see it. But apart from that,
no, not one word in all these years. The Empire broadcasts gave
them their sole news of him. He sang once a fortnight. He would
be singing tomorrow night. On the mantelpiece was a photograph,
cut from the *Radio Times* and pasted on a sheet of cardboard.
"He hasn't altered at all. He looks the same dear boy. I wish he
could find some nice girl and settle down." I examined the photograph. It had come from the file room, clearly. It must be at least
ten years old. Beside the rocking chair was an early nineteenth-
century spinet. Remembering how Louis had talked of the crowds
that had gathered under the banyan tree at sundown, I supposed

that his singing must be missed in Soufrière; his aunt shook her head. Louis had run away at twelve, signed on a French boat as cabin boy. They remembered him here, if they remembered him at all, as a no-account fellow, who would not work, who only cared for music. The parson's daughter used to give him lessons. But no one else had noticed him.

I was surprised, but I should not have been. It was in character that during these early months of struggle, first as a cabin boy, then in Paris as a waiter, the main spur to his ambition should have been the resolve to prove his real worth to the cousins who had despised him. And when he had fought his way to a position from which he could afford to remember their contempt of him with a smile, it was only natural that he should dramatize, should visualize his success in terms of a conquered, subject Soufrière.

I rose to my feet. Once the rough walls of this cabin had housed ambition of sufficient power to carry such an urchin as had besieged the motor launch that afternoon to the bizarre destiny of boastfully flashed silver cases. I looked about me, missing something. The clock: where could that have gone? A chuckle came from the vast nodded head. "So he told you about that? The clock with the soldier that beat the hours. Fancy his remembering. But of course he would. He'd sit and stare for minutes before each hour so as not to miss it."

"But where is it now?"

"Where it always was. The Rectory."

"Then it wasn't yours?"

"Could we afford a clock like that? Louis only went to the Rector's Bible classes so that he could look at it. We used to say that it was the only reason that he took music lessons from the Rector's daughter."

And that too was in the picture.

The next day my host took me for a ride over the mountains to Guilese, where the Government had established an experimental station for local agriculture. I understood during that ride what Louis had meant about the domesticity of the scenery round Castries. This, in comparison, was completely wild. A succession of intersecting valleys; no roads; just tracks, cut away by streams, winding round the side of mountains with a sheer drop on the far side, so narrow that every so often we would have to get off and lead our horses. Along the road, groups of peasants carrying huge bunches of bananas passed us on their way to the coast. An occasional youth with a shot-gun showed us a bag of pigeon. The path led us through Frond St. Jacques, a group of cabins with children playing under trees, women tending babies, hens wandering at large, pigs tethered against stakes. It was very simple; very primitive. It had a casual, South Sea atmosphere. The men would be lucky to work three days a week on the plantations: they would be paid a few pennies for their work: their daughters and their wives less. But they had their gardens, they had their allotments: they could raise their own crops, keep their pigs and poultry. They grumbled, but they were not unhappy.

It was from circumstances such as these that Louis's original ancestors had come. He was ashamed of that jungle background; and no doubt the house in Soufrière, with its two rooms, its furniture, its spinet, represented from one point of view an advance in progress. But there was no doubt as to which life was the cleaner, happier, healthier: the life of "civilization" in the narrow alleys of the town, or this primitive existence in the clear air of the bush. Nor could there be any doubt as to the way of living from which Louis, as every other colored artist, had drawn his strength. The depth and power in his voice had sprung out of nostalgia, was the cry of an exiled spirit. And as I rode on, I pondered such reactionary reflections as have fretted most of those who have been brought into touch with primitive native life. To what point, I asked myself, do we educate these simple people, unfitting them for the life to which the centuries have trained them, transporting them into an alien world, where even such a success as Louis's is purchased at a price whose payment must be in the end regretted.

At Guilese there was a resthouse where we ate our sandwich lunch. It was late in the day when we returned. It was several months since I had ridden, and I was grateful for the warm sulphur bath in the stone basin that Louis XVI had built there for his soldiers.

I wallowed lazily; so lazily that it was close on six before I was changed. And sundown in the tropics is the hour when club life starts.

But in Soufrière there is no club. Every morning the two main planters drive down to the wharf and, sitting in their Chevrolets,

transact there the majority of their business. Social life is confined
to the bridge four that meets every evening in the house of the
retired colonel who was my host and to the preprandial cocktail
proffered in turn by one or other of the other three. We were on
our way that evening to the house of the chief planter of the
district, an Englishman by fact of residence, but so French in
name and birth that half his older relatives could barely make
themselves understood in English.

Our road lay through the town, along the waterfront. The sun
was low in the sky. The air was cool. The work of the day was
finished. A large miscellaneous group was gathered in the square:
women sewing at the nets; fishermen puffing at their pipes; children tumbling over each other in the gutters; young men lounging
against the trees; old women on their door-steps in their native
costume, the French *madras*; girls in groups, chattering and gig-
gling; a couple of policemen, very smart and upright in their blue
tunics and white helmets. There was a buzz of talk. But louder
than the buzz of talk came the sound of music. "What's this?"
I asked. "A wake?"

My host shook his head. "Only a radio with a loud-speaker.
They often come out here in the evening."

Then I remembered. The Empire broadcast: Louis. "Let's
stop," I said.

We waited, listened. The organ voluntary concluded. The voice
of the announcer crackled through a blur of static: then the static
stopped. A rich, full voice came through it: a familiar voice. A
song that was ten years old. "That's my weakness now."

Did one person in that noisy group realize whose voice they
heard? Clear and full, it rang across the square.

> "I never cared for eyes of blue;
> But she's got eyes of blue,
> And that's my weakness now."

The buzz of talk subsided. A couple began to dance. It was
just such a scene as Louis had described to me.

I pictured him, three thousand miles away. It would be ten
o'clock in London. He would resent having to go out into the
cold of a January night. He would be taking it very casually: an
Empire broadcast; a small fee. He would resent having to accept
such work. He would be in his ordinary day clothes. Shabby

clothes, most likely, for he only needed to look smart at night: clothes cut to an earlier fashion, that fitted him too tightly. As likely as not he would be unshaven. There would be no audience in the studio. He would take off his coat and collar. Standing there, half-dressed, there would be nothing to distinguish him from these cousins of his grouped here under the banyan tree. Had he the imagination to picture them here, listening? I doubted it. His mind would already be upon the evening's work. The songs he would sing, the guests who would be there. His eyes would brighten at the thought of a blonde who had come there three nights running with a dreary and surely unimportant escort. As his eyes brightened, a new richness would come into his voice, so that three thousand miles away along a waterfront young couples across a cobbled square would smile into each other's eyes.

Here was his ambition realized: his boyhood's dream. The cousins who had mocked him were summoned to the square, to be held there, subjugated by his voice. Before me was the gay-colored throng, in my ears the rhythm of that rich full voice, before memory's eye a shabby, discredited figure by a microphone.

The music stopped. The announcer had taken Louis's place. Another performer was beckoned across the studio. I pictured Louis pulling a muffler round his throat, hurrying out into the cold, to the small bed-sitting-room in his Bloomsbury lodging-house, to bathe and shave and change, to take his place at the piano in the Alcove. A passage from an early Cannan novel crossed my memory—a passage to the effect that we always get out of life the thing we ask for, but never "according to the letter of our desire."

SNAPSHOTS : The West Indian Scene

Au Revoir, Martinique

Montserrat

Barbados

Anguilla

Trinidad

St. Vincent

Tortola

The West Indian Scene

from THE SUGAR ISLANDS

WRITTEN IN 1947

To THE BRITISH and American tourist the Caribbean has everything to offer at the time of year when our own climate is at its worst—between January and April. During those three months the islands provide varied types of sport—sailing and swimming, cricket and golf and tennis, fishing, shooting, riding. They can accommodate the dimensions and needs of the longest as of the shortest purse. The cost of living varies with each island and the various sections of each island. Jamaica is the most expensive in the group. Charges in Montego Bay are as astronomic as they are in Havana and Palm Beach. Yet even in Jamaica it is possible to live in very real comfort at a very reasonable cost, while life is as cheap in the smaller islands as it is anywhere in the world.

Fruit and fish are plentiful. Rum is a *vin du pays*, and when the sun is shining there is not a great deal to spend money on. By day you idle on a beach; in the evening you sip cocktails on a veranda. One day becomes the next.

Nor could the climate during those three months conceivably be better. It is hot to the extent that a man wears light or Palm Beach clothes by day and a white dinner jacket in the evening. He would feel overweighted by a flannel suit, but there is no equivalent for the overpowering dry heat of Iraq or for the exhausting damp heat of Malaya. Trinidad is the only island that has a sticky climate, but even in Trinidad there is a cool breeze

193

at night. There is very little malaria and mosquitoes are rarely troublesome. At one time in Martinique and in St. Lucia a very venomous snake—the *fer de lance*—made cross-country journeys inadvisable, but the introduction of the mongoose has removed that pest. There is a certain amount of rain, but the showers are brief and violent. You are quite likely to get soaked, but you are very unlikely to have your plans for a whole day ruined. It is prudent to wear a hat, but there is no need to worry about sunstroke. There is really no snag about the West Indian climate, its greatest merit for the tourist being that he does not need to take special precautions against anything. "Oldest inhabitants" may warn him against the dangers of drinking alcohol before sundown or of taking exercise between ten and four, but oldest inhabitants are always anxious to give one "the benefit of their experience." They are always urging the necessity of this and that. I have never been to a place in which I have not been assured by someone that I must avoid that, that I must take this precaution, and in most places I have found that by doing what I am in the habit of doing normally, with such modifications as in a different climate one's own inclinations will suggest, I have managed pretty well. Certainly I feel very fit in the West Indies in spite of cocktails before lunch and exercise between two and four. My advice to anyone visiting the West Indies is very simple: travel light and provide yourself with letters of introduction.

Letters of introduction are absolutely essential if the tourist is to get the most out of a West Indian trip. He can have, I will admit, a whole lot of fun without them. He can relax into an agreeable routine of sunbathing and picnics. He will make friends at his hotel and he will be unlucky if he does not in the course of a week make contact by chance with at least one resident who will invite him to his house and introduce him to the clubs. If he were to make a longish stay, that single contact would lead to other contacts, so that by the end of a month he would be leading a varied and amusing social life. But most visitors have not the time to spend as much as a month in any single island, and if you are limited to a fortnight's stay, it is essential, at any rate in a British island, if you are anxious to see what its real life is, to arrive with letters of introduction.

Colonies are usually, after all, more consciously national than a mother country, and life in a British West Indian island is a very family affair, reproducing the essential characteristics of English life. [The pattern of government is altering every year. This is how it was in 1947.] The British islands are all of them Crown Colonies, directly responsible to Parliament, and the responsibility of Parliament. The Crown is represented by a governor—or in the smaller islands by an administrator who is the Governor's representative. In most of the islands there is some slight difference in the actual machinery of government, but the general system is to have an elected house of assembly, which petitions a legislative council, half of whose members are selected by the Governor. The life of the island is centered round Government House. A letter of introduction to the Governor or Administrator is of the greatest possible assistance. It does not involve the visitor in tedious formalities. On the contrary, it saves him a great deal of time. The A.D.C. will be able to put him into touch with those of the residents who share his tastes and interests. Even if he has not a letter to the Governor, the visitor who plans to make a stay of a week or more should certainly in the case of the smaller islands sign the Governor's book on his arrival—in the same way that, if he is to make a stay in a French or American colony, he should call upon the British Consul. It is good manners and is also a prudent act. We all have our opposite numbers everywhere; the sooner we find them the sooner we can be introduced by them to whatever is most congenial to us in a new town or country. I have made stays long enough in most of the British West Indian islands to feel that I have got inside the atmosphere of the island's life, and Jamaica is the only one in which I do not feel that it is necessary to be introduced. I had a good deal more fun in Jamaica through arriving with such letters, but I could have managed quite well without them. Jamaica is a vast playground, with its golf courses and its beaches and its *grand luxe* hotels; the life of the residents is apart and separate from the tourist's world. In 1929 I spent ten days at Montego Bay which were as good as any ten days that I have ever spent, sunbathing and swimming and gossiping and dancing. And I am doubtful if I saw one resident during that whole period. Jamaica, however, is exceptional. In the other islands I am very sure that I should have had a bare quarter of the fun I did if I had not arrived with letters.

It is only natural, after all, that this should be so. The English way of life has been built round a tradition of entertaining inside

the home. The pre-war casual visitor to London, Continental or
American, rarely found much to attract him there. There were no
sidewalk *cafés*. Pubs closed at ten; only on extension nights could
he drink in restaurants after half-past twelve. There was no night
life in the sense that Paris and New York and the Berlin of the
nineteen-twenties understood the word. Everything closed early.
Such places as stayed open asked him if he was a member. The
only after-hours places that were accessible to the foreigner were
squalid, subterranean, furtive, and expensive. London has never
catered for the tourist. London belongs to Londoners. And to
those like myself who have been born there, who always, whatever their official address may be, regard London as their home,
London even in the drab and shabby nineteen-fifties has a dignity
and charm, a personal lived-in quality that no other city has. But
you have to be a Londoner or an adopted Londoner to appreciate
it. London is a city of clubs and private houses. You have to be a
member. And though there are those who will argue that London
is not England, London is the home of several million Englishmen. A national capital is the expression of national traits and
character. As London is, so, in my opinion, England is. And just
as I cannot understand how a tourist coming to London as a
stranger without friends could enjoy his visit, so should I be surprised if anyone who went there with appropriate contacts and
stayed long enough to get below its skin, did not find much to
like. To love London, the foreigner has to see it as Londoners
themselves see it, to become temporarily identified with the London way of life.

As it is in London, as it is in England, so is it in the British
colonies. The good times are centered in clubs and private houses,
with which one must get in touch, fully to enjoy oneself.

It is very easy to get in touch. The residents are invariably welcoming, invariably hospitable, invariably ready to take the visitor
into their homes. And it is a very pleasant life into which one is
introduced, a way of life whose particular charm is more readily
appreciated, or of whose nature perhaps I should say it is easier to
get a complete picture, in the smaller than in the larger islands.

In the smaller islands everything is more compact; it is easier
to see the working of the machine. During the greater part of the
second war I was employed in counter-espionage in the Middle
East. For most of the time I was a captain. When I was stationed

in Cairo I only understood the working of my own small section. It is one of the first rules of an intelligence organization that no one should be told more than is strictly necessary for him to carry out the particular task that he has been assigned. The work of military intelligence is divided up into a number of separate specialist sections. Employed as I was on a G.3 level, I did not understand while I was in Cairo how the activities of the various branches dovetailed so that the higher-ranking officers could form a complete picture of what had been found out, what had been deduced and what action was being taken.

In Baghdad, however, the General Staff was so much smaller that the work of a branch that in Cairo required a section of ten intelligence officers headed by a colonel could be done by a major and a lieutenant. Month by month during the three years I spent there, the establishments were reduced, so that at times the work of three branches would be concentrated in a single office. In Baghdad I not only knew personally every officer who was engaged in counter-espionage, but I had a rough, though not, of course, detailed, idea of what he did. By the time I left Baghdad I had acquired a sense of the general pattern of military intelligence that could not, I think, have been acquired in Cairo by anyone under the rank of colonel.

In the same way, it is much easier to get a sense of the West Indian pattern by visiting Grenada than Barbados, and I would recommend every tourist to make a stay of at least a week in one of the smaller islands. The inclination, naturally, is to see as many different islands in the limited time available—and the distinct differences that exist between every island make this a reasonable programme. At the same time, a too close following of that programme prevents him from recognizing the one common multiple of all these islands—the framework of English colonial life. Different though every island is, in this one respect they are alike. They have the same social framework, the same formula for living, so that were a prospective tourist to say to me, "But tell me, what kind of things should I be doing there?" I should be able out of my memories of many islands to describe for him a typical West Indian day.

He will wake, I should tell him, shortly after six in a large, bare, hotel bedroom. The sunlight striking through the shutters will be designing a zebra pattern on the walls and ceiling. He will throw back the shutters and walk out on to his balcony. The sun will be warm upon his cheeks, but a cool breeze will be blowing from the hills. In the street below, Negro women will be on their way to market with baskets of bananas on their heads. Across the road an untidy garden will be bright with yellow cassia. The road itself will be a narrow, mounting one, on the one side climbing into the mountains in whose shelter the town is built, on the other side running down towards the sea. Above its gray-tiled and corrugated-iron roofs he will see the gray-blue stretches of the harbor. Square-sailed fishing boats will be tacking near the shore. A launch carrying coastal cargo will be chunking its slow way between them. Shadowy on the horizon is the outline of another island.

The washing arrangements are likely to be primitive. At the end of a passage there will be a rickety and communal set of showers, but there will be no hot and cold running water in his room. After taking his shower, he will sit on his balcony, watching the slow parade below him of the island's life, savoring the day's freshest hour, till the maid arrives with a jug of shaving water and the coffee and fruit that is the invariable West Indian prelude to a substantial porridge and bacon and eggs breakfast taken in the dining-room.

It is possible that an expedition will have been arranged for him, and he is to be taken out into the country to see the working of an estate. The islands are almost exclusively agricultural. The Spaniards came to the New World in search of gold, but the gold that they found in Haiti had no depth or value and the mines they sank there were soon abandoned. Oil has been found in Trinidad in great abundance, but nowhere else; though when I was in Martinique in 1928, oil shafts were being sunk, without, I believe, encouraging results. Trinidad also has further mineral resources, through the pitch lake which provides a good deal of the world's asphalt. But the fortunes of the other islands depend upon agricultural produce, on sugar and rum and cotton, copra and cocoa, bananas, nutmegs, limes and cloves, grapefruit and arrowroot.

A car will be calling for the tourist shortly after breakfast on mornings when an expedition has been arranged for him. He will be driven by a mounting, circling road into the hills. The valleys will be bright with sugar cane. The bush will be dotted with wattle and corrugated-iron shacks. Here and there he will see the ruined masonry of an aqueduct or gateway. A steady succession of women with baskets upon their heads will pass him on their way to market: their blouses of red and yellow are vivid splashes of color against the deep green of the hills.

In Trinidad and Grenada he will be taken to see the working of the cocoa. He will be shown how in every island the laborers work in teams, husband and wife together, the man snipping off the pods with a long knife, the woman piercing them with a stroke of her pointed cutlass, carrying them in a basket on her head; then, when the basket is full, the man cutting open the pods and the woman shelling them. Eight baskets of pods supply one basket of seeds, and four baskets is a good day's work per team. The cocoa seeds are white and sticky, and they are put out to sweat for eight days under leaves. The visitor will see them being moved from one sweater to another. Then when they have been sweated, they are dried for a further period of eight days. The visitor will see them laid out on shallow trays that are run out on wheels. He will watch the trampling of the seeds for polish in large, circular cauldrons by laughing sweating laborers with their trousers rolled about their knees. [*The cocoa seeds are now, for the most part, polished by machinery, just as the treading of grapes has been abandoned.*] In just that same way, he will tell himself, was cocoa dried and polished two hundred years ago. A few estates have special drying devices which save time when the weather is wet, but ordinarily the methods of the old plantation days are still observed.

And the planter will point out to him, just as his predecessors would have done, the various odd chores that are required on an estate. He will show the women employed on weeding in specially measured plots, the men digging ditches and repairing roads, and the old women scouring for the "black cocoa," the dried and rotten pods that can be used for fuel. Just as in the old slave days, the laborers are allowed their gardens by which they supplement their meager earnings.

In St. Vincent the visitor will be taken out to see the working of the arrowroot on which, in addition to sea-island cotton, the island's prosperity depends. There is something very untropical about it all. You could fancy yourself in England. Arrowroot is planted in sloping fields. Rising to a height of four feet, it has a flower that you can scarcely see. Wild yellow flowers grow over and about it. In the late autumn, when the flower shrivels, the diggers start to work upon the roots. They are ground by a seemingly endless process of washing and of straining. The factories are as clean as dairies; there is a ceaseless roar of water as the arrowroot is passed from butts to strainers, then to the settling tables. In some factories a process of centrifugal force is used by which the white starch grows gradually dark as the impure matter is forced into a crust that can be cut away, leaving the starch clear, ready to be taken to the drying-house and stretched on wire.

In the old days the sugar plantations were adorned with windmills. Now busy bustling engines have supplanted them. The engines are less picturesque, but the general process is the same. There is the same squeezing and pressing of the canes between a row of rollers till the last drop of juice has been extracted, to run into the great clarifiers of the boiler-house to seethe under the heat of a fire that is maintained a degree or two below boiling point, till the white scum blisters to the surface and the coppers can be filled with the pure, almost transparent liquid.

As the traveller follows the planter from one group of laborers to another, it is not difficult for him to recreate the atmosphere of the old plantations.

He will at the same time have an opportunity of appreciating the conditions and nature of the planter's life. Usually the planter is a West Indian by birth. He is rarely the owner of the estate. He is the salaried or commissioned agent of someone who has a store in town and a large bungalow half-way up the hill, a man who is himself, usually, the salaried or commissioned agent of a public company with head offices in London or in Bristol.

In many ways the planter's is a monotonous existence. His day will begin at sunrise. By half-past seven, after a light first breakfast of coffee and fruit and toast, he will be at his *boucan* for the roll-call. His work is mainly supervisory. He walks round the estate, interviewing his overseers, gossiping for a few moments with his laborers. He is out till after eleven, when he returns to his bungalow for breakfast, a kind of lunch with coffee or tea taking the place of beer. He may find his mail there awaiting him and a newspaper from the capital. He will probably doze after his meal, but by two he will be again at work. When he returns at half-past four for tea, he will have had six and a half hours in the fields, and his day is not yet finished. There are his accounts, and his reports, and his correspondence. By the time dusk falls he is ready enough for his punch or swizzle.

There is unlikely to be a club within close range of him. He will either be expecting a neighboring call or he will be driving out with his wife to a friend's bungalow.

It will be to a friend, probably, that he has seen two or three times a week for the last five to fifteen years. Their friendship is one entirely of propinquity. They have no secrets from one another. They have nothing new to say to one another. They will gossip about the price of cocoa, the cost of labor, a party at G.H., the report of the last commission, their plans next summer for a trip to England; such gossip as he has exchanged with this or the other friend, in that or the other bungalow, every night for the last fifteen years; but as he sits there on the veranda, in the warm and scented dusk, with fireflies flickering over the tobacco plants, in the pleasant fatigue that follows on a long day's work, with the rich, heavy rum spreading its warmth along his veins, he will become minute by minute wrapped about in a sense of comradeship with this man who understands his problems, who shares so many of those problems, with whom he has no need to assume pretences, with whom he can be himself. And as he surrenders to the charitable influences of the hour, his personal plans show in a more roseate light. Surely, he thinks, the slump has reached its curve. Next year surely the boom—the long-prophesied boom— will come; there will be a bonus and dividends. He really will be able to take at last that trip to England that he has been talking about for five winters now. And the swizzle-stick will rattle against the ice. And he will sit there hopeful, confident, and happy, till his wife from the other end of the veranda reminds him that dinner cannot be served one minute after half-past eight.

Almost directly after dinner he will go to bed.

And the next day it will all be begun again, and maybe when he returns for his breakfast at eleven it will be to find among his mail a gloomy forecast of the next year's trading. The slump has not yet reached its curve. There will be no bonus and no dividends, and he would no doubt be wise to put off for another year his plans for that trip to England and, taking instead a shorter view, arrange to come into town for the next race meeting, staying on afterwards for a week or so. [*At the moment planters are doing well.*]

It is a monotonous and often a dispiriting existence. It is not surprising that the planter should grow despondent sometimes, as season follows season with the wearisome regularity of a climate that always does what you expect of it—so many days of the short dry period, so many of the wet, then the long dry season, then the hurricanes; with the slumps growing longer and more frequent, with the prospects of "that holiday in England" growing more remote. It would not be surprising if he did not lose heart sometimes and become defeatist. His welcome of the tourist will be no less cordial on that account, however; it will even be more cordial, since the arrival of a visitor from England is an agreeable break in a monotonous routine. He will make an occasion, a party of it.

On mornings when no such excursion has been planned, the tourist will have after breakfast a couple of hours to himself, to read or to write letters or to saunter down to the public library. Except in the three larger islands, there is no such thing in the West Indies as a leisured class. All the men are employed in some capacity, in stores or offices or in Government service. But usually by eleven o'clock a number of young women will be in the mood for an ice or a cup of coffee or a swim. [*Today there are very few idle young women. They nearly all have jobs of some kind.*]

In most of the islands there will be two clubs in the capital: a town club which is exclusively masculine, where the men will talk shop over their rum punches before going home to lunch, and a country club which is the main social center, which has tennis courts and perhaps a golf course, which is picturesquely sited often on the edge of the savannah. But it is in the evening that the life of the island is centered there. The tourist's eleven o'clock date will be in town.

About most West Indian towns there is a similarity of appearance. Their setting is invariably magnificent, a succession of high hills rising above a harbor with charming residential bungalows dotted along their slopes. But the shops and streets and offices that are grouped about the port are unattractive. Once they were stone-built and tiled and handsome. But they have been the victims, nearly all of them, of hurricanes and earthquakes. Today they are for the most part ramshackle improvisations of wood and corru-

gated iron, shabby where they are not squalid, with little sense of
dignity or of the past, with ragged beggars sleeping in their shadows. Most of the larger stores will have a teashop attached to
them, and it is probably in one of these that the tourist will find
himself sitting over an ice on mornings when he is not driving out
into the country. Perhaps, however, his friends will have some
special and unlikely rendezvous. My two chief friends in St. Lucia
used, for example, to meet every morning in a windowless room
opening out of a grocery which they called "Hell's Kitchen"; they
went there, they explained, because they were tired of seeing the
same people everywhere they went. Only some half-dozen of us had
the right of entry. We drank beer instead of coffee, and the girl
who was responsible for the idea presented each of us with a red-
painted cork. We were supposed to carry this cork with us at all
times. And if you met a fellow member in a neutral setting, your
production of your cork constituted a challenge. It was like "Seeing a hand" at poker. If the challengee had her cork, then the
challenger had to pay the first round next morning. But if the
challengee had not got her cork, then it was for her to pay. There
is a great lack of privacy in the tropics: Hell's Kitchen is symptomatic of the need one feels to be alone, or, rather, not to be overlooked.

Coffee will be followed by a swim. In practically every capital
there is an excellent bathing beach. I have never known better
bathing than in the West Indies. There are none of the coral and
sea urchins against which in Tahiti you have to be so much upon
your guard that it is foolish to bathe barefooted. The water is
fresher and has more bite than that of the Mediterranean. There
is no reason to be afraid of sunstroke, and the precautions that
you take against sunburn on the Riviera are adequate in the
Caribbean. An hour on the beach sends you back with a good
appetite to lunch.

The lunch, if it is taken in an hotel, will probably be a disappointment to the gourmet. The English as a race are not enter-
prising gastronomically. They are afraid of local dishes and ask
to be given abroad the same meals that they enjoy at home. Hotel
proprietors catering for this taste concentrate upon fried dolphin
and on joints. They usually overcook the meat, which would not
under the best conditions be very satisfactory, since, owing to a
lack of cold storage, it is usually eaten on the day that it is killed.

The local vegetables—yams, sweet potatoes, bread-fruit, plantains —are starchily flavorless. Only the fruit—paw-paws and soursop and avocado pears—is really appetizing. That is not to say that there are not a number of excellent West Indian dishes to be sampled: "mountain chicken," which is another name for bullfrog, can, if properly flavored, be delightful. In Trinidad admirable small oysters grow on marine trees. Barbados has its "pepper pot," and in private houses where the local spices are properly employed one eats extremely well. But lunch in the average small hotel, though ample and nourishing, leaves no memory on the palate, and it is not surprising that the early hours of the afternoon for those who do not have to work in offices are devoted to the siesta.

The three hours after tea are the most delightful of the day. It is then that the tennis courts are crowded, that nets are pitched on the cricket fields; that caddies are summoned to the links. The heat of the day has lessened, a breeze is blowing from the hills. There seems to be more color in the flowers; the leaves and grasses that by day had become polished surfaces to reflect the sunlight resume their own fresh greens. All day one has walked at the pace of a slow-motion film. At last one can move with freedom. One has the sense of having one's limbs restored to one. And later, in the swift-fallen dusk, it is with a contented feeling of languor that one sits out on the veranda of the club over one's punch or swizzle.

Rum is the *vin du pays* of the Caribbean. And there are two main schools of thought on the best way of serving it.

The planter's punch is famous throughout the world. It is made with heavy, dark rum—not the light Cuban Bacardi from which the Daiquiri is made—and the old formula of "one of sweet and two of sour, three of strong and four of weak" is the basis of it. Grated nutmeg is often scattered on the top. It is served in a tumbler and it is a drink to be sipped slowly. It is a picnic and a pre-lunch drink.

The swizzle, however, is a very different business. It has to be gulped in at the most two mouthfuls, to be enjoyed. It is made usually with a lighter rum, and whatever proportions of sweet and sour may be compounded with it, the prevailing flavor is of angostura bitters. In London a bottle of angostura will last you for six months. In the West Indies it will last a week. The swizzle is mixed in a jug. Angostura is added till the liquid is a pale pink;

then it is beaten, not stirred, with a swizzle-stick, a thin stick a foot and a half long, clustered at the head with a bunch of divided twigs. The stick is rotated swiftly between the palms of the hands till the mixture froths. It is pretty and pink and looks like liquid candy. But it is very sour. It cannot be sipped and it should be gulped when it is frothing. Dominica specializes in the swizzle. It is a matter of opinion as to whether one prefers punch or swizzle. There are two schools of thought. But it is safe to say that no drink can be anything but good that has a basis of West Indian rum.

A West Indian day ends as it begins, at an early hour. For the visitor arriving with letters of introduction the ninety minutes after sundown on the club veranda will often be followed by a dinner party—a formal party at which the women will wear long dresses and the men black ties, but such parties are exceptional in the general routine of a West Indian day. There is no night life in an urban sense, and except on occasions most residents who have been up since dawn, who have done a full day's work and taken two hours' exercise are glad to go to bed directly after dinner. The ninety minutes on the club veranda over the drinks short or long represent the climax of the day.

The conversation will follow an habitual pattern: there will be local gossip, there will be discussion of the latest party at G.H., there will be commercial talk of the price of cocoa, of the slump in sugar. Political talk will be concentrated on the policy of the Imperial Government. It is conversation in which the tourist can take little part. At the start of the evening, he will be asked, for good manners' sake, a number of questions about his trip. About "how things are in England," but unless he is an extrovert who wants to dominate the conversation and become its center, he will find himself gradually slipping into the background, which he will be content to do, since he is here to learn, to absorb an atmosphere, to receive rather than to create impressions.

He will sit back in his chair, watching and listening, sipping at his rum and soda, letting his attention wander, noticing sights and sounds that to the residents are too familiar to be remarked, noting how the dark green of the mountains changes into purple, watching the fireflies dart above the flowers, hearing the croak of frogs and in the hills the distant beat of drums; he will be conscious of the heavy smell of jasmine. How often during the war when evenings fell upon bomb-scarred London or on the brown burnt wastes of the Syrian desert have I not dreamed myself back onto a long veranda, looking on to the row of palms that flanks a broad, green savannah.

Au Revoir, Martinique

from HOT COUNTRIES

WRITTEN IN 1929

Boat days are of too regular occurrence in Fort de France to be the carnivals that they are in Papeete. But, even so, they are gay enough in the late days of spring when a French ship is sailing for St. Nazaire or Havre, and those who can afford to are flying from the parched heat of summer. On the *Pellerin* there was not a cabin vacant. The decks were crowded. The noise from the smoking-room grew denser as *coupe* after *coupe* was drained. But I was tired; too tired to join whole-heartedly in the revelry.

It was only ten days since Eldred Curwen and I had driven from Port au Plina at four o'clock on a late April morning. But those ten days, probably because they had come at the end of five months of travelling, had been intolerably exhausting. To begin with, there had been the long twelve hours' drive across the Haitian frontier into San Domingo, with the sun beating down through the thin canvas of the hood; there had been the heat and noise of San Domingo; the journey on the neatest of small ships, the *Antilles*, past Puerto Rico, past St. Martin and St. Barthélemy, those two forgotten little islands, only touched at by one boat once a month, half French half Dutch and speaking English; where cows and bullocks swim out at the edges of canoes towards the ship, to be drawn up by the horns on to the deck for shipment to Guadeloupe. Strange little islands. The arrival of the boat is the one incident in the life of a community which has no cars, nor motion pictures, nor newspapers, nor news. The whole island puts

207

on its smartest frocks, rows out to the ship for its three hours'
sojourn, to dance in the small saloon, to be stood liqueurs, to be
photographed, to take and leave addresses; then when the siren
goes to scamper back into their canoes for four more uneventful
weeks.

After St. Barthélemy there was Guadeloupe. The hurried rush
at Basse Terre to bathe in the hot springs at Dolé; at Pointe à
Pitre a casual investigation of the cyclone's damage, and afterwards there were four days of the noise and heat of Fort de
France. I was very weary when the time came to move my luggage
from the Hôtel Bédiat to the boat, so weary that I stayed in my
cabin unpacking slowly while the sirens went and the gongs were
beaten along the passage. It was not till I could feel the vibration
of the engines that I came on deck.

It was a colored scene. In the background the *charbonnières*,
black and weary, chattered together behind the stacks of coal.
Between them and the water half the population of the town was
gathered to wave farewell to friends and relations. The Frenchmen in their helmets and white suits, the colored people in their
bright print dresses, the Negroes with their handkerchiefs tied in
their hair. And hands were being waved and messages shouted,
and the conventional familiar thought came to me: What did it
mean, this parting? What was behind those waved hands and
shouted messages? Relief, excitement, sadness; to everyone it must
have a different meaning. Some heart must be breaking down
there on the quay. And I felt sad and stood apart as the ship
swung away from the docks, past the fort, into the Caribbean.

It was after six; in two more minutes the sun would have sunk
into the sea. And it would be against a sky of yellow hyacinth
that Belmont, leaning against the veranda of the little bungalow,
would see the lighted ship pass by on its way to Pointe à Pitre.
Through the dusk I tried to distinguish the various landmarks
along the road: the white church of Case Navire, the palm trees
of Carbet, the fishing tackle of Fond Lahaye. It was too dark.
Martinique was a green shadow.

A few minutes more and the sun would have set into the sea;
already it had set in the London that I was bound for. In the
suburbs people would be mixing themselves a nightcap. In Picca-
dilly the last act of the theatres would have just begun. At the

dinner parties that preceded dances there would be a gathering
of wraps and coats. But westward, in the colored countries, it
would be shining still; pouring in the full radiance of early summer over the Golden Gate; streaming southwards a hundred miles
or so through the open windows of a Spanish colonial house, on
to a long, low room with circled roof, on to black Chesterfields,
on to a black-and-white squared carpet, on to blue Chinese porce-
lain, on to walls bright with the coloring of old Spanish maps.
Lunch would just be over. The room would be filled with talk,
with talk of plans, of golf or tennis, or a driving under the pines
along the rugged Californian coast. There would be laughter there
and hospitality and friendship; a bigness and an openness of heart.

Montserrat

from THE SUGAR ISLANDS

WRITTEN IN 1948

Montserrat was discovered by Columbus in 1493 and named after the mountain monastery in Catalonia. Colonized by the British under Sir Thomas Warner in 1632, it came under French rule between 1664 and 1668, and 1782 and 1784. A number of Irishmen were settled here by Oliver Cromwell, and Sir Algernon Aspinall states that there were at one time three thousand Irish families in the island. A shamrock adorns the center gable of Government House. Its chief products are sea-island cotton and lime juice; it also exports tomatoes. It was very seriously damaged by a series of earthquakes in the early and middle nineteen-thirties, and when I paused there in 1938 for a few hours on my way up to Boston, the capital, Plymouth, had an air of St. Pierre with shacks going up among stone foundations. It has recovered, however, very gallantly, and with a population of fourteen thousand has a relatively balanced budget.

Montserrat is a port of call for both the Alcoa and the Canadian National Steamship Lines. But it has not an airfield yet. It is not often visited by tourists. If you were to plan to spend a week there, you would almost certainly have to make the trip at least one way in a small open motor launch. Myself, I had to take the launch both ways and one of the trips was exceedingly unpleasant. I should never indeed have gone there unless my old friend, Charlesworth Ross, who was at the time commissioner, had asked me to be his guest. Had I failed to accept his invitation, I should

210

have failed to see one of the loveliest islands in my experience, an experience including Colombo and Penang.

Montserrat includes within its narrow confines all of the separate and varied features that distinguish and adorn the other islands. Much of its sand is black, but it has white beaches too. Its interior is mountainous, its highest mountain being over three thousand feet; but the mountains do not jostle one another as they do in Dominica. They stand alone, with the ground sloping downwards, gently, through forest and coconut groves to the trim cotton fields and the rows of lime trees. The green upon its flanks is as vivid as in Dominica. But the whole thing has a designed, architectural effect that Dominica lacks. Moreover, because the mountains are not clustered close, you have a sense of breadth and distance. In Dominica you look down and you look up, but you never look across. In Montserrat you look from one plateau to another, over deep, broad valleys.

I made a trip on foot across the island; it took a bare four hours; and the paths were neither abruptly steep nor slippery. It was easy going. We passed the crater of a volcano. The air was sickly with the smell of sulphur. It was a vast vat of a cauldron, with its rocks stained green and yellow and the tepid steaming water cloudily, milkily white like Syrian Arak. St. Lucia can offer nothing more impressive. And when we crossed the center and could see the white line of foam along the windward beach, there was that same sense of entering a new barbaric kingdom that I had felt in Dominica.

At one time Montserrat was predominantly a sugar island, but the collapse of sugar was not followed by the collapse of a whole way of living. The planters, finding that they could no longer profitably market sugar, switched over to limes and cotton. Plantations were not abandoned nor the ground let run to waste. The old stone windmills stand now as picturesque relics over the countryside, and the houses are built among the ruins of old aqueducts and the round mills that the oxen worked. Only in Barbados will you find as well preserved the fabric of the old world of sugar. There is a good hotel in Montserrat.

Barbados

from THE SUGAR ISLANDS

WRITTEN IN 1947

For those travelling to the West Indies from Europe by the Elder and Fyffe line, Barbados is the first West Indian island and for many it must, as an introduction to the tropics, be a disappointment. It has none of the high-mountained splendor of Trinidad nor the luxurious foliage of Colombo. With its nickname of "Little England," it seems at a first glance another Isle of Wight; less foreign than Alderney or Guernsey. The Negroes who clamber on to the ship to dive for pennies seem as out of place, as inappropriate, as the white soles of their feet against the ebony of their ankles. It takes time to appreciate its particular and peculiar charm, its "lived-in" atmosphere.

Barbados is the most English of the islands. No other flag has ever flown there. Not once has it been invaded. Undiscovered by Columbus, it was visited by some Portuguese sailors in the sixteenth century, who christened it Los Barbados because of its bearded fig trees and considerately left some pigs behind them for the benefit of any sailors who might be shipwrecked there. When the first English settlers arrived it was to find themselves unopposed. Caribs are believed to have lived there once, but in February 1627 it was on an uninhabited island that the first English stores were landed.

The Barbadian story is one of a steadily maintained tradition, unbroken since the days of the first settlement. In a sense it has less "history" than any of the other islands. It was affected in-

212

evitably by the various wars with France, suffering considerably during the American War of Independence through its inability to trade with the Thirteen Colonies, and in the Napoleonic Wars it was only saved from invasion at the last moment. But it has been spared the sieges, the massacres, the riots of which practically every other island except Antigua has been the victim. Hurricanes and slumps alone have disturbed the rhythm of its existence. Its lack of drama is, however, due as much as other islands' excess of drama, to the caprice of history. It is the most eastern island. The prevailing wind blows from the east. It was very difficult in the days of sail for an enemy to attack it from the west. The defender was always at an advantage.

Its lack of history has made Barbados unique. It has also given it a personal intimate charm that none of the other islands have to the same extent. It may not be attractive at a first sight—or, rather, it may be disappointing at a first sight because it is not attractive in a particular, in an expected way. For although there is a very real beauty about the broad brown river that curves by the Da Costa warehouses, between the low wooden wharves, past the cluster of barges and of schooners, the tourist leaning against the taffrail may well grumblingly inquire where are the bright colors, where is the sense of spectacle by which the agency folders had lured him to the ticket counter.

And, indeed, for a twenty-four-hour stay it can hardly fail to be a disappointment. There is not a great deal to do or see. The island is mainly flat. There is a lack of fine views. There is a monotony about the endless fields of sugar cane. There are sandy beaches, and the aquatic club, which is open to visitors, has a good pier and a café, whose phonograph will play to you while you swim. But it is very crowded. If you ask the advice of a tourist tout, he will suggest that you drive across the island to the Crane or to Sam Lord's for lunch. It is an hour's drive. The sugar cane is so high on either side of the road that you will not see a lot. You will lunch well, sampling the local speciality, fried flying-fish; you will sit on a terrace and watch the Atlantic breakers beat against the rocks. It is all quite impressive, but it is not what you expected when you booked your ticket. I have heard more than one round-trip tourist say, "Oh yes, I had a grand time in the end, but I must say that I felt a little alarmed when I saw Barbados. If it's all going to be like that, I thought—" I have not, however, met anyone who has stayed there any length of time and who took the preliminary precaution of acquiring suitable letters of introduction who did not come to appreciate the intimate quality of the island.

Barbados has an integrated family atmosphere that the other islands lack. In many ways it is more prosperous. It is one of the most densely populated territories in the world—over a thousand to the square mile. The Blacks outnumber the Whites by nine to one. But though Barbados is almost the only island where the color line is still strictly drawn, [*In 1897 Barbados was the only island that would not include colored players in its cricket team against Lord Hawke's touring side.*] the loyalty of the Negroes to their island is very great. They have known no other masters, and when slavery was abolished they continued to work happily on their old estates as hired men, nor did their masters show any great haste to hurry back to England and invest their compensation money there. Barbados has few of the labor disputes that so constantly distract Trinidad and Jamaica.

There are many old-established families in Barbados. E. S. P. Haynes, when he heard that I was going out, gave me a letter of introduction to some cousins of his there. They lived some twenty miles out of Bridgetown in a fine Georgian plantation house; on one of the walls I saw a reproduction of the portrait of a venerable gentleman in eighteenth-century breeches and scarlet coat which hangs over the mantelpiece of my friend's London dining-room. "That's a very familiar picture," I remarked. My host nodded. "You've seen that in Ted's dining-room, of course. It's the head of the junior branch that went back to England." I have always thought of my lawyer with his long legal background as a direct scion of the eighteenth century. It was strange to hear him spoken of as part of a junior branch. It was strange, too, to hear of the elder son staying in a colony and the younger son going to England to seek his fortune. But that reversal of customary roles is not untypical of Barbados.

And indeed it is very appropriate that it should be in connection with a figure so Augustan as my lawyer that I should have had just that experience. For the eighteenth century marked the great period of West Indian prosperity, and in Barbados the eighteenth century is still alive. It was in that period that the majority of the plantation houses were built—thick-walled brick houses of formal, dignified proportions. The rooms are high and cool and rather dark as a protection against the sun; against the walls there is the glow of old, well-polished wood and the gleam of brass. On the desks are the inkwells of an earlier day and at night the tables are bright with silver. There is a parade, slightly starched atmosphere about it all that is very welcome after the general informality of the tropics. A planter from Jamaica arriving in Barbados would feel very much like a New Yorker visiting in Boston.

Barbados is very well provided with hotels, from the *grand luxe* of the Marine, Four Winds, St. Peter, and the Colony St. James, to unpretentious, inexpensive boarding-houses where the accommodation is invariably clean and the food well served. The bathing is excellent and the climate pleasant. The dry, cool season lasts from December to the end of May. There is no malaria. Sugar is the chief product, though cotton has recently become important.

Anguilla

from THE SUGAR ISLANDS

WRITTEN IN 1953

A SMALL BRITISH ISLAND in the Leeward Group, a flat arid stretch of land, very subject to drought, fifteen miles long and at no point more than three miles wide, it can only be reached by sloop from the French-Dutch island of St. Martin. It is a curious island. It has never known prosperity: its climate is too dry, its soil too stony. It has some extensive saltponds, it exports cattle to the French islands and a little sea-island cotton to Great Britain. But even in the eighteenth century it could only find employment for two thousand five hundred slaves. A traveller in 1825 could find nothing to compliment but the quality of its yams. The only white people there today are transients—priests, ministers, a doctor, government officials. The arrival of a white man is so unusual that I ought not to have been surprised when the boatman said to me on the way across, "I presume, Sah, you Jehovah's Witness."

Anguilla has no town. In a quarter called the valley, there is a concentration of houses but there is nothing resembling a main street, and there are only two shops, one of which because it houses a cotton gin is called a factory. Yet surprisingly enough five thousand people live there under conditions of relative comfort. Many of the small bungalows that smatter the landscape are built of concrete with cisterns under the verandas, while most of the others are solid wooden structures with shingle roofs and outside ovens. Over five hundred subscribers are registered at the public library;

216

the large Anglican church is packed on Sundays with a well-dressed congregation and High Mass is celebrated with an impressively smooth drill. The explanation of this apparently anomalous situation is that the island's intrinsic poverty forces its young men to emigrate to the rich Dutch islands of Curaçao and Aruba whence they send back gilders to their families. Some time ago complaints were made that the captain of one of the sloops was tampering with the mail bags and the authorities were surprised to learn from the extent of the claims submitted how much money was being posted home. Though Anguilla is an apparent liability to the British taxpayer, it is possible that in another ledger, in terms of hard currency, it is an asset.

Trinidad

from HOT COUNTRIES

WRITTEN IN 1929

Trinidad is a twelve-hour journey from Barbados. You feel as though you were coming into a different world when you wake in the morning and see, green and high on either side of you, the outline of the Bocas. You anchor a mile or so away from Port of Spain, and the hills are so high that in relation to them you fancy that there is no more than a village awaiting you at their foot. The size of Port of Spain astonishes you. It is like no other town in the West Indies. Straight, wide, and clean, the streets run from the savannah to the sea, their uniformity contrasting curiously with the polyglot population that throngs its sidewalks. Every people of the world seems to be represented here. There are Indian women in long white robes, their noses pierced with gold and brass decorations. There are Chinese signs over the shops. There are notices in Spanish. There are the inevitable Negroes. There are many French. Trinidad has passed through several hands. The outline of Venezuela is only seven miles away.

It is a rich and fertile island. Ninety-five per cent of the world's asphalt comes from there. The roads are smooth and wide over which you drive through landscape infinitely varied and infinitely lovely. There are cane fields and plains of coconut. In the hills the scarlet of the immortelle shelters and shadows the immature cocoa growth. In the south there is the barren stretch of the pitch lake and the wooden derricks of the oil-fields. From Trinidad comes all the angostura of the world.

218

Few products have a more romantic history.

A hundred years ago, in South America, a Dr. Siegert produced a blend of aromatic and tonic bitters that he called "aromatic bitters." It was produced as a medicine solely and it is as a medicine that it appears on the tariff of the United States, although ninety per cent of its contents are honest rum. It was made by Dr. Siegert for circulation among his friends and patients. It was not till its success led to exportation that it was christened "angostura" after the town where at that time the doctor was headquartered and where his factory remained till the unsettled condition of Venezuelan politics counselled a move to Trinidad. Today the concoction that was devised as a cure for diarrhœa is the flavoring of ninety per cent of the world's cocktails. A million bottles are exported yearly. The secret of its ingredients has never been divulged. Only three men, the three partners, know them. They do the mixing of it personally in their laboratory. Chemists are unable to diagnose its consistent parts. They recognize that one out of five drugs has been employed, but they do not know which. Till they can find out there will remain only one angostura. No history of the West Indies would be complete that did not contain a chapter on it.

In the West Indies it is employed as no one would think of employing it in Europe. In England a bottle of angostura will last about a year. In the West Indies they use a teaspoonful and a half at least to every cocktail. Every cocktail is colored pink. They are described as dry or sweet, and the Englishman who orders a dry cocktail will get the surprise of his life when he tastes the pale pink liquid with its creaming froth. Particularly if he sips at it; for the West Indian custom is to finish your cocktail at a single swallow. Perhaps that is the only way dry cocktails can be drunk. I never got the habit, and until I had learned to ask for sugar in my cocktail I used to maintain that the West Indian variety looked the best and tasted the worst of any in the world. If you want to know what one is like the colored barman at the small bar in the Trocadero will mix you one. He came from the Siegert factory. And to take the taste out of your mouth afterwards he will shake you a Green Swizzle, a Trinidadian drink that, as far as I know, you won't find anywhere else this side of the Atlantic.

Then there is the hotel. [*The sequel to this incident is told in Evelyn Waugh's Ninety-One Days.*] I am not sure that the Bar-

acuda does not deserve to be the subject of a novel as much as the
Grand Babylon. It is the hotel of legend, the hotel that people
have in the back of their minds as a popular conception when
they ask the traveller, "But the hotels—isn't all that part of it
rather unpleasant? The discomfort, the dirt, the noise."

At a first sight there is nothing to tell that it is going to be
that kind of place. It looks out on to the wide savannah and the
high hills that shelter it. It has a drive marked "In" and "Out."
There is a largish and cool veranda. There are notices of billiard
rooms, dancing rooms, and baths. There is a souvenir store. And
at the desk a large, brass-bound book that swivels round for you to
sign your name in. You are charged six dollars for an average room.
You are reminded of Raffles, of the Galle Face, and the E and O.
It is not till you reach your room that suspicion comes to you. It
is only a suspicion. Tropical hotels are furnished barely. There is
the bed with its white mosquito-net. There is a washstand, a
chest of drawers, a table, a couple of wooden chairs, a mat or so.
You cannot make much out of material of that kind. But there
was an ill-omened atmosphere of unkemptness about that room.
Two minutes later the suspicion had deepened.

"I'd better have a look at the baths," I said.

I was conducted down some hundred and fifty feet of passage.
There were a number of corners along the road. It was like being
taken through a maze. At the end of the passage was the lavatory
and two bathrooms that served some twenty rooms.

"But, look here," I said, "I'll never be able to find this again.
Is there nothing nearer?"

The bell boy shook his head.

"There's a shower bath downstairs," he said. "You go through
the billiard room and turn to the right past the bar, and then—"

But that was too complicated. "Never mind," I said. "You run
along and bring me up an inkpot."

I went back to my room and began unpacking. Quarter of an
hour later my clean linen had been separated from my dirty, but
I lacked the ink with which to prepare my laundry list. I rang the
bell. After some delay the door handle was rattled. There was a
pause; then a tap on the door. "Come in," I called out. "Door's
locked," the answer came. "It isn't," I shouted. Again the door
handle rattled: again ineffectively. "Oh, all right," I said, and
opened the door myself. A bell boy was standing in the doorway.

He looked at the lock resentfully. "Door stick," he explained to me.

"I know," I said. "Now run and fetch an inkpot."

He stared and repeated the word "inkpot." Then went out, leaving the door unshut. I got up and shut it. For five minutes nothing happened. Then there was a rattle at the door. "Come in," I called. "Door locked," the answer came. "Oh, no," I said, "it isn't. You try again." Again the handle rattled. Finally it gave. Another bell boy was standing in the doorway.

"That fellow new here," he said. "What is it you want?"

I told him. He nodded intelligently, then went, leaving the door open, to return two minutes later with an empty inkpot.

My room was in the corner of the wall, with Eldred's at right angles to it. It was quite easy for us to talk across to one another.

"What do you think of this place?" I said.

"That it's lucky," he answered, "we haven't the siesta habit."

It was. We should never have been able to sleep there during the day-time. The noise was incessant. Every car that passed in front of the hotel—and some two hundred passed every hour— honked its horn both at the "In" and "Out" opening of the drive.

"The less time," said Eldred, "that we spend in this hotel the better. Let's go for a drive."

We returned shortly after twelve to find every table in the veranda occupied, every passage crowded, and an alert custodian at the doorway of the dining-room with a demand for tickets.

We stared blankly. "Tickets? What tickets?"

"Lunch tickets."

It sounded like a return of the days of rationing.

"Lunch tickets?" we repeated.

"Yes, these," and he produced from a desk a number of green perforated slips across which had been printed "Universal Tourist Bureau. Trinidad. Lunch, Baracuda Hotel. Tips included." And stamped across it the name of the ship: S.S. *Reputed*.

Then we understood.

"But we're staying here," we said.

"Oh, in that case,"—he still looked dubious, however—"there's a tourist boat in, and when that happens we like our guests to breakfast early."

For in Trinidad meals follow the plantation routine. Tea between six and eight; breakfast between eleven and half-past twelve.

"I'm afraid," he said, "that you'll find it rather a squash in there."

That was not the way in which I should have described it. The dining-room looked like Pointe à Pitre after the cyclone had passed over it. Four hundred people had been or were being served with lunch. The few empty tables were covered with soiled cloths, dirty plates, dry glasses. The people who were sitting at the other tables were in tune with the atmosphere. Their faces were flushed; their manners boisterous; their glasses were half-full, which is to say that they were themselves completely. It took us a long time to attract attention to ourselves. Then the wine waiter bustled up.

"What would you like to drink?" he said.

"We want a table."

"I know, but what would you like to drink?"

During the twenty minutes that we waited for a clean table-cloth and clean plates to be set, five wine waiters approached us. On boat days all available bell boys became Ganymedes.

Eventually we were served with lunch. Personally, I thought the food less bad than popular report considers it. The menu varies little. There is grapefruit. There is a fish called salmon. There are some Venezuelan patties. There are cold meats. There is roast turkey. If you ask for anything that is not on the menu they will try to charge you extra. One evening I asked for three fried eggs instead of the set dinner, and found that forty-eight cents had been charged against me on the bill. The food is less varied and less well-cooked than at the small boarding-house hotels of the Leeward Islands, but, at the same time, it is not so bad as the majority of residents maintain it to be. The Venezuelan patties were quite good.

"How often do you have these boats in?" we asked our waiter.

"Every few days," he told us, "in the season."

Immediately after lunch we left the hotel. We did not return to it till half-past eleven. The noise had in no way abated. There was a tourist dance in progress. The hotel is constructed of thin wood: you can hear everything that is said and done in the room next door. Every beat of the foxtrot can be heard in every corner of the fabric.

"Heaven knows," said Eldred, "how we shall get to sleep."

I was so exhausted, however, after a night at sea, after a long day of sun amid the strain of new contacts, that in spite of the noise I was asleep within five minutes.

It was not for long: cars were still honking their horns in the street, feet were pattering down passages, whispered "Good nights" were being prolonged over banisters, when I woke out of a nightmare, my face stung and swollen. The briefest examination of my sheets sufficed. I rang the bell.

"Bed bugs," I told the boy.

He stared. "Such a thing has never happened in this hotel," he said.

"It has now," I said. "Look there!"

His sight convinced him. "I will fetch the maid," he said.

A weary-eyed wench arrived. "Bed bugs," I told her.

"Such a thing has never happened in this hotel," she said.

I pointed to the sheets, and sat gloomily by while they and the pillow slips were changed.

"It will be all right now," she said.

It wasn't. I had scarcely begun to doze before a fierce stab in the throat sent me raging into the passage. There was a bell boy collecting shoes.

"Hi!" I shouted. "Bugs are biting me!"

"Bugs!"

"Bed bugs."

"Ah!"

He stood staring, his arms full of shoes.

"I want another mattress," I said.

"Too late," he answered, and prepared to go downstairs.

"Then get me another room."

"Too late," he said, his foot on the top stair.

But I was not letting him escape.

"Either I am found a new room," I said, "or I will leave the hotel tomorrow, which will probably mean the sack for you."

By that time I imagine that any one in the hotel who was not snoringly asleep must have been aroused. I expected to see doors flung open down the passage. I wondered how the laws of Trinidad were constituted. I wondered whether there was such a thing as criminal slander; whether I could be sued for it on the grounds that my revelations on the bed-fed bugs had occasioned a breach of the public peace. The bell boy, however, had a dislike of scenes.

I was got my room. It was a reasonable room. An eight- or ten-dollar room. I slept deep and late. Eldred, however, who was kept awake by the music till after one, was waked every twenty minutes by different bell boys from half-past six onwards with the news that my door was locked and that no answer could be got to knocks.

"When," he asked, "did you say that the next boat for Jamacia leaves?"

That morning we discussed seriously the problem of searching for a new hotel. There were many disadvantages. We had sent a good deal of linen to the laundry. We had given the Baracuda as our address. By the time our friends had realized that we had moved we should have ourselves moved from Trinidad. After all, it was only for a week.

And there is a satisfaction, too, in making the worst of a bad job. When twenty consecutive June days have been spoiled by rain you are almost irritated when the sun shines upon the twenty-first. You want a record for bad Junes to be established. In the same way, we took the Baracuda as a grisly joke. We would have bets as to how long it would take to get anything we wanted.

"I am going to ring for my bath now," I would call across to Eldred. "You be timekeeper."

The game had to be played under strict rulings. If you asked simply for a bath, you could not claim a victory on the grounds that there was no water in it. It was a long job to get a bath. There was no system by which you rang once for a maid, twice for a bell boy, three times for iced water. When you rang, a bell boy arrived. He would take a minute or so to open the door. You would ask him to send the maid along. He would leave the door open when he went out, and time was wasted while he was being summoned back to close it. If nothing happened within five minutes the rule decreed that you must ring again. Almost certainly it would be a different boy who would answer you. You would explain that you had asked for your maid to be sent to you. He would explain that it was a new boy who did not know his way about whom you had asked. He himself would see to it. And he would leave the door open when he went. Eventually your maid would arrive. "Can I have a bath?" you would ask. Certainly: she would send the bath maid. Then there was a question of towels and of soap. A lengthy process. The worst time was thirteen minutes, the best three-quarters of an hour.

We relaxed. We never made an attempt to go to sleep before one o'clock. We danced as long as there was dancing. And when dancing ceased we would drive up Chancellor's Road, count the cars suspiciously parked in ditches, or race along the coastline to the little Church of St. Peter and argue as to the locality of the Southern Cross. We saw to it that our car should be the last car to honk by the savannah and our "Good-night" the last to echo down the corridor. We made the worst of a bad job. We were a-weary, though, at the end of it. And on the last evening we decided that, since we could not sleep early in the evening, we would try if we could not sleep late in the morning. Our own waiter was away, but to his deputy we gave the clearest orders that Eldred was to be called at nine and myself at eight. On our return from Chancellor's Road at two o'clock we repeated our instructions to the night porter. He assured us there should be no mistake. He took down our names and numbers. He chalked up the hours on the board. Eldred at nine; myself at eight.

Things ended as they had begun.

Keatings and a new mattress had cleaned my bed. They could not strengthen a feeble fabric. As I got into bed, three of the springs gave way, and with a loud crack the mattress collapsed on its iron support. There was silence. Then from Eldred's window came a cackle of horrid laughter. An instant later every one in that section of the hotel must have been awake. On my wall, and on Eldred's, fists were beaten and furious voices were adjuring us to remember that there were other people in the hotel besides ourselves. We refrained from arguments. It took us half an hour to make my bedstead possible. "Thank heavens I told them to call me late," I thought as I pulled the coverlet round me.

I ought to have known better.

Punctually at seven o'clock I was waked by a clattered tray.

I made no protest. I got up and drank my tea, ate my toast, and sat with my head nodding, my eyelids heavy, waiting for eight o'clock, for the tap upon Eldred's door, the clink of plates and for Eldred's indignant protest of "Oh, really!"

I did not wait in vain.

St. Vincent

from THE SUGAR ISLANDS

WRITTEN IN 1938

I FIRST SAW IT on a wet mid-November morning. I was on my way to Grenada. I was planning to return later to St. Vincent. I woke to the sight through my cabin porthole of a semicircle of jagged mountains banked with cloud. At the base of the mountains ran the wharf—a long colonnade, bisected by a wooden jetty. It was raining steadily. A dozen streams, pouring their silt into the harbor, sent a long tide of mud towards the ship. "Another wasted morning," the purser grumbled. Despondently, he leaned against the taffrail. We had lost two days already at Barbados. West Indians only work when it is fine. Today they had not even bothered to send out lighters. Heaven knew how many more hours we would not have to waste before we docked finally at Kingstown. Inaction fretted the purser. Impatiently, he tapped the top of his white buckskin shoe against the deck, answering at random the passengers' inquiries. St. Vincent? A poky little place. Pretty enough if you liked scenery, but nothing more. One of those small places that had gone to seed. One of the Empire's liabilities. What did they raise here? Oh, most everything. Sugar, coconuts, bananas, with arrowroot and sea-island cotton as their steady standbys. Was there anything to see on shore? Was there ever anything to see in the Caribbean except sunlight? And this was November: a month too soon for that.

His tone of denigration matched the scene. I never had seen anything less typical of a boat day in a tropic port. There was none

226

of the traditional noise or bustle; no boys diving for pennies; no boatmen plying vociferously for hire; no bargaining vendors of fruit and cushions; only a couple of silent salesmen standing in a corner of the deck beside a small store of local mahogany, bead bags, Coronation stamps, and shark's-bone walking sticks. The two anchored schooners in the harbor, motionless beside their moorings, were appropriate interpretations of the atmosphere of general inanimation. It was not till I was actually on shore that I found the explanation. During a long voyage one loses one's sense of the calendar. I had forgotten—everyone else on board had forgotten—that it was a Sunday morning.

The town of Kingstown was entirely deserted. Our ship, already two days late, had not been expected till the evening. Everyone who was not in church was sleeping late. The rain was falling with persistent heaviness. The chauffeurs of the four or five taxis that were drawn before the Customs solicited my patronage with no real expectation of success. The solitary guide, a tall, cadaverous African who presented himself with the introduction, "And what can Robert Taylor do for you?" soon wearied of following me through deserted streets, past shuttered windows.

Kingstown on that Sunday morning was the emptiest town that I have ever seen. It was also, in spite of the rain that puddled its pavements and flooded the runnels of its roads, one of the very cleanest. Perhaps, had the two been less empty, had its streets been crowded with chattering longshoremen and grubby urchins, with carts and lorries, with all the bustle of a West Indian day, I might not have noticed how clean it was and maybe I should have missed a clue to the true nature of St. Vincent's life. Perhaps cleanliness is more than anything a symbol of St. Vincent.

None of the other islands has a history at all similar. Where other islands were being occupied by French, English, Spanish, and Dutch settlers, the Caribs here put up such a fierce opposition to their invaders that St. Vincent was regarded as a no-man's-land, and in 1748 was declared neutral at the Treaty of Aix-la-Chapelle. Though the Caribs had repulsed their European visitors, they had welcomed, however, at the end of the seventeenth century, a cargo of shipwrecked Negro slaves. These Africans intermarried with the Caribs and their descendants were known as black Caribs in contrast to the original red Caribs. The black Caribs, who probably strengthened the stock and certainly introduced a cause of hatred against the Whites, gradually obtained supremacy over their red cousins. Whereas in the other islands the main issue through the eighteenth century was a conflict between the French and English, here in St. Vincent it was a conflict between White and Brown, and it was not till the end of the century that the Caribs were finally subdued.

During the last years they fought stubbornly against both the French and English. The first real English settlement was made in 1762, and though the French captured it in 1779, it was returned to England after the Treaty of Versailles and was in English hands at the time of the French Revolution. The Caribs ardently welcomed Victor Hugues' emissaries with their incitement "to break the chains forged for them by their English tyrants," and a Brigands' war broke out, as bloodthirsty and destructive as that which had ravaged Grenada and St. Lucia. When the revolt was crushed, it was decided to deport the majority of the surviving Caribs.

As one of the consequences of this long war against the Caribs, St. Vincent never fully shared in the eighteenth-century boom of the sugar islands. It had not the same long-established planter aristocracy. There was not so much to be destroyed during the Brigands' war, and when the slaves were emancipated there was not the same inducement to the settlers to brood over "departed glory." They were the product of a later movement. They did not feel the same compulsion to abandon their estates to overseers when the former feudal conditions were changed. In consequence, more purely white families are to be found in St. Vincent than in many of the other islands. On my return from Grenada I spent a week in St. Vincent and was struck in particular by a greater freshness, a greater youthfulness of outlook. There was less of a living in the past. I have a feeling that I was lucky to see St. Vincent in the way I did on that first empty, rain-washed morning.

The Botanical Garden in the capital, Kingstown, is famous, and it was here that Captain Bligh planted his cuttings of breadfruit trees after his second journey to Tahiti.

Tortola

from THE SUGAR ISLANDS

WRITTEN IN 1952

THE FOURTH PRESIDENCY in the colony of the Lee-wards, this scattered group of the British Virgin Islands is one of the most remarkable units in the Commonwealth and a parallel could be drawn with the New Hebrides in the South Pacific which is run by a British and French condominium. Here the link is with America. Across a few miles of water lies the former Danish island of St. Thomas, which has to import practically everything it eats and is grateful for Tortola's meat and vegetables. The entire trade of the British islands is with St. Thomas. The American dollar is the only accepted currency, and when the pound was devalued in 1949 the salaries of the officials had eventually to be readjusted, a Whitehall emissary who tried to argue that the British West In-dian dollar was legal tender being invited to go into the town and see what he could buy with it.

The British Virgin Islands are beautiful and fertile and though they are in the red to the extent that they cannot meet the costs of their administration, the islanders themselves are relatively pros-perous. They all have their own small properties, and when they are out of funds, they take advantage of the law that allows them to work for a period of twenty-eight days in the American islands. There is a constant "coming and going" that presents a continual immigration problem to the authorities on both sides.

At the end of the war there were very few white residents in the islands, but several British families have come out to settle and American capital has built on Guana Island a club much smaller than but similar to Milreef. It is not unlikely that in a few years the islands will become valuable as a tourist asset. St. Thomas becomes noisier and more crowded every year and there is a possibility that gambling will be legalized. The quieter kind of vacationist may well turn for refuge to Tortola.

I S L A N D S : The U.S. Virgin Islands

Saba

Antigua

An Island to be Explored

"Typical Dominica"

The U.S. Virgin Islands

from WHERE THE CLOCKS
STRIKE TWICE

WRITTEN IN 1950

THE CAR THAT MEETS you at St. Thomas airport will have a left-hand drive, but the chauffeur will hug the left side of the road. It is over thirty years since Denmark sold her West Indian islands to the U.S. Government, but the cattle cannot be trained to accept new traffic orders, so the old rule of the road holds good. That is symbolic of these islands—the persistence of old customs under a new régime; a persistence that makes each of the three islands—St. Thomas, St. Croix, St. John—different from its neighbors.

I can best indicate those differences by describing my first day in each of the three islands. I went to St. Thomas first. Through the windows of the circling aircraft I glimpsed a high green island, the hillside dotted with white bungalows, a land-locked harbor, schooners and yachts and sailing-boats at anchor; a township built over and between three rounded hills, and climbing back into the mountains. In the Customs shed a police official was organizing the chauffeurs and the porters in a sing-song British West Indian accent.

From the village shacks that flanked the road, the unmistakable but indescribable West Indian smell—a combination of heaven knows what olfactory ingredients—smote upon my nostrils. It was St. Kitts, Grenada, Guadeloupe again, but as we neared the town, Charlotte Amalie, there were signs of considerable and unfamiliar activity; roads were being built, construction companies were at work; half-way up the hill was the concrete skeleton of a vast hotel now open as The Virgin Isle, designed to accommodate a hundred and sixty guests. In the nineteen thirties, when the U.S. Virgins had shared in the general Caribbean slump, Herbert Hoover had dismissed the area as an orphanage, a poor-house; but there were signs of a boom now all right.

We passed through an outlying fishing section. The side roads were cleaner, the houses and gardens better tended than those of Castries, Georgetown, or St. John's, Antigua. The faces of the villagers were a good deal whiter. Later I was to learn the explanation. This was "French Town," a group of fisherfolk who, having come over generations earlier from St. Barts, had stayed together, intermarrying, retaining their language and their habits in true French fashion.

The car swung into the main thoroughfare, a typical West Indian street, with crowded pavements, honking horns, deep gutters; cleaner than most, perhaps, but typical except for this—there was a greater proportion of white faces, there were brighter colors, a greater air of elegance. At the end of the street was the fort that in some form or another you will find in every West Indian island. Built of rust-red brick, it bore the date 1671—the year of the Danish Occupation; from within its battlements rose a clock tower that had an Italian, a Mediterranean look, reminding me of Cagnes. It stood, this fort, as the backcloth to a kind of *place*—Emancipation Square—a garden running down to the waterfront, with a bandstand flanked by stores, the veranda of the Grand Hotel, and the imposing municipal façade of the Post Office.

Northwards, up the hill, a hundred feet or so above the main-street level, stood a colonial two-storied house, bearing beneath its roof the painted letters: HOTEL 1829. It was approached by two circular drives that met before a flight of steps leading to a veranda. The steps widened at their foot, the balustrade curving outwards. Most entrances are built upon this pattern. It is a style known as "welcoming arms." The veranda, that ran the whole length of the house, opened on to the main rooms; the narrow passage that divided them led to a stone-paved courtyard from two circular flights of steps mounted to a first-floor terrace. The steps enclosed a garden. It was a style of architecture, this enclos-

ing of a mounting series of terraced gardens, that I had not seen
in the West Indies or elsewhere, but that reminded me, as the
clock tower had, of Italy. Charlotte Amalie is built, it should be
remembered, on the sides of hills, and from the window of my
room I saw another architectural feature that was new to me—a
straight street of steps running vertically up a hill—steps that I
was to notice later were cut in some instances low and deep so
that a donkey could clamber up them.

I had reached St. Thomas shortly after breakfast. Letters of
introduction had gone ahead of me, and within three hours I was
sipping a very dry Martini on the balcony of a bungalow situated
on the far side of the mountain range that divides the island. A
thousand feet below me the bright blue meadow of a bay washed
in varying shades of green and turquoise against a long white-
sanded beach. Beyond it stretched an archipelago of islands, some
British, some American, some a bare grazing ground for goats.

It was a typically American kind of party; three-quarters of an
hour of dry Martinis with the talk getting gayer, the laughs longer,
with Christian names taking the place of "Miss" and "Mr." Then
there was an arrangement of dishes on a buffet table, a lobster
salad with hot rolls and cheese, coffee and a coconut-layer cake.
It was the American style of meal, the American style of entertaining transported to the Caribbean as I have seen it transported
to Antibes and Cannes. It was not the party itself but the guests
who comprised the party that for me made the occasion special;
something that I had not met before in the West Indies.

There were eleven of us. Two other tourists and eight residents;
Leo Riordan, the manager of the new hotel, and his wife were
the host and hostess; there was a couple who had come down from
New York to help him; the agent for Pan-American; a dress de-
signer who ran with her painter-husband a successful fashion store
called "Elverhoj," and finally the proprietor of the town's Ham-
burg Heaven.

There was not one of us, that is to say, who four years earlier
had had any links whatever with the Islands. It was that which
made the party different from any of those with which I had
grown familiar in the British and French islands. In Martinique,
St. Lucia, and Barbados—islands which have been inhabited con-
tinuously by Europeans for over three hundred years—there has

grown up a deep-rooted, integrated, residential life, of planters, business men, and the officials who administer their needs, a life into which the visitor seeks to be introduced—he would, indeed, have little social existence if he were not. But here in St. Thomas there had grown up, clearly, during the last few years a social atmosphere independent of the former colonial pattern. In islands where the French and Spanish influences predominate, the word "creole" is used to indicate anything or anybody born in and native to the islands. In the American Virgin Islands the distinction is drawn between "natives" and "continentals," and the distinction is not particularly marked between residents and tourist continentals. "States side" is a frequent phrase.

That night there was a Hawaiian party at Higgins' Gate, a recently reconstituted hotel that has become the rendezvous of the younger set. There were some fifty present, most of them in fancy dress. It was hot, the lights were dim, and clothes were scanty, with shoulders and arms sun-tanned. Round each guest's neck upon arrival was hung a wreath of bougainvillea. The floor of the main room was strewn with plantain boughs; there were low leaf-covered tables a foot high; you ate sitting on the floor. Business at the bar was brisk. Presently a buffet meal appeared: a South Sea Island meal, fish curry and roast pork and pineapple. It was as good a picnic, as good a fancy-dress party, as I remember. It was friendly, informal, gay, and no one drank very much too much. At least not at Higgins' Gate. When I went back to my hotel at midnight, half of the party were on their way to the town's chief hot-spot, the Hideaway.

My first day in St. Croix could not have been more different. St. Croix is in the main part flat. The airport is eleven miles from the capital, Christiansted, and the road runs through canefields. There was the same air of departed grandeur that I had seen so often in the other sugar islands—crumbling walls, abandoned windmills, stone gateways opening on to nothing. It was a Sunday and no one was at work. The town was as empty as the country. Those who were not in church were sleeping. I was staying on the Cay, an island—once the pilot's station—that lies a hundred and fifty yards off shore and is now entirely appropriated by a hotel. A central guest-house on the hill is surrounded by separate cottages. Tables are set under the trees; along the waterfront are beach umbrellas, white wooden chairs, macintosh mattresses, and backrests. A dozen or so guests were on the beach when I arrived. Some were reading, some gossiping, some sunbathing. They all said "Hullo," but there were no introductions. Very few of them, I fancy, knew each other's names.

The morning drifted by. Shortly before one, the lunch bell rang. There had been no Martinis. In St. Thomas I had found the meals rather meager. Those who eschew starch rise from the table hungry, but fruit and tomatoes are plentiful in St. Croix. There was a hot casserole dish, a lobster salad, a solid block of cheese to which you helped yourself as amply as you chose; black pumpernickel bread, iced tea, and soursop, with pineapple as a dessert. You could eat either at a long refectory-type table or at a small round table under a beach umbrella. It was a buffet meal. There were no fixed places. It was a very easy atmosphere in which to get to know your fellow guests.

After lunch I took a stroll into the town. In a sense it was a waste of effort. I could have seen all I needed from the Cay—the red-brown battlements of the fort, the clock tower above the school, the square and gardens, and the public library with its long flight of "welcoming arms," the schooners awash against their moorings. Or rather I could have had from the Cay the most picturesque view of it. There is actually more to it than you would expect; it has a greater depth than you would imagine in looking at it from across the water. But it is, in fact, a casual, haphazard kind of town with wide, untarmac streets, its pavements flanked by colonnades of low, very thick stone pillars: the kind of town that grew up casually to administer and satisfy the needs of an agricultural community. There was the same sense of departed grandeur that I had seen on my way in from the airport—crumbling walls enclosing untended gardens, flights of half-ruined steps leading to a colony of derelict native shacks. In an hour I had seen it all. By four I was back at the hotel for tea.

All day the sun had shone. The hotel time-table announced five to seven as the cocktail hour, but most of the guests lingered on the beach gossiping, playing bridge and Canasta, reading and taking dips till dusk fell. Everyone was exhausted by sun and exercise, by long hours in the open air. By nine o'clock "Good nights" were being said. By ten o'clock the lights in the lounge were out.

To the same extent that St. Croix is different from St. Thomas, St. John is different from St. Croix. I left St. Croix by the morning plane with a fellow guest who was returning to New York. Though I had seen from the hills above Christiansted the outline of St. John on the horizon, my fellow traveller was in New York before I had reached Trunk Bay. There are only two boat trips daily from St. Thomas, and the morning boat had already gone when I reached the airport.

The caprice of geography as of history has played its part in St. John's fortunes. Although separated from St. Thomas by only a few miles of water, it is so protected by islands that when you make the half-hour journey across to it by launch you do not feel you are in the open sea but in a large inland lake. Though in actual size it is only a little smaller, twenty square miles against twenty-eight, you have the sense, after making that short trip, of being upon another planet. Too mountainous to be suitable for agriculture or pasturage, cut off by that narrow channel from the commerce of Charlotte Amalie, St. John supported under two thousand five hundred even in the peak period of the eighteenth century, when St. Croix's population was twenty-eight thousand. When sugar slumped, as the result of emancipation and the discovery of beet-sugar, St. John folded up. Only eight hundred people are living there today.

It is as empty as any place could be. Not even in the interior of Haiti have the relics of former grandeur been obliterated more completely. The jungle has reclaimed it all—the canefields, the carriage drives, the slave quarters, the plantation houses. The old walls are buried deep in scrub and creeper. There are no roads now, only trails. There are no motor cars. You travel on foot or horseback; or by motor launch around the coast from bay to bay. You lead a completely rural life, getting up at sunrise, breakfasting at seven, going to bed almost directly after dinner; an open-air life of sailing, swimming, fishing. Everything is very primitive. Each house is responsible for its own supply of water. Rooms are lamp-lit. There is no town, there are no shops, no telephones. There are no cocktail parties and no newspapers. There is one quite substantial resort, at Caneel Bay. There is a guest-house or two; four or five private homes, and that is all.

Myself, I was bound for the Bulon Guest-house. Trunk Bay, which it overlooks, is a couple of headlands beyond Caneel, where the launch deposits you. A minute launch awaits you at the jetty. Before you have been in it five minutes you have very markedly the sense of being in the open sea. You no longer have the protection of the islands. The launch dips and plunges and vibrates, splashing water over you. On your right the hills rise, covered to their summits with trees and scrub. On one of the lower promontories is an abandoned windmill. Trunk Bay is a beach and nothing more. There is no projecting jetty. You change from the launch into a rowing boat, and then wade ashore. The Bulon Guest-house is half-way up the hill. It has a wide, deck-like veranda facing west and north. It was noticeably cooler than Charlotte Amalie or Christiansted. The veranda was lit by hurricane lamps, not electric light.

There were four or five guests on the veranda. It was shortly after six. Most of them had a glass beside them. "Do I ring for a drink?" I asked. There was a laugh at that. They had the honor system, they explained. You could buy your own bottle or you could mix your own drinks by the glass. You signed for them in a book. Limes and ice and sugar, but not soda, were on the house. Beer and Cola were in the icebox.

It was Sunday, and supper took the place of dinner, a cold meal served on the veranda. Conversation turned on the next day's activities. A party was going round the island in the launch. The trip was to start at half past seven. I had known many picnics scheduled to start at least an hour before they do. I was more than surprised next morning, before sunrise, to hear footsteps below my room. As I went down to the beach to swim shortly after six, I met one of the guests coming up from the cottages fully dressed. I was the last arrival at the breakfast-table at five to seven. By a quarter past seven I was on the veranda, my manuscript before me.

Rarely have I felt myself more surrounded by peace and beauty than I did as I sat writing on that high deck-like veranda with a white, palm-line beach below, with the mountains climbing green behind, with pelicans gliding above, then diving suddenly into the shallow water, with sloops from Tortola drifting across the middle distance, with the whole horizon littered with the shapes of islands, with the water every shade of blue, and with the trade wind cooling the sun's heat. St. John was certainly as different from St. Croix as St. Croix had been from St. Thomas.

Those first three days illustrate not inaccurately the differences between the islands, though as regards St. Thomas and St. Croix those first days are less typical than symptomatic. It was on a Saturday that I reached St. Thomas, and normally Charlotte Amalie is not all that gay. It was on a Sunday that I reached St. Croix, and St. Croix is not normally that quiet. On the contrary, it has a very active social life. There are probably more cocktail parties in St. Croix in a week than there are in St. Thomas in a month, but they are a different kind of party.

St. Croix was originally an exclusively agricultural community. Its early history is involved; at one period or another it was owned by practically every European power, including the Knights of Malta. Under the French it failed for a time to prosper. For a few years it was practically uninhabited, and the French in 1733 were glad to sell it to the Danes to prevent its falling into British hands. The Danes invited planters from other islands to undertake its cultivation, and under Danish rule, with Denmark a neutral throughout the succession of eighteenth-century wars, it prospered so rapidly that within twenty years every acre of the island was under cultivation; it supported a population of thirty thousand. Today that population has been halved. The sugar industry, as bankrupt in St. Croix as in the British islands, is subsidized, as a form of poor relief. All the cane is ground at a single central mill under Government control. Only about half the island is under cultivation. The sugar is not particularly good. There is so much unsold Cruzan rum under Federal seal that the manufacture of it has been abandoned. None of the Continentals who have settled in St. Croix during the last four years are planters to more than an amateur extent, though some of them run small five- to ten-acre estates as a hobby. They have come to paint, to design furniture, to write, to sail. But though the patrician planter aristocracy exists no longer, the traditions of an agricultural community have been maintained. Agriculturists are always vaguely contemptuous of townsfolk, and Cruzan society is centered in the country. It is a residential society, existing independently of tourists. It does not depend on tourists for its amusement or support.

It has its homes, its parties, its private beaches, where groups of friends take picnics out on Sunday and play volleyball afterwards on the sand.

On the west coast of the island, fifteen or so miles from Christiansted, is Frederiksted. It is an even quieter town than Christiansted, and it suffered heavily during a workers' riot in the eighteen-seventies; but it has a definite life of its own. Just as one part of the island treats Christiansted, so does another section treat Frederiksted as its market town. Eric Hatch has organized a Jonkey Club, which holds donkey races on the baseball field. The five-days' visitor to the Cay or to the Buccaneer who did not arrive with letters of introduction to any of the residents might imagine that not very much was happening in St. Croix. He would have an enjoyable and healthy life, bathing, sailing, fishing, taking motor trips, but he would interpret the absence of restaurants and bars and night-clubs to mean a lack of social life. He would be mistaken. A great deal is going on, only it is going on in private houses; it is a life built up by the residents among themselves, carrying on the original traditions of the island.

Just as, in their different way, are the Thomasians.

From the earliest days there has been that essential difference between the islands—St. Thomas is commercial, St. Croix agricultural; St. Thomas is urban, St. Croix is rural. The soil of St. Thomas is as poor as that of St. Croix is rich. The sole industry in St. Thomas in all its history was the manufacture of bay rum, and the bay leaf was grown upon St. John. Most of its food has always had to be imported. Only in its north-west corner, and to a small extent, have the descendants of French colonists been able to exploit their hereditary capacity to wring sustenance from the most barren soil.

St. Thomas is a port. That is its history. That is its significance. Not only has it a fine natural harbor but it is the first landfall for ships sailing west from Europe. Denmark's neutrality during the eighteenth century made it the perfect rendezvous for the ships of warring nations. For a time it was a hide-out for the buccaneers, and two of its forts are known respectively as Blackbeard's and Bluebeard's Castle, though there is little historical evidence to support the legend that it was the home of the fierce Edward Teach of Bristol, who tucked the ends of his great black beard behind his ears and justified his habit of suddenly snuffing

242 LOVE AND THE CARIBBEAN

the candles over dinner and firing his pistols at his guests with the retort, "If I don't kill one of you now and then, you'll forget who I am."

Perhaps the legend grew because there was so little other scope for legend. The people is happy that has no history, and St. Thomas has been a happy island. While the others—St. Lucia, Grenada, Haiti, Martinique—were the scenes of war and massacre, St. Thomas followed its pacific way, sheltering, succoring, and gathering the fruits of its immunity; becoming, as soon as the brief Napoleonic interregnum, when the Union Jack flew from Christian's Fort, was over, once again an open port and the exchange center of Caribbean trade. Only by slow stages did it lose that fortunate position, as the other islands—in particular Puerto Rico—came gradually to realize that through the power of steamdriven vessels it was not only possible but profitable to deal direct with Europe; one by one the main steamship lines began to move their headquarters—the R.M.S.P. to Barbados, the C.G.T. to Martinique. In time, so far as Denmark was concerned, an asset became a liability. But the slump came slowly. For Thomasians themselves there was always a modicum of prosperity.

Charlotte Amalie is St. Thomas. A fact which might sound a condemnation. It is a safe rule in the tropics to get out of town as soon as possible. In essence no matter how superficially dissimilar, tropical cities are the same—hot and noisy, with honking car-horns, the air stale and fetid, juke-boxes playing, a restless vibration in the atmosphere; you feel that something is going to happen, but it never does; your head aches, you sleep too little and you drink too much. A much-travelled friend wrote to me from New York, "St. Thomas doesn't sound like the ideal place for you to re-establish your communication and respect for islands. From all I've heard, St. Croix will be more like it. I've always imagined that St. Thomas would have a pathetic honkeytonk atmosphere about it, which is bearable when it's a place like Marseilles or Christobal that has a waterfront culture to go with it all, but I prefer my islands straight and hot, without blues notes. . . ."

And she was right: dead right, or rather she would have been right nine times in ten. St. Thomas is an exception. What Juan-les-Pins is to the Riviera, Charlotte Amalie is to the Caribbean. It has admittedly a restless, gaudy, night-club atmosphere; and it has, in addition, the exacerbation of its divorce mill. Not so many people come down "to take the cure" as is generally supposed, four hundred a year is a rough average. But each of those appeals involves a six weeks' visit. Each appeal involves a personal problem. Each applicant is in her own particular way worried, lonely, at a loose end, uncertain of her immediate future; not sure, now that it has come to the final point, whether she has done the wise thing, after all. The presence of those four hundred plaintiffs is a highly flavored ingredient in the general atmosphere. Yes, Charlotte Amalie is a restless place, just as Juan is, but it has also, just as Juan has, an air of elegance.

John Vandercook in *Caribbee Cruise*, the outcome of a trip in the late 'thirties, described the shops in Charlotte Amalie as being "more useful than alluring." That would not be true today. The old wharves running down from the main street to the sea, that mouldered and crumbled during the depression, have been converted into art galleries and stores by experts in the art of showmanship. Most shops have bars attached to them. You sit at Elverhoj's over a cool Rum Collins and look down a large, high-arched, stone-built warehouse supported by red pillars, its walls painted light pink and green. At the far end of the room there is a constant movement of bright fabrics, wide-sashed belts, wide-swinging skirts, blouses low-cut over sun-tanned shoulders. I can think of no more acute inducement to extravagance.

Everywhere in Charlotte Amalie the eye is caressed and charmed. Built as it is over and between three rounded hills that run as spurs into a harbor studded with islands, it is the ideal setting for a town. From the veranda of every villa you get a new and charming view. Years ago Sir Frederick Treves described it as the most picturesque town in the whole sweep of the Windward Islands, and that was before modern skill had developed its possibilities; before the two forts, Blackbeard's and Bluebeard's Castles, had been made hotels; before Ira Smith had converted a ruined street of steps into a guest-house studio and bar.

This, indeed, is how I should sum it up. It is a question of the mood you are in. St. Croix, St. Thomas, St. John, they have each something very special to give you, provided you are in the right mood for it.

They say that the British colonies are more British than Britain is. In a way they are. An American would learn as much about

England by dividing three months between Grenada, Barbados,
and St. Lucia as he would by spending a year in London. He
would see a microcosm of English society. He would observe its
formalities, the dressing in the evening, the punctuality, the
parade atmosphere of dinner. The leaving of cards with the left
hand top corner of the pasteboard turned over has now been in
the main abandoned, as it has in London. But in Siam in 1926 I
should have committed a grave solecism if I had not hired a car
and driven out four miles into the bush, at quite considerable
cost when I was short of money, to leave a card upon my host of
the previous evening whom I knew I should be seeing at the club
three hours later.

That is over now. But there remains the concentration upon
clubs, the ritual of Government House, the signing of the book
on arrival and departure, the signing of it after you have been
entertained there. "The sun never sets on Government House."
So ran Noel Coward's satire, and though in a large island like
Jamaica or Ceylon a foreign visitor might not be aware of the
extent to which the social life of the colony takes its tone and
color from the personality of the King's representative, in Grenada
or St. Lucia he could not fail to realize how every activity is concentrated upon Government House, how integrated is the social
life and how he himself must, if he is to have any fun at all,
become a part of it. English colonial life is a direct corollary to
the old pattern of feudal life, with the various concentric circles
radiating outward from the court to the far circumference of the
artisan and peasant.

In the U.S. Virgin Islands there is no such concentration. It
may be that it is an impertinence for an Englishman to dogmatize
about a country that he can necessarily only know at second-hand,
but, just as I learned a lot about France from a two months' stay
in Martinique—the extreme conventionality of French family life,
the almost purdah-like imprisonment of its womenfolk, coupled
with the freedom of its menfolk to mix without embarrassment
with the native population—so by spending five weeks in the Virgin Islands I feel that I am now better able to understand certain
aspects of American life and history.

The Continentals, as I see it, came to the Virgin Islands in the
same spirit that their ancestors came to the United States. The

nineteenth-century emigrants escaping from conditions that had grown irksome, in search of a new and fuller way of life, arriving as strangers, looked about them for friends who would think as they did, with whom they could share their tastes, their interests, their ambitions; with whom they could form a group, self-contained and self-sufficient, whose strength and preservation would depend upon the existence of other groups whose rights would be maintained by a central authority acknowledging not only the privileges but the obligations of each separate group. The direction of the individual emigrant, that is to say, was a search first for the group, then through the group towards a central authority. While English life based on its feudal system represents a growth outwards from a center, American life represents a growth inwards towards a center. I think history would show that this principle was at work in the whole "manifest destiny" operation of the nineteenth century, and I think it is in operation in the boom that has struck the Virgin Islands in the last few years.

There is no centralized social life here in the sense that there is in a British island. There is instead a succession of different groups. Tourists to St. Thomas and St. Croix need not arrive with letters of introduction to enjoy themselves. They do not feel out of things if they do not belong to clubs. In the strict sense of the word, there are no clubs; though The Constant at St. Thomas tries through its Thursday buffet suppers and Sunday beach parties to provide for resident Continentals a common meeting ground for one another, a recent anti-discrimination law has practically, though, I suspect, unconstitutionally, made the forming of a private club illegal. The tourist who has letters of introduction will have a better time, but there is no need for him to have them. The majority of hotels are run on the American plan; it is a system that has some disadvantages, but it has the advantage of making each hotel a kind of club, and indeed each hotel in St. Thomas has its own particular *cachet*, its own clientele, so that it is wise for the tourist to find out in advance the hotel that suits his tastes.

Nor will the tourist feel out of things if he is not invited to parties at G.H. G.H. is not in any sense a social center. I was surprised to find when I went to sign the book there that a column headed remarks was filled with testimonials like "Had a wonderful time," "Everything splendid," "Hope to come again," as though His Excellency was less the President's representative than a public-spirited *hôtelier*.

In another respect, too, I found a considerable difference between the American and the British islands—in respect of the color problem. As the United States have a domestic color problem whereas Britain has not, I had expected that I should find this issue more acute in St. Thomas than in St. Lucia. I found the contrary.

On my last evening but one, Jeanne Perkins Harman gave a party for me. It was an unusual party, as any party that she gave would be. Young, handsome, Amazonian, she had gone down to the Islands a year before as a *Time-Life* reporter to write up the Divorce Mill. Within a few hours of her arrival a proportionately outsize Lieutenant-Commander in the U.S. Navy fell in love with her. He pursued her across four islands, and on the twenty-fifth day of their acquaintance persuaded her to marry him. He retired from the Navy, she resigned from *Time*, and they acquired a yacht-type launch that they christened the *Love Junk* and anchored on the edge of French Town, beside a glass-bottomed boat in which he takes tourists round the harbor at two dollars a trip. Rarely can a more expansive and extensive couple have set up their *ménage* within narrower confines.

One would not expect an ordinary cocktail party from the Harmans, and I did not get it. It was staged in the grounds of a partially disused hotel. It began at half-past seven. The large courtyard was dimly lit with torches. A couple of largish tables were covered with small dishes. It was not light enough to see what you were eating; it was mainly shellfish, excellent and nourishing. The Commander moved among his thirty guests, carrying a pitcher of rum punch. It was powerful and fragrant, and cold enough to kill its sweetness. On a terrace behind the courtyard a vast cauldron was steaming above an open fire, against which long-skirted natives with broad-brimmed floppy hats moved in silhouette like the witches in *Macbeth*. The cauldron contained a thick fish soup. It was not in the least like *bouillabaisse*; it had no saffron and no garlic and it was more substantial, but was in its own way as pungent. We sat down when it was ready. Three tables were laid and there was no fixed seating. The soup was followed by a dessert and cheese. Liqueurs accompanied the coffee.

Before the war, the Wine and Food Society issued in its quarterly journal a record of memorable meals. This party was certainly my most memorable meal in the Virgin Islands. But it was not so much the actual food, the rum punch, and the setting that made it memorable, as the guests themselves. Half of them were of African descent.

I am very sure that such a party could not have taken place in a British island, except at Government House. G.H. does not recognize racial distinctions, but socially, at informal parties, a Governor has to respect the prejudices of his guests. The Administrator of an island once said to me when I was the guest of a planter, "I'm afraid that I can't ask you to meet the most interesting people in the island, because they are colored. I can't ask you without asking the ——'s too, and except on official occasions I can only invite members of the club to meet them."

"I see," I said. "But suppose I was staying in the hotel and got to know the local politicians, would the plantocracy want to meet me?"

"No," he said, "they wouldn't."

It is a vicious circle. I remember a tennis party at G.H. on one of the smaller islands, at which the Administrator was at pains to arrange his doubles with partnerships of Africans and Europeans. As soon as each set was over, the partners regrouped themselves according to their color. Late in the afternoon a heavy thunderstorm broke over the court and we scampered for shelter to the veranda. As a recently arrived visitor, it was easy for me to find in this change of plan an opportunity to gather round me over cocktails a mixed group of the younger people. We were some eight of us and had a pleasantly animated talk, the Europeans and Africans mixing naturally. When the party had broken up I asked the Administrator if he thought that those young people who had seemed so friendly together were likely to meet again. "Not till they come here next. Their parents will see to that," he said.

"The parents on both sides?" I asked.

"The parents on both sides," he answered. [*The incident described here took place in 1948. Racial discrimination is rapidly disappearing in the Caribbean. The administrator of a small British West Indian island would not make the same remark today.*]

Even when they meet at official parties, the Whites and the Africans try to keep apart; they are reserved and cautious, unnatural with each other. It was only because a thunderstorm had broken the pattern of that particular party, because the guests were young, and because I as a stranger had acted as a catalyst, that that easy talk took place.

And that is why the Harmans' party was for me so memorable. Though there was no fixed seating and no stage-management beyond general introductions on the part of the host and hostess, the guests of European and African descent mixed easily, grouping themselves at tables irrespective of color. The conversation was spontaneous and general.

I remember four of the guests particularly—a Federal Court judge, a minor local politician, a youngish married woman who had spent several years in Harlem, and the Chief of Police. They all behaved exactly as their opposite numbers would in Europe. The judge was urbane, relaxed, courtly, a little conscious of his importance. He was accorded the same kind of deference that in London at Pratt's the Lord Chief Justice receives from his fellow members. The lady from Harlem was definitely more polished and better dressed than the others, whom she impressed in the way that an international socialite who is dressed by Hartnell dazzles a provincial gathering. The policeman was rather silent, as men who have had a security training invariably are. The politician talked just a little bit too much, as local politicians tend to do, arguing parochially on the need for Federal funds to stimulate relief work and discourage the spread of Communism in the islands. They all behaved in character. They were not different through being of African descent, whereas I have usually found in British and French colonies that certain types of behavior are indicative of African descent. In a British or French island it is difficult for a man of European origin to be natural with a man of African descent. I did not find this difficulty in the Virgin Islands.

I would not, however, dismiss this difference with the explanation that Americans are more democratic than Europeans. The reason lies, I think, in the history of the islands. An American, an Englishman, a Frenchman, and an Italian can meet, at a normal time, at dinner on equal terms. But if they meet in wartime on neutral territory, when one is a non-belligerent and another a potential enemy, there would be embarrassment. In the British and the French islands there is still a certain wartime element. The planters were once slave-owners who distrusted and feared their slaves. There were revolts and massacres. All that is a long time ago, but the white landowners are the heirs of the men who once lived on terms of enmity with their laborers. The atmosphere is not yet wholly cleared.

The landed proprietors in the Virgin Islands are not, however, the heirs of slave-owners. They are Americans who have come down from the north to make their homes here, in the same spirit that New Yorkers moved north into Connecticut and Iowans moved west to California. They have no ingrained, inherited feeling of distrust; they have no sense of guilt; nor equally have they any sense, as many planters in the British islands have, that an injustice was done them at the time of emancipation and that their case has been misrepresented by the abolitionists. The American residents in St. Thomas and St. Croix have not those particular reasons for feeling ill at ease with men and women of African descent. The Africans equally need not on those grounds feel ill at ease with them.

America has many problems to face in the Virgin Islands, but she seems to me to have been spared that headache. If friction ever arises between the natives and the Continentals, as some think it may, the cause is likelier to lie in the resentment that is invariably felt in a small community when "strangers from the north" buy up its property.

Saba

Published *in* HOUSE AND GARDEN

WRITTEN IN 1952

IF ONE CANNOT TRUST the *Encyclopaedia Britannica,*
where can faith begin? Because of a reference to it in that august
authority, I had long been anxious to visit the Dutch West Indian
island, Saba. The reference is brief; but how it whets the imagination! Saba, I was informed, produced the finest boatmakers in the
Caribbean, but since it has no beach, the boats had to be lowered
over the side of the cliff. I was most curious to observe this industry.

Saba was, however, hard of access. Small as it is and a Dutch
colony, there is no economic reason why the British and French
islands should maintain contact with it. Unless you were a yachtsman, the only way of getting there was from St. Kitts—itself a
little off the map—in a thirty-five-ton two-masted schooner, the
Blue Peter, which made a weekly five-day tour of the Dutch Windward Islands to deliver mail. I had often seen Saba, shadowy on
the horizon, a single cone-shaped mountain like Vesuvius, but I
had failed to fit a visit there into my schedule. So when I wrote
a comprehensive book about the West Indies, and came to Saba,
I had to content myself with copying from the *Encyclopaedia.*

To my surprise I received a letter from a correspondent assuring
me that there was no truth whatsoever in that paragraph and calling my attention to an article contributed by Charles W. Herbert
to *The National Geographic* magazine in November 1940. "Saba,"
Mr. Herbert wrote, "has no natural timber and if the material

250

was imported, it is hard to believe that men would struggle to
carry the massive timber fifteen hundred feet up to the top and
then be faced with the colossal task of getting the completed
schooner down to the salt water." It was very clear that whatever
else I might miss on my next trip to the West Indies, I must not
skip Saba.

Now, having kept that promise to myself, I am convinced that
Mr. Herbert was right and that the *Encyclopaedia* was wrong. I
asked a number of the oldest men and women in the island if they
could remember a time or had heard their grandparents talk of a
time when boats had been lowered over the cliff by ropes. Nobody could, though one man did recall that in recent years a
film company had arranged an exhibition recreating for the screen
the scene as it had been described in the *Encyclopaedia*. Having
been all over the island and examined its remarkable geological
conformation, I doubt whether boats have ever been built on
Saba. It seems far likelier that they were built on the neighboring Dutch island of St. Eustatius and sailed across.

That may sound a very negative result for a visit that involved
considerable planning, but in fact I have rarely spent five days
more profitably. Saba is unique, and the life that has been built
up by its thousand or so inhabitants on this barren rock with its
area of less than five square miles has no counterpart in my experience.

From a distance it looks like several other islands, Nevis in
particular, but as you approach you see where the difference lies
and why Père Labat two and a half centuries ago described it as a
natural and impregnable fortress. It has no foreshore, no flat
cultivated land at the mountain's base. It seems uninhabited; and
it is not until you are quite close that you see high in the hills a
red smattering of roofs. Saba is an extinct volcano, and the Sabans
have perched themselves round the lip of the crater. There are
many uninhabited islands in the Caribbean, and it must be assumed that the only reason why a settlement was made here was
because as a natural fortress it presented complete immunity at a
time when the Caribbean was the cockpit of constant conflict.
At that time the settlements round the crater could be reached
only by a single narrow passage cut in the stone, too narrow to
admit more than one person at a time, and the Sabans heaped
stones over the passes in such a way that by the pulling of a string,

they could be catapulted onto an invader. Saba was able to survive, and built up its own personal way of living while all its neighbors were the victims of attack and siege and plunder.

When the danger of invasion passed, that narrow passage was replaced by a flight of steps, traces of which you can see today beside the steep, winding road that, built since World War II, runs from the crater to the one point in the island where landings can be effected all through the year. On the northern side, a flight of five hundred and thirty steps connects the crater with a second beach, Ladder's Bay, but the seas there are generally so rough that it is rarely used.

Landings at Saba are notorious for their discomfort if not their danger. The beach is narrow, and between it and the open roadstead where you anchor there is a line of rocks. Myself, I arrived shortly after sunset; the sea was moderately rough, there was no moon, and I did not find it easy to transship from the schooner into the rowing boat that bobbed beneath it. When I was finally settled in my seat, the boatman wrapped a tarpaulin round my shoulders. I could not think why, as it was not raining, but I was soon to discover the reason. In the dark I could not see how the boat was maneuvered between the rocks, but suddenly the keel struck on pebbles; as it did, a wave went right over the boat. I scrambled over the side into the water and reached the shore soaked to the waist. It was in very much that way that Père Labat landed there two and a half centuries ago.

Much has been changed since then, but the main changes have all taken place since the second war and it is easy for the visitor to reconstruct for himself the curious existence that was led on this barren rock during the eighteenth and nineteenth centuries.

In Labat's day Saba was inhabited by forty to fifty settlers and some hundred and fifty Negro slaves. The plantations, he tells us, were small and well-cultivated, and the whitewashed houses very pretty and well-furnished, the settlers living as it were in a large club and frequently entertaining one another. He was, he said, received there very kindly.

In essentials Saba is not so very different now. Today the visitor to the island will be met at the beach by the Dutch Administrator in person. He will be treated as a guest. He will be driven in the Administrator's jeep to the Government Rest House. Though he will pay five dollars a day for excellent meals, service, and accommodation, he will have the sense of visiting in a private house. No record is kept of his raids upon the icebox. When he leaves, a rough calculation is made of his consumption of beer, Cola, Dutch gin, and dessert wine. The Administrator will ensure that he is "shown the island."

There is a great deal to be shown that will interest and amuse and at times surprise him. It is surprising, for instance, for a village that you have reached by a climb of eight hundred feet to be called "The Bottom," but as far as Saba is concerned the administrative center of the island is situated on the floor of the crater whereas the other villages are perched round the lip. Though Saba is a Dutch colony, the purest English in the Caribbean is spoken there; though there is a genuine feeling of loyalty for the Dutch royal family, scarcely a Saban has any links with Holland. The young men go to the oil islands, Aruba and Curaçao, to earn their livings. In New York there is a Saban colony at Richmond Hill, and the island is almost entirely supported by the savings sent back to it by emigrants from these places.

Though few new settlers come to Saba, though practically all the old inhabitants are interrelated, there has been no intermarriage between the descendants of the original settlers and of the original slaves. Sabans are pure African or pure European. The two races live on terms of the greatest amity, dividing the co-operative duties of administration; but they live in different sections of the island. The Africans live for the most part in The Bottom since they prefer the warmer air inside the crater, while the Whites chose the outer, exposed edge of the crater, where the air is cooler. There are curious customs in the island: a family in one of the villages, for instance, is allowed the highly prized privilege of burying their relatives in their own backyard.

The island's life has developed calmly and peacefully in terms of the islanders' own needs and wishes. In general appearance the island probably does not look very different from what it did in Labat's day. There are no plantations, but the streets are clean, and the houses now, as then, are white and trim; the Sabans with their sailor training are experts in the use of paint, and the red shingle roofs look as though they were tiled.

The houses on Windward Side are built so close together, and on so steep a slope, that it has been said that you step from the front door of one house onto the roof of the house below. That is an exaggeration, but it gives an idea of what the village looks like.

The West Indian climate is on the whole the most equable in the world. It is never cold, and it is rarely too hot; but in all the mountainous parts it rains a great deal, and when you look across at Saba from Nevis, its peak is often hidden by cloud. In the autumn heavy rains sweep the Caribbean; the gales of wind are so frequent and so strong that an ingenious method has been adopted of preventing the windows from rattling. There are no fastenings, but long nails, fixed obliquely, hold the frames rigidly in position. It must often be very bleak in the houses of Hell's Gate and Windward Side. A romantic novelist might well regard it as the setting for somber dramas of hate and jealousy, born out of isolation and propinquity. But in actual fact the history of Saba contains no such drama. The official religion of the island is Protestant. Until very recently divorce could be obtained easily, but there were very few divorces.

The only story I heard of trust betrayed had a comic atmosphere. One of the chief figures of the island had been engaged for several years to a pretty girl several years younger than himself. On the eve of her marriage she went up to New York to buy her trousseau. She never returned. A few weeks later her marriage was announced to a young American who for several years had visited the island in a yacht. The girl had worked in the post office and for five years she had conducted a correspondence with him unknown to anyone. She had put the official stamp on her own letter and locked it into the mail box, and when the mail from New York came she had extricated his letters to her before they could be delivered at her parents' house. She had not broken off her engagement, because she was not sure if she would ever see the American again, but she had been resolved to take the first opportunity of deciding how they still "felt about each other." Her Saban fiancé has never married and in his cups bewails the perfidy of woman.

There are few quarrels in Saba; as in Labat's day there is the feeling of living in a club. There is frequent entertaining. But there is no club and there are no cocktail parties as there are in the other West Indian islands. A store on Windward Side has a frigidaire and a call to buy a packet of Chesterfields may easily lead to an hour's gossip over a glass of beer. There is a lot of call-

ing in on friends after dinner. Scotch whisky and London gin are
rarely seen in Saba, but Dutch gin, which is free of duty, is available in two-liter bottles, and from the neighboring French island
of St. Barthélemy sweet dessert wine is imported. The visitor is
offered his choice of these, and his choice is accompanied by a
sweet biscuit or a cake.

No opportunity for a party is overlooked. I arrived on the day
of a wedding, on a Wednesday. That afternoon there had been a
considerable party, but the festivities did not end when the bride
and groom drove away. The honeymoon was being spent in Saba
and on the Saturday a dance was given for the young couple. It
was held in the second Government Rest House. There were
some fifty guests; there was no one present who was not completely
white. Nowhere else in the Caribbean have I seen girls with such
fresh complexions. They all wore flowers in their hair, and the
young men were resplendent in New York ties and tie clips. There
was a five-instrument string band. The men took off their coats to
dance. There was no supper, but in the entrance hall was a two-
liter bottle of Bols gin. It was a very gay occasion.

In Labat's day the principal trade was in boots and shoes, and
Labat regretted that the island did not belong to Catholic shoe-
makers who would doubtless have called it St. Crispin. Today
there is no shoe trade; there is really no trade at all except their
special kind of embroidery, and it is in less and less demand now
that Americans and Europeans no longer fill their houses with
small round tables over which they can spread elaborately decorated cloths. There is little agriculture. Such labor as is available
is employed by the Government in public works, mainly upon the
roads.

This road-making was begun shortly after the Second World
War, and these roads created more changes in the island's life in
five years than had taken place in the previous two hundred. In
1940 there was no transport in the island at all except a few donkeys, and no roadways except the steep flight of steps from the
sea to The Bottom, and from The Bottom a narrow path up the
inner lip of the crater to the two villages, Windward Side and
Hell's Gate, that are perched on the outer rim of the crater. Every
beam and brick that was used for the building of the houses had
to be man-handled from the beach. It is not surprising that Sabans
are very proud of their homes. Before the war, when a dance was

held in the Rest House, the young people used to walk over from Windward Side carrying their evening clothes with them. They changed in The Bottom; then after the dance they undertook the long ninety minutes' climb back to their homes. Soon after the war a road ran from the beach to The Bottom. Two years later it was extended to Windward Side. It is planned to continue it to Hell's Gate. As soon as the first road was built, the first jeep was landed. Now there are seven or eight. No other kind of car could manage the steep gradients of the roads. The jeeps are owned by the Government but can be hired out as taxis.

The arrival of these jeeps has completely altered the life of the islanders. The jeeps naturally were enthusiastically welcomed, and a regular feature of the contemporary Saban scene is a Government jeep crowded with young male employees in long-peaked caps and bright American sports shirts honking round the corners. At a first glance it would seem that the life of the islanders had been enormously embellished by the march of progress, but I am inclined to doubt it. It has made everything too easy. Girls who have once been taken to dances in a jeep are not going to take a ninety minutes' walk both ways. But jeeps are expensive to hire; the young men have very little money; they can afford to hire them only upon special occasions; in consequence, the practice of holding regular dances at the Rest House has been abandoned. The young men do not think they are worth the cost of a jeep and the girls will not go without one. There is less fun on the island now. I also wonder whether the health of the Sabans will not begin to suffer now that they take less exercise.

Children in Victorian England who had no radio and motion pictures, who had to rely upon their own devices, had busy and happy Christmas holidays organizing nursery theatricals; modern children become bored unless they are constantly entertained. I think this will happen to the Sabans. What kept them happy occupied and healthy was the difficulty that was presented by every project. Everything had to be worked for. It is hardly worth while hiring a jeep to visit a friend that you will most likely run into anyhow in the course of the next few days; but a glass of wine and an hour of talk in a friend's house were very enjoyable when you had to climb an hour for them. The Sabans had always been entirely dependent upon their own resources. It is for that very reason—though, too, it is part of the Dutch heritage—that their roads are so clean, their houses so pretty. They felt they had been set a challenge. They were happy because they had a lot to do. Now they are all working for the Government.

It will be curious to see what happens to Saba in the next generation. The administration of every West Indian island has its eye upon the tourist trade, and Saba is no exception. If a helicopter service could be maintained—so it is argued—tourists would be attracted to the island: this argument is fortified by the frequency with which yachtsmen put in there. But the very difficulty of reaching Saba and of landing there makes Saba a scalp upon the yachtsman's belt. I can't see how Saba, which has no bathing, no sport, could attract any type of tourist but the recluse.

I foresee the future of Saba in terms of the hill villages in the South of France, Eze, and St. Paul, that are tending more and more to become museums; the young people break away to Nice and Cannes. By day Eze and St. Paul are visited by charabancs, and the squares are crowded with bright dresses, but in the evenings they are dark, gloomy, and deserted. I should not be surprised if in fifty years Saba is uninhabited. The young people will get restless and go away.

I wish that I could have seen Saba before the jeeps arrived; but I am glad that I have seen it when it was still possible to reconstruct the life that was lived there for two centuries and a half. Saba is unique in many ways and in this particularly that curiosity should have been aroused in so many travellers by an apparent mistake in the one authority, the *Encyclopaedia Britannica*, that is normally held to be above suspicion.

Antigua

Published in HOLIDAY MAGAZINE

WRITTEN IN 1951

"I NEED A COMPLETE BREAK from the daily grind, and I don't want to spend too much," he said.

"Make for the West Indies," I advised.

"But isn't it ruinously expensive?"

"Only in certain islands; there are plenty others."

"For instance?"

"As of now, Antigua."

Antigua (it is pronounced An-teega) the seat of Government of the Leewards, a scattered group of British islands, with an area of a hundred and eight square miles, is very beautiful. It raises sugar and to those who associate the tropics with mountains, lush foliage, and ravines, sugar may sound an unexciting crop, but there is an intimate and appealing charm about broad green valleys that curve through a landscape dotted with abandoned windmills, between low rounded hills with the spearheads of the cane stalks waving in the breeze.

In several West Indian islands the sand is gray; in others the beaches are a stretch of pebbles; but in Antigua the sand is white and the coastline is indented with such a profusion of coves that the smuggling of cigarettes from the neighboring French islands is a profitable industry. The bathing is unmatched.

Architecturally it has much to offer. There are the naval dockyards, still in reasonable repair, where Nelson in his youth was stationed for three years and to relieve his boredom, conducted the

258

courtship of a widowed lady to a conclusion disastrous for himself.

Above the dockyards is Clarence House, where William IV lived in his sailor period. St. John's, the capital, may appear at a first glance "just another collection of two-storied wooden shacks" but a closer inspection will detect example after example of exquisite colonial craftsmanship, finely moulded cornices, unusual fanlights, gracious and harmonious lines.

Antigua has been British for close on three hundred years, and has none of the French atmosphere that you find further south. This is, for the visitor, an advantage, since the natives do not speak the patois which in the country districts of St. Lucia and Dominica makes conversation with them difficult. The Antiguans are a fascinating mixture of imported Africa and colonial England, and still retain the fetishes of the bush. "Is good moon for planting tannias," they will tell you. The moon rules their lives. If a girl cuts her hair when the moon is waxing, it will grow long and thin; at full moon it will grow short and thick. The best time is between the moons. Then it will be long and thick.

Their belief in obeah—a kind of necromancy—persists. When I arrived at the sister island of Nevis, my hosts and I were met on the wharf by their cook in a state of near-collapse. The child of a neighbor had been drowned in her daughter's company, and the neighbor had had obeah put on her. She must return at once, she insisted, to Antigua, the island of her birth, to seek protection. Next morning we woke to find white feathers scattered high over the window netting and in a semicircle round the steps. Later the dogs discovered a neatly dismembered duck with the head and carcass missing. We presumed it was counter-obeah, placed there by the gardeners now the cook had gone.

Antigua has no local handicrafts, no wood carving, and no weaving; but such local eccentricities provide ample recompense. You are in another world there.

There are no obvious snags about Antigua. The climate is dry; there is none of the humidity nor are there any of the maladies that are expected in the tropics. The temperature rarely rises above eighty-five degrees. Mosquito-nets are in general use; but you are not worried when you sit on a veranda in the evening. A trade wind is blowing and you need a jacket. There is no malaria. I have never heard of a white man catching elephantiasis—that plague of the South Seas. There is no regular wet season; there is a slight danger of hurricanes between late August and early October, but Antigua has an all-round climate. Hotels charge tourist-season rates from Christmas to the end of April, not because conditions are pleasanter then but because that is the time when Americans, Canadians, and English are anxious to escape from their own unpleasant climates. Antigua is pleasanter in June than it is in February.

It is accessible: in 1940, as part of the exchange treaty for fifty battleships, a section of the coast was ceded to the U.S.A. on a ninety-nine years' lease as an army and navy base. The troops have departed now but they have left as a hostage an excellent airfield which serves as a main junction for P.A.A. and B.W.I.A. (British West Indian Airways). Antigua is an easy overnight journey from New York and is the jumping-off stage for an entire area.

There is no lack of accommodation for the visitor. Near the airport and on the shore has been built a modern hotel—The Beach—with showers and toilets in every room. In St. John's [*My friend Charlesworth Ross—one-time controller of Montserrat—now runs the White Sands Hotel.*] a member of the Plantocracy operates in the Kensington Hotel, a fine colonial house with a quiet garden. His wife, a French Creole from Martinique has introduced a Latin flavor into the cuisine.

One does not associate provincial England with inspired cooking, and colonies tend to reproduce the characteristics of the mother country. But you can eat as well in Antigua as anywhere in the Caribbean. There are no special delicacies, no dishes that you can get nowhere else, but the fresh fruit and vegetables that are imported from Dominica and Montserrat have a flavor that canned commodities inevitably lack.

Antigua has something of the best of everything that the other islands can offer and at half the price, a third of Cuba and Jamaica. Sterling was devalued in 1949, but a pound is still a pound to an Englishman; and wages and the cost of labor have kept their level. A maid is paid three-and-six a day, and feeds herself on that. She will steal a little, but within reason.

The following prices are indicative of the cost of living.

You can get a good single room at the Beach Hotel at two pounds a day, American plan. There is a ten per cent reduction if you stay a week. After 30th April—and May is a delightful month—there is a further fifteen per cent reduction. Extras need

not be excessive. You can keep your bar bill low by drinking rum.
Bourbon is hard to obtain. Heavy duties are paid on Scotch and
gin, and Scotch is sometimes in short supply. French wine in a
restaurant costs a pound a bottle and is rarely worth it. But
Barbadian rum costs four shillings a bottle. Barbadian rum is little
known outside the islands: it is lighter than Jamaican, heavier
than Cuban rum, and it is excellent. Monotony can be avoided
by following the West Indian custom of drinking a punch at
noon—long, sweetish, and cold, it is excellent after a swim—swizzles before dinner—they are sharp, bitter, highly flavored with
angostura, to be gulped rather than sipped at, and in tune with
the heightened tempo of an evening's conviviality; after dinner a
rum and water highball. Rum drinks average a shilling.

Transport presents a problem for there are no practical forms
of public transport. There are no trains. Buses are crowded, un-
punctual, smelly, and hardseated. It is too hot for bicycling. The
Beach Hotel runs a ferry service into St. John's, at fixed times;
from the Kensington you can hire a taxi to the nearest beach—the
St. James and one of the very best—at ten shillings the round trip.
But with picnicking, one of Antigua's first attractions, far and
away the best plan is to hire a drive-yourself car. The cost is a
question of bargaining. The West Indian always asks a fantastic
price at first, but he is very amiable and comes down without
rancor. I had a long argument with a boatman who wanted to
charge me six shillings when the fare was three and six. At first he
refused to accept my three and six; but at the last moment, just
as my launch was sailing, he returned to take my money. "Thank
you very much," I said. "Don't thank me, thank yourself," he
answered. He had a broad grin on his face. You should be able to
hire a car for one pound a day.

For the visitor who decides to make a longer stay, there should
be little difficulty in renting a bungalow; there are several on the
Beach estate; they are modern, stone-built, with modern plumb-
ing, and they vary in size. The weekly rent for a family bungalow
should not exceed five pounds. The cost of living is conditioned
by the low rate of wages.

Much of the traveller's enjoyment depends on his ability to
mix in the local life and to recognize and appreciate the national
characteristics that make the country he is visiting different from
his own, and it is a great help in visiting a British island to arrive

with a letter of introduction to one of the residents. It is said that
the English are inhospitable. I hope that is not true, but we do
all live so close to one another that we are chary of making new
acquaintances; every acquaintance is practically a neighbor, so we
do not speak in trains to people whom we do not know. But one
letter of introduction to a resident will introduce you to half a
colony. As I have told before, it is also a wise precaution to sign
the book at Government House. It is a courteous gesture and may
lead to something.

It is not of course always possible to arrange for such letters of
introduction, and it is possible for a visitor to feel lonely in a
British colony. But this is unlikely to happen in Antigua. So much
coming and going has created a readiness to welcome the bird of
passage. There is, moreover, an admirable social catalyst in the
person of Nick Fuller, a young Chicagoan who came down during
the war, acted for a while as American Vice-Consul and when the
post eventually folded, decided to stay on.

Facing you when you land by air is a large army hut welcoming
you in faded letters to the Coolidge Airport. Once a recreation
room for enlisted men, it is now, as a bar, one of the many irons
in Nick's well-tended fire. You might well do worse than pause
there for a punch or Cola before you drive on to the Beach or
Kensington. Nick has already converted the old officers' club into
the island's single "hot spot" and as of now he is busily creating
a guest house out of an abandoned barracks. Anyone with a gre-
garious nature who introduces himself to Nick should soon find
himself caught up into the island's life, and the agreeable succession of picnics and of punch parties that form its framework.

Sooner or later almost certainly you will find yourself included
in an invitation to Mill Reef. You will be very foolish if you do
not accept it. Mill Reef is very special. It is a private club for
American membership only, where a large guest house provides
resort facilities for a rapidly increasing group of bungalows—at the
moment there are over twenty and the terrain can accommodate
sixty. Its members are hospitable and during the season from New
Year to 15th April, stage innumerable lunch and cocktail parties,
at individual bungalows and at the central guest house. The actual
members are for the most part retired and middle-aged, but they
invite down their children and their children's friends. There is a
youthful and gay atmosphere about the Saturday night dances.

Antigua, as an air junction, is, moreover, an excellent jumping-off place for amusing short expeditions. I took one this spring that I can heartily recommend. It lasted five days, the transportation cost twenty-five dollars and it included visits to two of the most discussed and least visited islands in the West Indies: the Dutch island of Saba and St. Martin which is half French, half Dutch, whose disputed ownership was settled two hundred years ago by setting a Frenchman and a Dutchman to walk round the island in opposite directions and drawing the dividing line from the point at which they met.

St. Kitts is by air half an hour distant from Antigua and every Wednesday afternoon the Dutch mail boat, the *Blue Peter*, starts on a tour of the small Dutch islands. The *Blue Peter* is a schooner with an auxiliary engine. It has cabins and is compact and comfortable; from its deck you get an excellent view of the St. Kitts canefields and the vast fortifications of Brimstone Hill on whose defence in 1782 the fortunes of the British in the West Indies hinged. You reach the Dutch island of St. Eustatius as dusk is falling. You can go ashore if you like and eat in the rest house a poor dinner for two dollars, and for an extra two dollars you can stay the night. But it is cheaper and cosier to bring sandwiches and stay on board. At six in the morning you sail for Saba, which you reach at 10 a.m. and where you disembark.

On the Saturday morning the *Blue Peter* calls back to take you to St. Martin. From St. Martin on the Monday a K.L.M. plane will return you to St. Kitts. You have two days at St. Martin to compare the difference in atmosphere between colonial France and Holland and also, since St. Martin is a free port, to stock up on perfumes. For seven shillings a bottle you can drink good claret on the French side of the line but you will be better housed on the Dutch side. On both sides they will confuse you by explaining that the Dutch gilder is the currency they prefer—a type of coin you are certain to be without. You will come off a little badly with taxis and with boatmen, but not so very badly. It is by and large a bargain trip.

You will not meet café society in Antigua, nor are there any night-clubs. But apart from that—and is that so heavy a disadvantage?—you can get there the best of what the Caribbean has to offer and at half the price.

An Island to be Explored

from WHERE THE CLOCKS STRIKE TWICE

In February 1951 Hamilton Wright took a party of journalists to Puerto Rico, to celebrate the hundredth of the new industries with which "operation bootstrap" was trying to bring prosperity to the island. I was invited to join it, on the verbal understanding that I should "Some day write something, somewhere." This is the only occasion on which I have not paid my own passage money and I hope it will be the last. The undertaking to "write something, some day" put me in the position of a guest delivering himself of a bread-and-butter letter. I did not feel that I could say all I wanted, as I could and did when I was describing St. Lucia, Grenada, and Martinique. The writing of this piece convinced me of what I should have known before, that a travel-writer must never put himself under an obligation. I have, however, included this piece because it contains some background material about Puerto Rico.

WRITTEN IN 1951

A̲IR-PASSENGERS FOR S̲T. T̲HOMAS change planes at Puerto Rico, as do most passengers who are bound for or across the Caribbean. San Juan has become the most important provincial air junction in the world, but its airport is all that the average tourist sees of the island of which it is the capital. A Frenchman once wrote a book called *England; the Unknown Isle*, and the same sub-title could serve for an essay on Puerto Rico.

The third largest island in the Caribbean, it was for centuries the most neglected. When the Spanish-American War broke out
264

in 1898, the war correspondents who hurried to the public library "to read it up" could find practically nothing on it in the English language. Discovered by Christopher Columbus on his second voyage, its first Governor was Ponce de Leon. On sighting the harbor of San Juan, he exclaimed, "Ah, que Puerto Rico!" (What a rich port!) And it was prophetic of the island's destiny that that name should have been chosen; its subsequent importance to the Spaniards was simply that—its value as a port.

The Spaniards crossed the Atlantic with a triple-pronged objective, "Glory and Gold and God," and they soon lost interest in the colony that had no mines. But though Puerto Rico had no rich minerals, the prevailing trade winds gave a strategic value to San Juan. The country that owned its harbor was well placed to control the convoys of bullion flowing east from Panama, and its citadel was highly fortified to resist attack. John Hawkins lost his life there. Drake failed to land. Cumberland held it for a little, but fever killed off his troops. Through the long wars of the seventeenth and eighteenth centuries, when Barbados alone among the British islands was uninvaded, the Spanish flag flew from the ramparts of the Morro Castle. It became the Gibraltar of the Caribbean.

Puerto Rico was a garrison, no more and no less than that; a fact that presumably explains the distinctive nature of its population. Only a small proportion of its natives have marked African strains, the crinkled hair, thick lips, and nose that you will find in Guadeloupe, Antigua, and Jamaica. The average Puerto Rican has a darkish skin, but straight black hair and delicate European features. This cannot be due to the original Indian strain, for here, as in Hispaniola, the Indians were eliminated within a few years of the occupation. Very few Spanish women came out to the colony during the first decades, and it must have been with imported Africans that the Spanish troops formed their alliances. The plantation system was, however, not developed in Puerto Rico to the extent that it was in the Sugar Islands, in Jamaica, Barbados and Martinique. The number of slaves imported was limited to the needs of a garrison rather than an agricultural community. As a result, the Spanish strain predominated over the African.

Spain valued Puerto Rico for the protection it provided for its commerce; a value that was not to be assessed in terms of a credit and debit balance-sheet. It was not expected to pay dividends, and its successive governors appear to have been more liberal, more beneficent, than those who were appointed to Peru and Mexico. There was little civil disorder; little resentment against Government, and the eighteen-twenties found Puerto Rico, with Cuba and San Domingo, still loyal to the Spanish Crown; a loyalty that was increased by the recruitment from Haiti and certain of the new Republics, of colonists who did not wish to lose their link with Spain. Puerto Rico was nicknamed "Ever the loyal isle." Its relations with Madrid were cordial, and in the very year that the Spanish-American War broke out, Spain, through the diplomacy of Luis Muñoz Rivera, the father of the present Governor, ratified a constitution that granted the colonists a high measure of autonomy. The majority of Puerto Ricans were as contented with their lot as any group of inhabitants in an imperfect universe. It was merely the caprice of history that made them citizens of the United States.

When the *Maine* was exploded outside Havana, few Americans can have visualized the acquisition of Puerto Rico as a war objective. Yet, in point of fact, when peace was signed Washington had no alternative. Spain could scarcely be allowed to retain a possession in the New World. Puerto Rico was in no position to conduct her own affairs as an independent republic. Moreover, since the Civil War, Washington had recognized the need for a naval base in the Caribbean. For some time it had been negotiating with Denmark for the purchase of the Virgin Islands. San Juan provided an immediate solution to that problem.

It was not at the start a change of régime that the Puerto Ricans themselves particularly welcomed, and little was to happen in the immediate future to engender filial feelings. Washington was no more paternal than Spain had been. The Union is in large part self-built, its citizens have been encouraged and trusted to conduct their own affairs. The Puerto Ricans were allowed an equal latitude; in consequence, the island returned to the long obscurity that had shrouded her activities since the Morro Castle had rendered her impregnable. It was not till after World War II that Americans as a whole, through a slow process of gathering awareness which was startled into full recognition by the attempt organized by Puerto Ricans on President Truman's life, came to realize quite what a problem they had on their hands.

It was slowly, very slowly, that that awareness came. It was not till the middle nineteen-thirties that Eleanor Roosevelt was to be shocked by the conditions under which so many of her fellow citizens were living. Later the spread of the Pan-American network was to convert San Juan into an airport, where many Americans were forced to spend an hour or two in transit. The experience annoyed them and disturbed them. They were subjected to Customs inspections which seemed unnecessary, since they were in U.S. territory, and which were conducted by officials who spoke little English; they took a drive through a city supposedly American where they could not make themselves understood; they saw a slum quarter that matched in squalor anything that Kingston, Havana, or Port au Prince could offer, a slum quarter which was not even built on solid ground, but in one of the lagoons that skirted the main city: poles being stuck into the mud to support wooden shacks. A sense of responsibility was aroused, and Puerto Rico crept into the news. By the later 'forties she was in the headlines. Continued unemployment had led to mass emigration into the United States. Puerto Ricans were citizens, and immigration and quota regulations could place no check upon their movements. They were going up at the rate of a thousand a month, speaking little English, unused to cold, to find themselves huddled into Harlem tenements, with no more security of employment than they had known at home; to drift, many of them, into crime.

In synopsis the problem is this: two million American citizens speaking little English, trained in a Spanish tradition with little if any appreciation of American standards and ideals, living in an island that never has been self-sufficient, that never has paid dividends; an agricultural community the extent and nature of whose soil cannot find full employment for its population; a territory in which there is a strong enough nationalist minority to stage a revolution and attempt the assassination of the President. That is the problem, or rather that is the dark side of the problem. For there is a bright and hopeful side. There is the immense effort now being made under the inspiration of Luis Muñoz Marin, the son of the Luis Muñoz Rivera, who arranged the original treaty of autonomy with Spain, to reorganize the financial and industrial life of the island under a scheme that he has labelled "Operation Bootstrap."

My visit to the island coincided with the opening of the one-hundredth new industry that had been started to implement this policy. In a speech at the inaugural ceremonies, its Administrator, Teodoro Moscoso, explained the scope and purpose of the project.

"There is," he said, "an average of six hundred and forty-five of us crowded on each square mile of land, and we are laboring under a lack of balance between resources and population density to a degree which is present in few areas of the world. Nowhere in the world can six hundred and forty-five persons per square mile subsist on a purely agricultural economy except at an extremely low level. The island is suffering from an industrial density of population and an agricultural production pattern. The land problem is something which we cannot change. We cannot stretch our land nor put into it minerals which are not there. What we can do is to adopt new techniques and learn new skills. The task in which we are engaged is to create the conditions for industry to develop and prosper, and a financial and social climate favorable for rapid economic development. We have brought a hundred new factories to the island."

There are at the moment of writing some hundred thousand semi-employed persons in Puerto Rico. For only some fifteen thousand do the hundred new industries provide full employment. Another seven or eight hundred industries will be required. In order to attract capital from the mainland, there has been a remission of Federal income-tax for fifteen years. A great, great effort is certainly being made.

To attend the celebration of this one-hundredth industry, some sixty pressmen, publicists, and bankers were brought down from the mainland. I was invited to tag along. The junket was arranged to show us the type of industry that was being undertaken, and the type of island for whose benefit the project had been devised. It was also intended that we should enjoy ourselves. There were no customs formalities at the airport. On the contrary, while the baggage was being sorted out, frothing *daiquiris* were served. In our rooms awaited each of us a leather zip-fastening brief-case containing a great number of brochures and tourist literature, stamped with our own names, and in the center, above the island's seal, with the title *Operation Bootstrap*.

It was a three-day program. On the first day a nine-thirty start sent us off to a china factory forty miles west of San Juan. An early lunch was followed by a second forty-mile drive in the opposite direction for the opening of the one-hundredth industry—a blanket factory. Five names appeared on the list of speakers and I anticipated a full two hours of oratory. To my surprised relief no speech lasted more than seven minutes, and we were at liberty to examine not only the plant itself but an exhibition of the other ninety-nine new industries. Some excellent fish *hors d'œuvres* accompanied a rum-based swizzle. That evening there was a reception at the Governor's palace, where we drank sweet champagne under the stars.

The next day was given over to a picnic—a pig-roast at the Louquillo beach. Swimming and sunbathing, cock-fighting and local dances had been arranged. Ed Gardner was to stage a show with members of his Duffy's Tavern. Fate was unkind. The weather could not have been worse. It was one of those gray, windy days that contradict more often than one would suppose the unqualified superlatives of the travel folders. It actually did not rain a lot, but it was no day for sunbathing and scarcely one for seabathing. Our hosts' time-table was ruined. We had been invited for eleven, but it had not been planned to serve the meal until three o'clock. Owing, however, to the wind, the cold, and the gray skies, every guest on arrival made straight for the *daiquiris*. Ed Gardner lured us to his bandstand on the beach, but we went with glasses in our hands. It was soon apparent that by two o'clock at the latest an assault would have to be made on the six pigs that, transfixed on stakes, were roasting over open fires: those pigs had needed another hour.

For the Puerto Ricans, to whom pig-roasts are a part of their routine, it was no doubt a disappointing afternoon, but to a visitor like myself to whom it was a new experience, the occasion was both enjoyable in itself and interesting as an indication of the kind of life that Puerto Ricans lived.

For me that picnic was typical of the ten days I spent in Puerto Rico. Without getting the full enjoyment out of a pig-roast, I recognized how enjoyable one could be; in the same way, though

I did not see the people or the place in the way that would have enabled me to write with any authority about the island, I recognized what there was to see and what I missed.

During the long week-end while the Press representatives were being entertained, I took a number of drives into the country. With the junket over, I attached myself to a documentary film team that was preparing a picture on the sugar industry. The expedition took me round the north and west of the island, and south as far as Ponce. I returned to San Juan by air. I saw the actual terrain; I saw how intensively each section capable of agricultural exploitation had been developed; I realized the necessity for "Operation Bootstrap"; I saw how the north of the island differed from the south; I saw also how much the island had to offer to the visitor, the extent and beauty of its beaches, the picturesqueness of its mountain villages. I realized how little of the island you have seen if you have only seen San Juan. You might as well judge Ceylon from Colombo.

There are indeed certain resemblances, socially, between Colombo and San Juan. Each is a port. The lounges of its hotels are littered with the bustle of arrival and departure. Each is a large, prosperous, and important city whose residents have built up for themselves a personal and individual life, independent of and indifferent to the comings and goings of these visitors. In San Juan, as in Colombo, the tourist is conscious of an animated, busy life going on around him in which he has no part. San Juan possesses a number of hotels, at least two of which are classified de luxe. They were both booked solid. A number of the visitors were holidaymakers, staying some of them for a month. At the same time there is no resort atmosphere in either the Caribe Hilton or the Condado; each is self-contained, a world of its own. My room faced not upon the sea but upon a minor thoroughfare. All day long horns honked below my window. I looked out upon a series of apartment houses. An alien city lay about me. In Charlotte Amalie, Miami, Cannes, and Montego Bay the tourist feels that the whole locality has been built up for and is devoted to his tastes and needs, that the beaches, the bars, the night-clubs, the flowered terraces, the pools, the smart expensive little shops have all been put there for his pleasure. As indeed they have. There is no such atmosphere in San Juan. Though San Juan can sell you anything you need, it has no shopping center. The smart shops are scattered through the town. On occasions, such as New Year's Eve, the old families of Puerto Rico will attend at the Condado, sumptuously attired in silk and taffeta and brocade, of an unmodish cut but beautifully embroidered; young Puerto Ricans will bring their girls to dine and dance there, but the real life of the city is staged in private houses.

A considerable effort is being made to develop the island as a vacation center, but the effort, very wisely, is not being concentrated upon the capital. San Juan with its two or three first-class hotels is the most comfortable airport with which I am familiar. A couple of days can be spent there very profitably, loitering through the narrow streets of the old city, visiting the Morro Castle— which is so capacious that a freak nine-hole golf-course has been laid out within its walls; as you lay the basis of a sun-tan, you can enjoy the best long rum-based drink that I have ever tasted, a fruit punch based upon the local Don Q rum and flavored with pineapple. In the small restaurants of the old town you can sample excellent colonial dishes. If you have letters of introduction to any residents, you will be introduced into a pleasant social world of picnics and clubs and cocktail parties. But to get the distinctive flavor of Puerto Rico you need to get into the country and the country towns.

Once out of San Juan, America seems a long way off. Everyone speaks Spanish. Everyone looks Spanish. Every township with its plaza and cathedral has the feel of Spain. The houses are built on a Spanish pattern. When I was in Mayagüez, I visited the owner of the saltponds industry. His home could not have been less American: a bare wall with shuttered windows faced the street; a long narrow house ran through to the next block; the courtyard was open to the sky; there was a pianola.

Spanish customs are still maintained. In a town like San German you will see on Saturday and Sunday evenings the young men and women strolling in couples round the plaza, in opposite directions, eyeing one another. The double standard is maintained. While upper-class girls are strictly chaperoned, Ponce at least maintains quite openly a highly adequate *bordello*—a dancing floor with bungalows set round it, attractive hostesses and a bar that is unexpectedly embellished, not only with *Esquire* pin-ups but photographs of the New York Yankees—a rival ball team, as my cicerone put it. In Ponce I was entertained by one of the

heads of Don Q rum. Born in Puerto Rico, married to a Puerto
Rican, the son of a German immigrant, tall and blond, speaking
with a German accent, he told me that as a young man, raised in
a tradition that was half German and half American, he had re-
belled against this system of strict chaperonage, but now as a father
he endorsed it. Puerto Ricans may be American citizens, but they
are leading a Spanish life.

There lies for the visitor the attraction of the island. If Cer-
vantes were to return today, he might find himself less lost in
Puerto Rico than in Barcelona. For over fifty years the Stars and
Stripes have flown over its squares, but those fifty years have to be
set against four hundred years of Spanish rule.

I spent ten days in Puerto Rico. I did not, as I said, see either
the places or the people that I should have done. But I saw
enough to know what I had missed and whom there was to see.
The island has a great deal to offer to anyone who gets into the
country. It is an island to be explored. It provides another good
reason for learning Spanish.

"Typical Dominica"

from WHERE THE CLOCKS STRIKE TWICE

WRITTEN IN 1948

For a long time I had felt curious about Dominica. I had been there twice—in 1929 and again in 1938. Of all the West Indian islands that I had visited, it was the one that I had liked the least; at the same time it was the one I was most anxious to see again; a contradiction that is typical of Dominica, whose saga is a long succession of inconsistencies.

Every fact about it is self-contradictory. The third largest of the British West Indian possessions, it supports one of the smallest populations. Though its soil is extremely fertile, only a small proportion of its surface is under cultivation. Though it possesses in Rupert's Bay a superb natural harbor, its capital stands at Roseau in an open roadstead. One of the loveliest islands in the world, its beauties are hidden for weeks on end by cloud. Its beauty has, indeed, proved a liability. Its beauty is an effect of mountains, and its mountains by attracting rain have deluged the interior with such floods that no road has been built across the island [A *road has now been built.*] and no road has been built round the island. Two-thirds of the windward coast is cut off from the capital.

For many years the island has been in the red. Its ill-luck has been persistent, and its ill-luck has been accompanied by ill-management. In the middle of the eighteenth century, the island was put up for sale in lots by the British Crown. The sale realized a quarter of a million pounds. Not one penny of this sum was

273

reinvested in the island. It was used instead for Queen Charlotte's dowry. In the eighteen-forties coffee was a highly successful product, but disease destroyed the crops. Limes were planted, and Rose's Lime Juice became an internationally accepted label, while planters on the windward coast produced a concentrated lime juice from which citric acid was extracted and which could be stored safely until an opportunity came for shipping it. In the nineteen-twenties, however, wither-tip disease damaged, in many cases irremediably, the lime plantations, and the discovery in Italy of a synthetic method of producing citric acid made the marketing of the Dominican product no longer profitable. When the Panama Canal was opened, Dominica by its geographical position should have become the coaling-station for British ships, but because the capital had been built at Roseau instead of Rupert's Bay, owing to the malarial nature of the northern section, St. Lucia got the contract.

Before World War I, a Royal Mail steam-packet toured the island weekly, collecting cargo and carrying passengers. The service was not resumed after the war, and planters on the windward coast had to rely on schooners and on canoes. For weeks on end the sea would be too rough for schooners to put in to shore.

Work was begun on what was imposingly christened the Imperial Road, a broad-surfaced thoroughfare that was planned to link the windward and the leeward coasts. Heavy rains, floods, and mounting costs delayed, curtailed, and finally liquidated the enterprise. Then came the hurricanes of 1928 and 1930.

The windward coast never recovered from these hurricanes. One by one the big plantations were abandoned; there is not now a single plantation house between Hatton Garden and Pointe Mulâtre. The estates are worked spasmodically by peasant proprietors who "head" their produce across the mountains, supply local needs, or await the caprice of schooners.

During World War II, the saga of ill-luck continued. It was typical Dominican luck that the island through lack of a suitable air-base should have been cut off completely from the general atmosphere of war, should have made no direct contribution to the war effort, should have been so isolated from the main currents of American and English thought, receiving none of the mental stimulus of being allied with great events. At the same time, it suffered very definite war damage. It was also typical of Domini-

can luck that, situated as it is between two French islands, it
should have had to accommodate several thousand refugees, only
a very small proportion of whom were honest adherents of the
Free French cause, who, demanding a daily meat meal, created a
cattle shortage that still continues. The interior economy of the
island, a very delicately adjusted organism, was seriously disturbed.

Ill-luck was accompanied by ill-management. The blockade of
Madagascar created a market for vanilla, but the traders profited
so imprudently in this unexpected boom that they shipped inferior and unripened pods. American buyers now distrust Dominican produce.

It was decided finally that Dominica should be linked by air
with the other islands. So an expert on aeronautics was sent to
locate an airfield. He selected a strip on the north-east coast. The
immediate disadvantages of this site were obvious. Not only was
it already occupied with a valuable coconut plantation, but it had
no direct communication with the capital. Passengers would have
to motor to Portsmouth, then go by launch to Roseau, a journey
that would take at least four hours. The expert maintained, however, that no other site was suitable, so the coconut palms were
felled, a vast quantity of stones collected by hand labor, and
simultaneously, so that there should be direct access from the
airport to the capital, work was resumed on the Imperial Road.
The labor and capital of the island were concentrated on these
two projects. For a year the work continued. Then, when the air
strip had been cleared and a valuable plantation ruined, a second
aeronautic expert decreed that the site chosen was unsuitable for
aircraft. Simultaneously, it was discovered that the sum of money
voted for the completion of the Imperial Road was quite inadequate, so that today, for the expenditure of a hundred thousand
pounds and the slaughter of several thousand palm trees, there is
nothing to show except a track of cobbles through the jungle, and
on the flanks of the mutilated Melville Hall estate three or four
admittedly impressive piles of hand-gathered flints.

"Typical Dominica," was the comment in St. Lucia.

"Typical Dominica." It is a comment and a criticism that you
will often hear made in the other islands.

They will make it laughingly on a note of mockery, of affectionate, fraternal mockery. There is a Dominica legend in the Caribbean.

"Everyone goes crazy there," they say. "All that rain and those mountains shutting them in and everything going wrong. Did you hear about that fellow who tried to dig a hole through the center of the earth because his wife was buried in Australia? He dug it with a cutlass, carrying the earth up in a calabash. You can still see the hole. That's typical."

It is typical, they will also say, that the island should have attracted so many English and American eccentrics, that square-pegs after long efforts to fit themselves into round holes should have made their homes there. Dominica is the only small island with an expatriate colony. It has been called "The Tahiti of the Caribbean."

I visited Dominica first in February 1929, a few weeks after the first hurricane had struck it.

I stayed a week. It rained incessantly. Roseau even in the sun-light is a scrubby little place. It is clean, but that is the most that can be said for it. It has no harbor; it happens to be the capital only because it is there that the chief valley meets the sea. Seven block long and eight blocks wide, it is a cluster of small two-story houses built on stone foundations which have contrived to resist successive hurricanes because, it is claimed, at the time when they were built it was the practice to mix syrup with the mortar. Un-painted wooden balconies project over the pavements; there are no gardens, no trees, no flowers.

There are admittedly a few attractive corners, particularly in the south, where a number of fine trees stand on a slight promi-nence of ground and police headquarters are housed in an old fort. The veranda of the library has a charming view of the bay and of Scotts Head. Beyond the Botanical Gardens, which are really fine, you can climb to the summit of Morne Bruce and see in the Roseau valley the lime trees of the Bath estate, stretching in even rows to be divided every so many yards by the windbreaks of the galba trees. There are attractive corners. But in a morning you can see them all.

I made a trip by foot and horse across the island. The moun-tains were concealed in cloud; incessant rain symbolized adversity.

I was there for the carnival. There were cocktail parties every night. I was meeting for the first time the "sour cocktail" of which angostura bitters is the chief ingredient, which I have described before. I had not yet acquired the knack of gulping swizzles. Round followed round, exhaustingly and bewilderingly. It was the only time in my life when I found myself defeated by straight-forward run-of-the-mill drinking. In a sense, it was all extremely gay, but beneath the gaiety I was conscious of an almost desperate defeatism. Dominica seemed to be flinging up the sponge; the hurricane was being accepted as the final straw. There was no point in trying any longer. The island was in the red for keeps. It was up to the Imperial Exchequer to take care of it.

I had some good times in Dominica. I made two real friends there. But even so I was glad to get away. I was depressed by the all-pervading apathy. Yet in retrospect, in continuing terms of that framework of anomalies and contradictions, out of all the islands I had visited, it was of Dominica that I found myself thinking most. I kept feeling that it was my own fault, that it was due to some deficiency in myself that I had got so little from my visit. Dominica had something, I suspected, which the other islands lacked, something which I had failed to find.

I was to hear much talk of Dominica during the nineteen-thirties. In London and New York, the Dominica legend was taking shape. The expatriate colony was growing. Stephen Haweis, for example, went there, and Elma and Lennox Napier and John Knapp. Stephen Haweis, the son of a distinguished Victorian clergyman, is an excellent and well-known painter. Lennox Napier held a gallant military record, and till his death during World War II played a prominent part in the island's political and social life. Elma, the daughter of Sir William Gordon-Cumming, one of the chief figures in the Tranby Croft baccarat scandal, widely travelled and the authoress of several books, is very much a person in her own right. The name John Knapp will not convey anything to those who did not know him personally. A scholarly, well-bred American, at one time a schoolmaster at Groton, he never at-tempted to make anything of his life. He was a complete escapist. But he was a gifted and a charming man. I had met him in Tahiti. Outside his house a notice-board announced in high white letter-ing visitors were not welcome. He sought solitude and privacy. He failed to find them in Tahiti. He did find them in Dominica.

In England I was to meet Jean Rhys. Her novels have not

reached a large public, but they have a personal flavor. Jean Rhys
in her writing is herself and no one else. There are no echoes.
The central character in her best-known novel is a composed and
assured person, unable to fit herself into organized society, who
recognizes this idiosyncrasy in herself and is undisturbed by it.
She told me she had been born in Dominica. Re-reading *After
Leaving Mr. Mackenzie*, I could see how many flashbacks to Dominica—imperceptible to the unacquainted reader—occurred in it.
I could see how Dominica had colored her temperament and outlook. It was a clue to her, just as she was a clue to it. People who
could not fit into life elsewhere found what they were looking for
in Dominica. Jean Rhys, who had been born there, chose as her
central character one who could not adjust herself to life outside.

Dominica clearly had something which the other islands lacked.
When I came back on this first post-war visit to the Caribbean, I
was resolved that whatever else I might be forced to miss, I would
not hurry my second visit there.

It is not easy to get to Dominica. The amphibian air service, a
six-seater plane based on St. Vincent, calls there, at the time of
writing, only once a week, and you have to get to St. Vincent to
connect with it. There are fewer ships now on Caribbean routes;
[*The French Line now makes a brief stop there.*] by no means all
of them stop at Dominica. The ships sailing from the north are
booked solid with round-trip passengers. Inter-island passengers
have to travel "deck" unless the casual sailing of a schooner or a
motor launch coincides with their time schedule. It is idle to pre-
tend that travelling in a small motor launch, in the open sea on a
rough day, is pleasant.

I was lucky in that I was making the journey from St. Lucia,
an island so close that there are those who claim to have seen it
from Scotts Head. I was lucky, too, in that mine was a morning
sailing; I had not to spend a night aboard. It was a bright clear
day. From the decks of the *Lady Nelson* I could pick out the bays
and valleys of Martinique; Diamond Rock glittered in the sunlight. For once there were no clouds over Mont Pelé; its jagged
summit lifted over the skeleton of St. Pierre, the deep track of its
lava running brown towards the sea. As we passed out of the
protection of the land, the ship began to rock. There is a heavy
swell in the twenty-mile channel between Dominica and Marti-

nique. I was grateful that I was not making the journey in a schooner. Slowly the tall shadows of Dominica became distinct.

Always before, I had arrived in darkness. I had never seen how cosily the little villages of Soufrière and Pointe Michèle cluster about their churches. It was the first time I had seen Dominica in the sunlight. I had not believed that anything could be so green. I had never thought of green as being a color that could dazzle you. I had not believed there could be so many shades of green, that a single color could combine so many varieties of tone and texture, could achieve such an effect of patchwork.

Very often one's first hours in a place set the tone for an entire visit. This happened now. As I was about to clamber down the gangplank, a young man in shorts and an open shirt pushed his way towards me.

"You are Mr. Alec Waugh?" he asked.

"I am."

"Fine! I was afraid I'd missed you. I'm taking you up to Springfield."

"Where's Springfield?"

"John Archbold's place."

"Who's John Archbold?"

"A planter here. He's expecting you for cocktails."

I had never heard either of John Archbold or of Springfield. The man who was proposing to take me there was white and an American.

"There must be some mistake. You must have got the wrong man," I said.

"Not if you are Alec Waugh."

Even so, I was unconvinced. I have a namesake—in no way related to me—who works in pictures, and whose bills, love-letters, and income-tax returns have constantly found their way into my mail box over the last twenty years. It was not impossible that John Archbold had confused us, but I did not see any reason on that account to decline what would probably prove an agreeable invitation.

We set off in a station-wagon. I was not the only guest. Three other passengers had been collected off the *Lady Nelson*. They were making the round trip and were continuing north that night. My escort believed that I, too, was a round-trip passenger. He seemed surprised and possibly a little disconcerted when I told him that I was planning to stay a month.

Springfield is seven miles out of Roseau on the Imperial Road. From its veranda you can see a narrow triangle of horizon, framed between two cliffs. The mountains rise on either side of it, high and vertical, but not so close as to make you feel shut in. In the immediate foreground is the deep gorge of a river with banana plants climbing up its sides. The long living-room behind has the solid, practical comfort of deep armchairs and substantial tables. My host was in the middle thirties, tall, fair-haired, clean-shaven; he was wearing a recently pressed Palm Beach suit and a canary-yellow foulard tie. He fixed us drinks and we sat on the veranda. The air had cooled rapidly as we swung up the abrupt, steep curves. I was glad that my socks were thick and that I had brought a cardigan. I do not imagine that even in midsummer it would be really hot.

One of the party was asking John Archbold how he had come to settle here. He gave a typical beachcomber answer. He had come on a cruise, meaning to leave that evening, and suddenly, like that, had bought himself an estate. He was specializing now in oranges. He was concerned about finding a suitable label for his produce. At the moment he could think of nothing more effective than "Liquid Sunshine," and that, he recognized, was not satisfactory.

Presently his wife Lucie joined us. She was tall, dark-haired, and very lovely, in white linen trousers and a white silk shirt. She was clearly too young to be the mother of the studious ten-year-old girl who was reading in a corner of the veranda. I learned later that John had been a widower, and was now, remarried, on his honeymoon.

"Time for your supper, Anne," said Lucie.

Nothing could have been more "typically beachcomber" than this story of a man who had come to an island for five hours and stayed fifteen years; yet nothing could have been farther from the beachcomber atmosphere than the domesticity of the scene and the keenness with which John Archbold was planning his estate.

Slowly the night darkened round us and the air got colder.

"Time to be moving," said the man who had met me at the boat.

I rose with the others.

"No, no," said Archbold. "You're staying on for dinner, if you can manage it."

It was the first chance I had had of explaining my predicament. "Didn't you get my letter then?" he asked.

I shook my head. I was travelling "deck"; the letter explaining that an old friend of mine, Charlesworth Ross, the present Commissioner of Montserrat, had cabled an introduction, had remained in the purser's office. I was to get the letter the next day.

"You'd better stay on. We've got a duck," said Lucie.

By the time I was back in Roseau, I had made two new friends.

That first evening at Springfield set the tone for my entire visit. As it was with John Archbold, so was it, I soon found, with the rest of the expatriate colony. Two other Americans live on the Imperial Road, one married to a compatriot, the other to an English girl. Both work their plantations seriously. There are also two American boys recently released from uniform who have started a lumber business. One of them has an American wife, the other while I was there married the daughter of the manager of the Royal Bank. It was the most charmingly intimate wedding I have been to, with the planters bringing down from their estates great sprays of orchids and gardenias, and with half the native population peering through the windows of the church and lining up in the road outside to roar with laughter at the surprising headgear of the guests.

John Archbold is in a slightly different position from his compatriots, in that he is a rich man with many responsibilities in the United States, [*His brother was the late Armour Archbold.*] who can only devote three or four months a year to Dominica; throughout the entire war he was away on active duty with the U.S. Navy, but he has this in common with the others—that he is working his estate seriously, and by his presence on the island is contributing substantially both to its congeniality and its prosperity.

Nor is the situation so very different in the case of an English expatriate like Elma Napier. A widow now, in the later fifties, she has two properties, one on the leeward coast, which she has let, the other in the north-east corner of the island at Pointe Baptiste. Though she does not work either of her estates, she is a busy woman. There is nothing escapist about her life; not only has she written three or four books there, but she is active in local politics. She was serving then on the Legislative Council, as an elected member, a thing that no other woman, white or black, had ever done. There are no proper roads in her district, and it took her five days to cover it. She took her obligations very seriously.

Eccentric things can happen and do happen in Dominica. [*Since I wrote this piece, three of the people whom I met during this trip have committed suicide.*] Yet the life led there by those English and Americans who for reasons of choice have made their homes in Dominica is very remote from the somewhat sinister legend of irresponsible folk, cultivating new, strange vices while the rains wash away their roads. Yet even so I could not see at first what it was that had attracted to this island so many persons of charm and of distinction who could have lived almost anywhere else in the world if they had wanted.

I spent a full month in Dominica, and a month is ample time in which to examine the resources of an island twenty-seven miles long and thirteen broad. It is not a tourist's island. It has two hotels—the Paz and Cherry Lodge. They are clean and comfortable, but they are located in the very center of the town. They are hot and noisy. And the first requirements of a hotel in the tropics are a view and a feeling of fresh air. In addition, there is Kingland House, where I stayed myself, which is really not an hotel at all but the old home of Dr. Nichols, with whose work for the island every student of Dominica is familiar. His daughter now takes in a number of paying guests. It is at the top of the town, it is not particularly noisy, it has a charming garden and a clear view of the hills; it has no bar nor any licence to sell wines and spirits, but guests are permitted to supply their own. I was extremely comfortable there myself, and I had the good fortune to find myself in a group of highly congenial fellow guests.

Dominica needs a good hotel, but it would not pay to build one. There is little to attract the tourist. There is no bathing beach, for instance. The aquatic club is housed a mile out of town, in a small bungalow—one of a row—facing a six-yard stretch of pebbles that shelves into the sea. There is a certain amount of undertow, so that the scramble up after a swim is awkward. Sunbathing on pebbles is not comfortable, nor is there the slightest privacy. There are only two alternatives to the aquatic club: the rivers, where there is no space to swim; and Scotts Head, which is four miles away at the extreme south of the island, and where a long thin thirty-yard strip of sand runs out from Soufrière to a rocky promontory that once held a strategic fort.

There is no road leading to Scotts Head, and it is an hour and a quarter's run in a motor-launch. Land breezes can be abrupt and strong, particularly on the journey home, and you are usually well soaked by the time you are back in harbor. A picnic at Scotts Head is a popular Sunday expedition. A fishing-line may be towed behind the boat. The sand is white, and there is the shade of palm trees. From the summit of the rock among the ruins of the old fort you get a fine panoramic view of Martinique and the wide curve of the bay of Soufrière. There is an agreeable village feeling about the place: fishing-nets are hanging up to dry, fishing-boats are tacking in the bay and in the rough waters of the Dominica channel. Sooner or later a boat will put in to shore, and a group of infants will eagerly gather round while a couple of fifteen-pound dolphins are disembowelled. As you wait your turn to drive a bargain with the fisherman, it is by no means improbable that one or two of the villagers will offer you for ten shillings a bottle of French brandy that shows no signs of having paid tribute to the British Customs. As you return to Roseau in the late afternoon, the sun will be shining on the church spire of Pointe Michèle and the abandoned factories of Soufrière. It is a pleasant expedition, but with the exception of Trinidad no island in the Caribbean offers fewer facilities for bathing.

There are, in fact, few facilities for sport of any kind. There is little shooting; the fishing is poor; there is no golf-course; the roads are so rough that if you take out a horse the opportunities even of trotting will be few; any motor trip involves a return by the same route that you took out. Unless you play tennis, it is hard to get any exercise in Roseau.

There is no night life of any kind. The bar of the Paz closes at nine o'clock. I once came into Roseau by launch shortly after eight at night to find the waterfront so dark that I felt sure the pilot was in error. I could not believe that any place so unlighted could be the capital of anything.

There is no leisured class in Roseau. Everyone is there for a specific reason. The adult white community of the island is a hundred strong. It has one club, the Dominica, a mixed club with a tennis-court, a bar, a billiard-table, and a bridge room. It is here that the social life of the island centers between five and eight, Wednesdays and Saturdays being the big club nights. There is no other meeting place apart from an ice-cream parlor, which is also a circulating library, a grocery store, and a sales counter for local handicraft. There is no restaurant. The returning of hospitality constitutes, indeed, quite a problem for a visitor. It is difficult for him to throw a party anywhere except in his own hotel. And if he does, an embarrassing situation is likely to be caused in a building which contains only one small sitting-room, unless he invites to it all his fellow residents.

The club in Dominica is very much more the center of the island's life than are similar institutions in the other islands. There is less social life outside it. There are fewer cocktail parties, and not only the life of Roseau but the life of the estates is centered there. Pointe Baptiste, where Elma Napier lives, is at least five hours away. There is first of all a four-hour trip to Portsmouth by a launch that stops at every valley, where there are passengers and cargo to be landed and collected; then there is a three-quarters of an hour drive across the northern tip of the island; yet Elma Napier, who often has to come into Roseau for council meetings, is in touch with the life of Roseau in a way that in St. Lucia the residents of Soufrière are not in touch with the life of Castries. Castries is an administrative center, and its life is as much cut off from the life of the estates as was, in World War II, G.H.Q. Middle East at Cairo from the formations in the desert. In Dominica, on the other hand, the planters along the Imperial Road come in for tennis two or three times a week, and are invariably invited to any large parties that are held in town. The life of the estates is far more an integral part of Roseau's life than is the life of the estates a part of Castries' life in St. Lucia. Life in Dominica is more compact, is more of a family affair, the threads are more interwoven, the fortunes of one are in a sense the fortunes of all. For residents of Roseau, life is reasonably full and varied, but the visitor to Roseau is likely to be bored unless he undertakes expeditions.

On my first visit to Dominica I had crossed the southern tip of the island to Pointe Mulâtre and had seen something of the interior. This time I crossed the center of the island by the mountain lake and travelled along the windward coast from La Plaine to Hatton Garden, the section along which no motor road has been even planned. The agricultural adviser, Louis de Verteuil, was making a tour of his experimental sections. John and Lucie Archbold, and John's daughter Anne, were going, too, with Mrs. Lewis, a Dominican friend of Lucie's. I made a sixth. We expected to be away six days. It was one of those trips on which nothing turns out as it is planned, but on that very account I got a clearer insight into the island's problem.

We started from the Botanical Gardens at nine o'clock; driving by truck to a point at which travel by road became impossible. We were met there by guides and horses. We were travelling light, but we had to carry a large proportion of our provisions. Crossing to the windward coast is an operation. F. A. Ober wrote in 1928: "There are no hotels on that coast, nor even boarding-houses, so one is compelled to share the hospitality of the planters (who are becoming scarce) or of common cultivators." Mr. Ober was prophetic. The planter caste is now extinct. And I doubt if there are any "common cultivators" who could provide possible accommodation. There are police posts along the coast, there are also two agricultural experimental stations. But one has to feed oneself. One guide, however, can carry several days' provisions on his head. Six guides and three horses were considered adequate for a six days' journey.

The journey to La Plaine from the point at which the trucks were forced to stop is, measured on a map, some eight and a half miles. We had travelled eighteen miles before we finally arrived. We started to walk at half-past nine, we took half an hour's rest for lunch and three-quarters of an hour off for a swim in the Rosalie River when we reached the coast, but we did not arrive at La Plaine until after five. At the point where we left the trucks, we were at a height of a thousand feet. Before we began to descend we had reached a height of two thousand five hundred feet, and we were travelling, it must be remembered, by the easiest track. The highest point, Diablotin, scales five thousand feet.

It is impossible, however, by looking at a map or studying facts and figures to appreciate the interior of Dominica. That is where the bureaucrats of the Colonial Office, sitting at their London desks, find themselves at a disadvantage when they blueprint Dominica's future. There is only one way to understand Dominica. You have to walk across it and along it. You have to realize just how long it takes to get from one place to another. Your feet need to be sore from walking on cobbles. Your calves need to ache from climbing slippery paths. You need to have been soaked by rain and chilled by falling temperatures as you climb. You have to see how sharply the cliffs rise above the paths, you need to note on this and the other mountainside the brown bare path of a landslide that would have cut away any road that had been attempted there. From a photograph you might be able to realize to what height the mountains rise. You might even recognize the vertical nature of those mountains, of how they stand up before you like straight and solid walls. But what you would never realize from a photograph is the third-dimensional nature of it all. To the right and left and straight ahead you will see what appears at first glance to be a solid range of mountains; you look more closely and you realize that it is not one range but two, not two but three. You cannot be quite certain whether it is not four or five. Range after range with its leaf-domed summit merges into the background of successive ranges, with each shade of green merging into another, and the passing of the clouds across the sun sending fresh waves of shadow into that seemingly solid background. You may guess how far away it is in terms of time. You cannot tell how many valleys lie between you and it. Valley after valley, gorge on gorge. Arithmetic may show the area of an island twenty-seven miles long and thirteen broad, but no arithmetician could compute how big an area would be covered if a giant hand were slowly to press down and smooth out the whole thing flat.

Dominica has been called the loveliest of the West Indian islands. It depends on what you mean by lovely, or rather it depends on what kind of beauty most appeals to you. A taste for one type of beauty often precludes that for another. I would not say that Dominica was the loveliest island I have seen, but I cannot believe that in terms of grandeur and majesty there can be found anything in the world to rival Dominica's succession of forest-covered mountains. The forest is so thick that you cannot distinguish tree from tree. You cannot tell how tall they are nor how widely their branches spread. It is all a tangle of bamboo and ferns and vine, of palms and mahogany and mango, of cedar and bay and breadfruit trees. It is green, all green. At certain times of the year a tree in blossom will stab the mountainside with yellow or white or scarlet. But when I made this trip there was not a tree in flower. There were no butterflies, there were no birds, though as we climbed we heard the single shrill note of the *siffleur montagne*, the bird that seeks solitude and is rarely seen.

There were few signs of habitation along the way. Scarcely a single village; barely a dozen bungalows. Occasionally, high on a mountainside, would be the brown scar of a clearing where the trees had been felled and the undergrowth burned. Every so often there would be a regular patch of cultivation, coconut or banana. Quite often we would pass small groups of peasants carrying on their heads the waterproof fiber baskets that the Caribs weave. Many of the peasants were of Carib stock. Their faces had a Mongolian cast, their black hair was straight, their lips were soft and full, their cheeks not so much brown as yellow. In the stream women were washing out their clothes. They greeted us as we passed, and their smiles were friendly.

A journey across the island is a succession of sharp climbs and sharp descents. There is no walking along the level. You are either sliding on a clayey surface or bruising your soles on pebbles. It is an open point as to whether sand shoes or thick-soled boots are the less impractical. Hour after hour, that is the way it is, with the air getting cooler as you climb, with rain clouds intervening; but all the time, as you look back, you will continue to get sudden tremendous vistas of the Roseau valley, with the houses of the horizon very faint beyond.

It is a journey which has in a sense no landmarks, or rather it would be more true to say that its landmarks are incidental. An expedition has to set itself some objective, some target or other to be aimed at; so one talks of walking out to Laudat or to the waterfalls, to the Boiling Lake or to the freshwater lake. From the village of Laudat, which is about two thousand feet high and an hour or so's climb from the point where we left the trucks, there is a plateau raised above the valley, but the view was no better than it had been a mile farther back or than it was to be a mile farther on. It is the same with the mountain lake. It is three-quarters of an hour beyond Laudat. There is nothing remarkable about it, except that it happens to be there. It is simply a stretch of water. It makes a good full day's picnic in the same way that the waterfalls make a good morning or afternoon excursion, but it is not a spectacle. The waterfalls and the freshwater lake are alibis, excuses for seeing the scenery of Dominica. It is not what you see when you arrive but what you see along the way that matters.

There is only one really dramatic moment as you cross the island—the first view of the Atlantic. You see it in a glimpse and for a few yards of roadway, from a distance of four miles and of two thousand feet, a brief shot, between the mountains, of the bay of Rosalie, a vivid triangle of white-edged blue, a line of surf such as you will not see anywhere along the leeward coast, a warning, as it were, of how different a world is awaiting you on the farther side, as though the great architect of the universe had intended to flash upon the original Carib settlers from the leeward side this premonition of another way of living.

We arrived at La Plaine on a Monday evening; Louis was to devote the Tuesday to his section; we planned to move on northwards on the Wednesday, but, as I said, this was a trip on which nothing turned out as it was planned.

It was to end very nearly in cruel tragedy.

On the next day, the Tuesday, we went down, the six of us, to bathe. We had all of us, tired though we were, slept badly, as one so often does in strange surroundings. We were in a lazy mood. It was good to lie out on sand instead of pebbles. I stretched myself on my face; Lucie ran past me to the water; she was wearing a white and green two-piece bathing dress. She looked very slim and lovely.

"The sun seems to smooth away every trouble that one has ever had," I said.

"As the Greeks said about the sea," she answered.

They were so very nearly the last words we were to exchange. I lay forward on my face and let the sun beat on to my back and legs; rarely had the the world seemed pleasanter. And then. . . .

But it all happened so quickly that I am not sure even now what happened. I became conscious all of a sudden of a commotion somewhere. I raised my head and turned. Mrs. Lewis was shouting something. Louis, up to his waist in water, was signalling to the shore. He was shouting, but the wind was too strong for us to hear. Beyond him and to the right and some way ahead I could see John and Lucie. "They're in trouble," Mrs. Lewis said. I ran into the sea. Before the water had reached my knees I was aware simultaneously of a tremendous current that was pulling my feet from under me and of the power of the incoming waves that nearly knocked me backwards. I realized then that it was not to me that Louis had been beckoning but to a couple of grooms who had just brought the horses down to water. One of them was running down the beach, the other was still fiddling with the bridles. "Both of you. Both of you," Louis was shouting. "Fetch a rope, a bridle rope," he said to me.

Before I had reached the shore the second groom had left the horses. Anne, bent forward on her knees, her forehead pressed upon the sand, was howling hard. I tried to comfort her. "It's all right," I said. "Don't worry."

By the time that I had brought the rope, the first of the grooms was on his way back with Lucie. Louis and I waited in the shallows to take her from him. "Get back to the other one," Louis told the groom. Lucie was conscious but a dead weight. It was not easy to carry her back to shore, even with the water below our knees, in that current and against those breaking waves. By the time we had got her into the shade, John was already rescued. He was in far worse shape. He had swallowed a great deal of water, but he was breathing. It ought to be all right.

How long had it all lasted? Two minutes, five minutes, a quarter of an hour? Not more than three minutes in all, most likely. It had happened so quickly that I could not tell.

I sat by Anne in an attempt, by appearing myself unconcerned, to set her mind at ease while Louis worked on John and Mrs. Lewis on Lucie, kneading their backs, forcing the water out of their lungs. It was by the merest chance that those grooms had happened to be there at just that time; it was equally by the merest chance that men instead of boys should have been sent down for the watering of the horses; just as it was the merest chance that those grooms had been exceptionally strong swimmers.

Within a quarter of an hour Lucie, though in pain still, was coherent. John, however, was giving cause for some anxiety. Two years earlier he had been involved in a serious motor accident and his heart was weakened. It was necessary to protect him against shock. The beach was twenty minutes' walk from the rest house, the village of La Plaine was a further fifteen minutes' walk away. At the time of the accident the beach had been completely empty, but by now we had an audience of half a village. Every minute brought a new arrival, briskly swinging his cutlass, asking what he could do to help. Assistants were despatching themselves bewilderingly by every path. "Get a jelly nut," said Louis, and two bands of urchins scattered to collect green coconuts. There is no doctor on the windward coast, but emissaries were on their way to every possible locality in which the dispenser from La Plaine might be at work. Another party went back to the house for a rug and brandy. They were very thorough. About everything West Indian, even about an accident as serious as this, there is a quality of comic opera. A Bedouin tribe could have encamped under the supply of blankets that they brought. Every bottle in the house was requisitioned, not only brandy, crème de menthe, and whisky, but brilliantine and Aqua Velva. They brought everything except the swizzlestick. Finally, the parish priest came cantering up to perform last offices.

At length both John and Lucie were strong enough to be lifted upon stretchers. We were followed by a procession sixty strong. It was after one o'clock when we arrived to find as much to our relief as to our surprise that the wife of the dispenser, a trained nurse, was waiting in white linen and with two beds prepared. The cook, however, had not even started upon a lunch. At that point for the first and only time during the expedition Louis failed to control his patience.

"No food, and it's after one. What do you think army cooks do in a battle? They cook for the men who fight."

Later in the day the cook broke out to Mrs. Lewis and myself in a fine explosion of self-vindicatory rhetoric. "What I do? Death is coming to the house. In they come. Blankets they take. Bottles they take. What I do? Death is coming to the house. Who think of eating? Who want food? What I do?"

That night as I sat out on the veranda, watching the fireflies flickering above the crotons, I tried to reconstruct the scene, to remember the exact sequence of events. But I found myself, as I have on the two or three occasions when I have been caught up in unexpected drama, unable to recall in detail what had happened. If you are sent to report a football match, the antennae of your perceptions are alert, but it is quite a different matter to be the witness of a car crash when you are walking down a London street thinking of the lunch party that you are on your way to, your thoughts concentrated somewhere else. There is the sound of a horn, the scream of brakes, a sudden cry, and there before your

eyes is a machine mounted on the pavement and a pedestrian
bleeding at your feet. But you have no idea, at least I haven't,
what happened first, what happened next.

Had I had to give evidence in a court of law, as well I might,
on what had happened on the beach that morning, I should not
have been able to answer accurately such questions as: "What
made you realize first that anything was wrong?" "When did you
realize it was serious?" "How long did the second groom delay?"
"What did Louis do when you went back to get the rope?" My
answers, if they had been given honestly, would have been stum-
bling and uncertain. An incredulous look would have come into
counsel's face. "Do you seriously ask the court to believe that
every detail of such an episode was not photographed upon your
memory?" Yet in point of fact I could not remember what warned
me first that anything was wrong, whether it was Anne's tears or
Louis's waving or Mrs. Lewis's shouting. I only know that some-
how or other I became conscious of commotion.

I wonder how often in a court of law a man's life or reputation
has not been endangered by a witness who, having in all innocence
produced an inaccurate sequence of events, has subsequently
maintained his story through fear of appearing foolish in the box.
During the later part of World War II, when I worked in counter-
espionage in Baghdad, I frequently had to interview enemy agents
whom we had taken into custody. Before we had taken
them in, I had anticipated that these interviews would clear up
points which had long puzzled me; but when the time for examination came, I was surprised to find that very often the agents
had forgotten what they had done on days so dramatic that I
would have expected their least detail to have been imprinted on
their memories until the day they died.

It was, as I said, a trip in which everything went wrong. But
it taught me more about the windward coast than the trip which
we had planned originally could possibly have done. In no other
way could I have learned quite how completely cut off it is from
the leeward coast. Gossip travels fast in Roseau, yet it was forty-
eight hours before anyone rang us up. The dispensary did not
stock the medicines that were required and a man had to be sent
on foot to fetch them. That took thirty hours. It became soon
apparent that Lucie could not continue the journey on foot or

horse, and that the sooner she was got home the better. But neither to north nor south was there a motor road within ten hours of us. There was nowhere for a seaplane to land. There was no beach where a launch or schooner could put in. There was nothing to be done but wait.

I remained at La Plaine four nights, and when you are stationary you have an easier chance of appreciating a surrounding atmosphere than when you are on the move, when you are conscious of personal direction, of purpose, of an immediate objective. I learned during those extra days how completely stagnant was the life there, as much cut off from Roseau as during the war Roseau had been from the world. There were no newspapers. No one had a radio. A Test Match was in progress in Jamaica, but there was no means of finding out the score, and anyone who knows how intense is the West Indian passion for cricket will recognize what that meant. At the head of the village street was a notice-board containing a single typewritten sheet giving a summary of the world's news. But it was two weeks old.

La Plaine is a self-contained community consisting of a single wandering street, with the Roman Catholic church the center of its village life. We called at the presbytery to arrange for a Mass in token of John's gratitude for the sympathy which the villagers had shown and the help which they had given. The parish priest was a youngish man, a member of the order of F.M.I., from La Vendée, which has for many years supplied the churches of Dominica and St. Lucia. He welcomed us with a glass of wine. He had only been out a year. After six weeks' instruction from his predecessor, he had been left on his own. He had spoken no English when he arrived, and though he was taking lessons from the local schoolmaster, his opportunities of speaking English were extremely few. He declined consequently to speak French with us, which made conversation difficult. The patois he had learned more rapidly and it was in patois and in French that he addressed his congregation. It is not surprising under such conditions that the use of the French patois has been maintained, though it is nearly a century and a half since the French owned the island.

We visited the church. Though it had been rebuilt only eighty years ago, stone weathers fast in the tropics, and it had already an air of age. It had dignity and charm and color. It was easy to see why in a village of two-room shacks this building and its presbytery, now that the planter class and the influence of the big house have vanished, should serve as a symbol of authority and why its incumbent should be the most respected person in the neighborhood; easy to see why the Church should be for the isolated villages along the coast the solitary link with Western culture. Outside one of the village shops was a thing that I have never seen before, a wooden blackboard on which had been inscribed a four-line text from the New Testament.

Once the agricultural station had been part of a prosperous estate. At the foot of the valley stood the ruins of an old sugar factory. The machinery was rusted over. A tree was growing from the chimney-stack, pushing out the brickwork. Portions of the stone channel of the aqueduct remained, and from a line of cabbage palms you could track the course that it had followed. A further cluster of palms marked the site of the old plantation house, no trace of which now remains. No one seemed to know when the plantation had been abandoned, whether or not it had survived World War I, to have its limes hit by the withertip disease in the early 'twenties, and its sugar cane destroyed by the later hurricanes.

It was all as though it had never been. Today the peasant proprietor cultivates his own small garden, relying on local sales and goods that can be "headed" across the mountains. Vanilla is the easiest crop to handle, but the price of vanilla has recently slumped badly. A root called *toutlemoi*, from the French *tous les mois*—meaning that it is available every month—is on the whole the favorite product. There was a one-man mill by the stream that divided the station from the village. The owner trod a pedal which operated a wheel on which a grater had been fixed. He fed the roots through a hole in a wooden frame. A beige yellow-brown pulp fell into a trough below. His wife collected the pulp. She had a barrel over which a reddened cloth was spread, she poured a stream of water over the pulp, wringing it out, straining it through the cloth. When all the starch had been extracted, the pulp was thrown away, and the starch left to settle in the barrel. It was washed again, then it was ready to be sold.

A one-man river-mill looks very different from the elaborate arrowroot factories of St. Vincent, but the principle is the same.

I stayed on at La Plaine until the Friday. Then, when it was finally decided to carry Lucie back to Roseau on a stretcher, I arranged to push on by myself along the coast to a point where I could cut in across the interior to the Imperial Road. It was a three days' journey. One night I stopped at the police post at Castle Bruce, one night I spent at Marigot, back in civilization to the extent that I was in a village from which a surfaced road ran to a point from which I could take a launch to Roseau, to a point, that is to say, from which communication could be maintained with the outside world.

I was six hours on the road the first day, seven hours on the second. During the second morning I passed through the Carib reserve, where survive, now peacefully making their canoes and plaiting their waterproof baskets, the thousand relicts of the once-warlike race that not only exterminated the original Indian settlers but resisted the British and French forces so effectively that the contesting powers agreed for a time to treat Dominica as neutral territory.

In many ways the journey along the coast was a repetition of what I had seen already at La Plaine—a series of rivers running to the sea past ruined factories. Once Rosalie rum was famous; now at the river's foot there is just a chimney and a crumbling aqueduct and a slatternly cluster of untended cottages. It was the same at St. Sauveur. It was the same at Castle Bruce; with the cliffs between the valleys rising straight out of the sea, their vegetation crushed and beaten by Atlantic gales, and the shrubs that crown them combed back tightly against the rocks like the crinkled hair of a mulatto girl. I saw nothing that I had not seen already at La Plaine or that from my four days at La Plaine I might not have guessed that I would see; but Matthew Arnold said of Byron's poetry that to appreciate it you must judge it in the mass. The same thing is true of Dominica. You have to see it on foot and by the hour. Then, in terms of your own physical exhaustion, you can recognize how extensive has been the ruin there and how complete; how much, moreover, there was there to destroy.

Economically the windward coast lies prostrate; at the same time it is not possible to travel day by day and hour after hour along its lovely valleys without being attracted to the casual friendliness of the life that is lived there now. No one bothers anyone. No one is rich, but they all get along, cultivating their small gardens in the mountains, working their one-man mills. The smallest village has its cricket pitch. It all had a garden effect, such as is rarely seen in villages on the leeward coast. The villagers are house-proud, as though the farther they had got away from the alien Western conditions to which they had been transported, the closer had they returned to the cleanliness and order of the bush. Native peoples are invariably clean in their own surroundings. Everyone that you pass along the road has a smile and a good morning.

The police sergeant at Castle Bruce showed me his monthly charge-sheet. He had little crime, he said. In a large district he had had only one case of manslaughter in three years; there was little battery and assault; rape was unknown; robbery of houses rare; officially the worst and most general crime was praedial larceny, the robbing of crops and produce; but the chief entry in the ledger was the unusual offence of stupefying fish. The villagers rub bark over the streams, which has the effect of drugging the larger fish and making them easy prey. The shredded bark did not poison the large fish; but what merely drugs a big fish kills off the smaller fish and those forms of water life on which the big fish live; if the process were not discouraged, the rivers would soon be fishless.

I arrived at Castle Bruce in the early afternoon. I had brought with me for my supper a tin of corned beef which I was proposing to embellish with produce from the local store. The police sergeant looked doubtful when I told him this. It was a Friday and I could get no bread, he said. "What about fruit?" I asked. "Jelly nuts or pawpaw or bananas?" Again he shook his head. He was doubtful, very doubtful.

He sent his constable with me into the village. Its only store was run by a retired cricketer. Behind the shop was a freshly painted bungalow. Standing half-way up the hill, it was clearly the "Big House" of the community.

"You have heard of course of Mr. T. O. Murphy," said the constable. He spoke with awe.

Murphy was coal black in a way that only a Barbadian can be. Such teeth as he still possessed were very white. He was powerful and short and stocky. His shop was adorned with relics of his career. A pair of batting gloves dangled above his door like scalps over the entrance to a Red Indian's wigwam. There were pads in one corner of the veranda, and a bat leaned against the desk. It was an old bat, bound and pegged, but it told its story. There was a lovely spoon in the middle of its drive. That bat had hit many balls hard and far.

It was by now half-past four. "What about a punch," I said. It was two punches later before I told him about my ungarnished supper. It is very rare for two cricketers not to like each other, and by then we were good friends. He shook his head, however, when I asked about buying jelly nuts. It was doubtful, very doubtful, he insisted. He turned towards the kitchen and shouted something out in patois. There was a scuffle of youthful feet. Anything that could be done would be done, I felt very sure.

He took me round his property. It was very small, less than an acre, but it was thickly planted with every variety of local produce. His chief source of income, apart from his shop, was a mill for manioc. In many ways it was like the *toutlemoi* mill at La Plaine. There was the same one-man pedal for a grated wheel against which the root was fed through a hole in a wooden frame, but it was a more elaborate construction. There was an amateurish but apparently effective balance by which the pulp was pressed under the weight of stones. There was also a furnace composed of a large flat *tayche*—originally a cauldron from a sugar factory— broken in half over a charcoal fire. Here the dried starch was spread and sifted. Murphy did not cultivate manioc himself, but rented out the mill to his fellow villagers.

We went back to the bungalow for a final punch. As we sat there sipping the white local rum, his emissaries one by one returned with news of failure. Three hours earlier I would not have believed it possible that the chance visitor to a West Indian village, however small, would find it difficult to buy local produce. I suppose the explanation is that not one visitor would pass that way a week, that not one visitor a month would not provide himself with all the food he needed, and that local economy was so accurately balanced that they only produced exactly what they needed for themselves. I could understand how their domestic economy must have been dislocated during World War II by those Free French from Martinique and Guadeloupe who insisted on a daily meat meal.

On the next day I went through the Carib section. It looked no different. On the surface the life led there is identical with that which exists on either side. At one time they had a language of their own—or rather they had two languages, for the men spoke one language and the women spoke another, but very few of the original words are now in use. At one time they built a slightly different kind of cabin with a second floor under the roof on which they slept, but now they have adopted the familiar style. They are Roman Catholics, and they play cricket.

They are very pacific nowadays. The corporal in charge of the police post at Salybia told me that he had very little trouble with them. They enjoy their rum as much as the next man does, but they keep their squabbles to themselves. When a Carib feels the need to let off steam, he calls a friend across and exchanges a couple of punches with him, without rancor or ill temper. That and no more than that, and he feels a great deal better.

They still make excellent canoes. I saw one under construction. Long and narrow, scooped from a single trunk, it was being dried over a fire with the inside filled with boulders to prevent the wood from shrinking. I also saw a local craftsman at work on one of the baskets that are in universal use throughout the island. They are made in two layers, with large leaves arranged between to make them waterproof. The cover is decorated by the weaving of different-colored fibers. Their only disadvantage for the northerner is the weakness of the handle, which is, of course, no disadvantage to the islander, who carries his luggage not by the handle but on his head. I bought one of the baskets, a 2 ft. 6 in. by 1 ft. 6 in. affair, for seven shillings. I tried to talk to the man who made it, but he spoke only patois. I was equally unsuccessful with the councillor to whom the corporal introduced me. A short, dapper little man with a drooping black mustache, he looked like a Maupassant character out of the original Albin Michel edition. He spoke a little English, and I could understand what he said to me. But his vocabulary was small, and I could not be sure he was understanding what I said. He was a courtly, gracious man, and he appeared to be in agreement with me. His replies, however, rarely bore much relation to my original enquiries.

On my return to Roseau I was to learn that an English motion-picture company was planning to stage in Dominica a section of a film about Christopher Columbus, starring Fredric March, for which two galleons, exact replicas of the *Santa Maria* and the *Pinta,* had been constructed in Barbados at a cost of thirty thousand pounds, and that a team of experts had selected as the most photogenic a beach near Castle Bruce. One of the experts, Basil Keyes, was an old wartime friend with whom I had often swum in the Bain Militaire at Beyrouth. He told me that Dominica had been chosen as the site of Columbus's first landing in the interests of historical accuracy, since it was the only island in which the Carib population still survives; a decision which shows that film executives grow to pattern, and that J. Arthur Rank's London studios are related by ties closer than those of blood to Goldwyn's Hollywood. Since his arrival, Keyes had realized that complete historical accuracy was unlikely to be achieved, since the mid-Bahamas, where Columbus landed, were dead flat, whereas Dominica's cliffs on the windward coast rise sheer, since the coconut palm had not then been introduced in the Caribbean, and since it was not by the warlike Caribs but the docile Arawak Indians that the Spaniards were made welcome. Keyes was accepting these facts with equanimity. He had made films before; he knew that historical accuracy is a question of what your audience knows. On one point only he insisted. On no account must a breadfruit tree appear. All the world had seen Charles Laughton as Captain Bligh. Everyone knew about the *Bounty's* business in Tahiti. He was also concerned as to whether the Catholic priests would allow their flocks to appear in the attire in which Columbus had been received. *"Tellement nue"* had been Labat's startled description of a seventeenth-century Carib. Keyes asked the opinion of the officer in charge of the police. "There is only one way to deal with Caribs," he was told. "Don't give them any rum until they've done their job."

A few months later I received the following letter from Elma Napier's daughter—Daphne Agar:

I realize with horror that I promised to write you if the "Columbus" company came here—well, they did come and I didn't write! Neither did I go round to Woodford Hill and watch them at their antics, which were considerable. I was a little shocked at the "goings on" and at the untold gold which was scattered around the Northern District—fine for the Northern District, of course, but no one out here will ever believe again that England is in any financial difficulty. The Caribs made an average of 12 pounds per day per family, so were only too delighted to take their clothes off or do anything else anyone wanted—they don't see money like that from year's end to year's end. Every car in the district was commandeered, so no private individual could travel at all. The people who catered for the sailors made fortunes; also the purveyor of Cola, for every actor averaged about five a day, and not one of them had an opener so the beach was strewn with broken bottles. They had perfect weather and the shots they took are reported excellent, but as the conclusion everyone reached was that they would never pass the censor, all the effort is probably in vain. The galleons never came here, and as I expect you read, the *Santa Maria* got burned the other day.

The Carib section is bounded on the north by a stream so trivial that you would not recognize it as a boundary. The landscape is no different after you have passed. Valley succeeds valley. You climb and you descend. There is a cluster of cottages at each valley's foot and the creeper-covered chimney of an abandoned factory. There is a church and there is a cricket pitch, and women are washing out their clothes beside the stream. Villagers pass you on the road, each with his basket on his head. Mile after mile it is the same, and then suddenly at the foot of a sharp descent there is a river broader than the rest, across which is flung a very narrow one-plank-wide suspension bridge. You cross it and you are in another world; a broad and surfaced road stretches on either side of you.

To the right the road runs to the coast, turns north at Marigot, skirts Elma Napier's property at Pointe Baptiste, cutting across to Portsmouth. To the left it leads to the unfinished road.

A car had been ordered to meet me at Hatton Garden, the point where the track joins the road. I was on time; the car was not. I was tired and I was thirsty. On the opposite side of the road was a large plantation of grapefruit trees. My guide pointed it out to me. He also pointed to a group of girls who were coming down the road, "When they pass, I get fruit," I thought he said. I hoped I had misheard him. But I had not. The moment the girls had passed he made for the plantation; he looked disappointed when I called him back, his face bearing an expression which seemed to say, "I thought you had more sense."

Presently the car arrived. I was spending the night in Marigot in a hotel rest-house. I arrived in the late afternoon. A fleet of fishing-boats had just come in and the bay was crowded. To my surprise everyone was talking English. By one of those caprices of history which make the study of the islands so perpetually fascinating, Marigot is as English as Barbados, with no French patois spoken, and a Methodist church upon the hill. Charlesworth Ross suggested as an explanation that a number of Antiguans who had originally come across to work at Portsmouth on a forestry project had later moved to Marigot to avoid malaria. Certainly there is little of the atmosphere of Dominica there.

Not that it is, by any means, without its charm. Like every village on the windward coast, or for that matter like every village throughout the whole West Indies, it carries its own relics of departed glory—the walls still stand of the stone house that once stored sugar, and, thirty yards out from the waterfront, project the flight of steps which once supported the jetty which fed the ships. But Marigot even now has a prosperous air of bustle. It has a motion picture house, and a local industry in the form of pottery, which supplies the island with earthenware. Its store was well stocked with liquor; girls were selling cassava cakes and bread and grapefruit. There were men playing dominoes along the sidewalk.

The site of the abandoned airfield was a mile away. I walked across to it. There it stretched, a broad, long avenue cut through a coconut plantation. Beside it in broad, high piles were the stones with which it had been intended to pave the runway. The tangle of grass and weeds was already ankle-high. There was as little to show here as there had been fifteen years earlier in Coral Gables that many thousands of pounds had been wasted. On the near side of the airstrip were the ruins of a sugar factory. There were the familiar chimneys, the rusted machinery, the crumbling aqueduct. There was an ironically symbolic contrast in this juxtaposition of an ancient and a modern failure.

I returned by road. I could have motored to Portsmouth and taken the launch to Roseau, but I had already made the trip by launch. I was curious, moreover, to go over the unfinished section of the Imperial Road. It was all cut out, I had been told. Much of it was already paved. There were only five miles to be completed.

Peter Fleming had been over the road with Louis de Verteuil a short while earlier. He had remarked to Louis that it was "a nice little walk," but then Peter Fleming is not a person to magnify discomfort. He looks at discomfort through the large lenses of his glasses. He is a younger and a much fitter man than I am; what I would regard as downright dangerous would be merely inconvenient to him. He went, Louis told me, on a rainless day. He also followed for the first part of his journey not the line of the modern road but the old Carib trail; and the Caribs were sensible people who did not cause themselves any more trouble than they needed. They knew that the longest way round can often be the quickest in the end. I look forward to reading what Peter Fleming has to say about the unfinished section of the Imperial Road, if he considers the details of so puny an expedition worth recording, but nothing he may say about "a nice little walk" will alter my own opinion of that road. It was worse than a duckboard track at Passchendaele through a waste of shell-holes.

It took me two and three-quarter hours to do five miles. It was raining all the time. I lost count of the rivers that I waded through and slithered over. Down the sides of the valleys, where it is planned eventually to bridge the footpath, it is so narrow, so overgrown, and with so deep a drop on the other side, that you have to consider each step with the greatest caution or your foot will land on the green roof of a ravine. It is hard to distinguish between a solid root and a broken branch. The planned stretch of the road is either a greasy surface or a weed-covered accumulation of sharp stones. "The road is sliding," the guide kept saying, and he spoke the truth. Every so often the road had been blocked by landslides. We did not pass a single villager. In the solitude it loved, the *siffleur montagne* emitted its sharp, shrill cry. There was one superb spectacle along the road, an avenue cut straight as a ruled pencil line right through the forest. On either side of it the tall trees towered as it stretched in narrowing perspective towards the succession of mountain ranges that form Roseau's background. But I would not for the sake of it make that journey twice. I have never felt more personal emotion for an inanimate object than I did for John Archbold's station-wagon when I saw it waiting for me at the point where the track became a road again.

As I drove through to Roseau, I thought back over the last three hours. I am not an engineer. I could not gauge the amount of skill and labor that would be required for the bridging of those five main ravines and all those minor valleys; I could not estimate the pressure of the mountain torrents that those bridges would have to bear. I could not measure the various problems of transport, equipment, and accommodation that would be involved, nor the cost and difficulty of maintaining a road that would be subjected to an incessant cascade of rain and the consequent inevitable landslides. I am, however, familiar with the inherent laziness and inefficiency of West Indian labor. I know how numerous are the demands now being made in other parts of the British Empire on skilled labor and equipment, how diminished are the resources of English capital, and how profitable are the uses to which, in other sections of the Empire, capital and labor can be put. I had heard so much talk about that road. I had heard so many people say, "Of course it will be all right once the road is finished." But if that road is completed in my lifetime, I shall be astonished. [*This prophecy has not been fulfilled.*]

I arrived in Roseau soon after lunch. The day had cleared and the sun was shining now. The garden of Kingsland House looked very restful, very domestic after the barbaric scenery of the windward coast. Mangoes were ripening; the plants bordering the lawn were studded with blue blossoms; the tulip tree was still in flower, its bright red mellowing to orange; beyond the convent a poui tree whose presence before I left I had not suspected was now a brilliant splash of canary yellow against the deep green of the Morne; a hen was shepherding four infant ducks beneath the bay tree; an old woman in a sloppy, broad-brimmed straw hat was sweeping leaves up with a broom; the wind kept blowing off her hat, and once she lost her temper with it, beating it fiercely with her broom, abusing it with savage oaths. Soft vague clouds drifted across the sky.

I had another two weeks to spend in Dominica. They would be a pleasant two weeks, I was sure of that. There was the Anglo-American wedding of which I have already written. A number of parties had been arranged in honor of it. There were old friends to be seen again; acquaintanceships to ripen into friendships. There would be picnics and expeditions; I should work during the mornings on the early chapters of a novel, I should bathe in the afternoons, and gossip in the evenings on the club veranda. It would be a happy time. At the same time, I knew that as far as this book was concerned my visit to Dominica was at an end.

I could understand now why it was that Dominica should have exercised so powerful a fascination on so many people.

There is nothing to be done about Dominica. That is the crux of the whole issue. In every connection there is that constant vicious circle, that cancelling out of contrasting factors. It will never be possible to restore to cultivation the estates on the windward coast unless there is a means of transporting the produce to the leeward coast. Roads have to be built or a coastal service has to be supplied, but the rains will destroy the roads and a coastal service cannot operate until the estates have been restored to their old prosperity.

Geologically, Dominica presents a problem that no one has yet learned to solve. Its mountains are just that much too high for an island measuring twenty-seven miles by thirteen. At the actual moment of writing there is a banana boom, and as a result of some disagreement with the Azores, a Scandinavian line is maintaining a monthly boat service direct from Dublin; but the essential problem still remains.

On my first visit I had been depressed by the defeatism that underlay the gaiety of carnival. I was not mistaken in recognizing that such an attitude existed, but I had not then seen far enough, I had not then seen how logical was such an attitude and how inevitable; nor that in the acceptance of it lay the island's charm.

John Archbold told me that Dominica had appealed to him because it was a place where he could do what he liked; a remark that would seem at first to confirm the Dominica legend of crazy people cultivating peculiar vices in the rain. But John Archbold is not the kind of person who would want that kind of atmosphere, nor are the other Americans who have made their homes there. They are all of them leading organized domestic lives, working hard on their estates. John Archbold was attracted to Dominica because it was a place where you are not fussed by busybodies, where you are not interfered with, where people generally assume that you mean well because otherwise you would not be there.

Having realized that there is nothing to be done about its basic problem, Dominica has developed a rather large broad-mindedness. It recognizes the rights of the individual; it recognizes the rights of the individual to be individual, to be eccentric if he chooses. There had existed, for example, for quite a while between two of the chief planters one of those ridiculous quarrels—it has now been healed—that break out inevitably every now and then in small communities. It had been going on for so long that no one knew any longer how it started or what it was all about. When one of them moved into a new house on an estate that was relatively adjacent to his enemy's and the question of installing a telephone arose, it was found that far the most economical way of installing a party line—and practically every country telephone in Dominica is on a party line—was by placing the two adversaries on the same extension. This clearly was impossible, and the postal authorities recognized it. With an admirable indifference to red tape and at a cost of several thousand extra feet of wire, three or four connections were relinked so that only friends could be listening in to friends. That is just as much "typical Dominica" as digging holes to the center of the earth to reach one's wife's grave in the Antipodes.

There is one aspect of Dominica's particular and peculiar appeal. There is, however, much more to it than that. There is an intrinsic quality of otherworldliness about "the fatal gift of beauty." What Matthew Arnold said of Oxford in his famous "impossible loyalties" preface to *Essays in Criticism* is apposite to Dominica. In the beauty of her valleys and her mountains she stands both as a witness and a reproach, testifying in her perfection and defeat that many of the finest things in life are not for sale, that many of the finest things have no market value, that there are standards other than that of being in the black.

Stephen Haweis, to whom I have referred already, is spoken of in the other islands as a typical Dominica character, and in a sense in the truest sense, but not in the way they mean, he is a part, very much a part, of the Dominica legend.

A much-travelled man, close now on seventy, an Englishman, educated at Westminster and Oxford, bearing an honored name, he came to Dominica in the nineteen-twenties, to buy an estate, just as John Archbold did, in a moment of caprice. He was then at the height of his reputation as a painter. But a few years later, when the stock market crashed, his small West Indian estate was his only tangible possession.

That was his story as they had told it to me in St. Lucia.

"But he had his painting," I objected.

I had seen several of his pictures; one in particular had struck me—a cluster of coconut palms, sinuous, feminine and graceful, with each palm individualized, each palm seeming to have a distinct and separate existence of its own.

"The man who can paint like that doesn't need to be worried by a Wall Street slump," I said. "His capital is his hand and eye. He only has to go on painting."

"That's what he said. He'd come down to recuperate. As soon as the slump was over, he was going back to New York to have a show. He talked about it quite a lot, at first. But he never went."

"I suppose there was a girl involved."

"No, no. There is nothing like that about him. He's a widower. He's always lived alone."

"What does he live on?"

"Partly his estate, partly on his pictures. Sometimes he sends a few to New York. He usually sells a fair proportion of them. Sometimes he sells a picture to a tourist. He could sell all he wanted locally if he'd care to, but he puts a price on his pictures that is beyond the means of most. He's a pretty eccentric character, you know."

So eccentric that during the war, they told me, he had come into serious conflict with authority. He had written an article criticizing and attacking the Government's agricultural policy. Authority unwisely took offence, and imposed a fine both on the printer and the author of the article. Haweis refused to pay the fine on the ground that freedom of speech was one of our war objectives. After weeks of argument and correspondence, a policeman presented himself outside Haweis's house with a pair of handcuffs.

"What happened then?" I asked.

"His friends bailed him out as soon as they heard of it. 'Typical Dominica.'"

Was it? Maybe it was. But it seemed to me that it was authority, not Haweis, that had been made to appear ridiculous. By any ultimate standards, Haweis was in the right.

He was one of the first people that I met when I arrived in Dominica. I had expected that he would have become, as old bachelors so often do, ill-kempt and scrubby. He hadn't. He was a short, neat figure, with thin white hair and an even, grayish-brown complexion. Without indulging in any sartorial eccentricities, he looked an artist. Just as the sitting-room of his house looked like an artist's. It had the practical untidiness that an artist's studio should have. It looked a workshop.

He showed me some of his pictures. He had once specialized in fish, but now he was concentrating on vegetation. The chief thing that struck me about his paintings was their sense of movement. They were representational, though occasionally he adopted a cubist technique. There was one canvas of a man planting cane. The body did not join up with the legs, but there was movement there. In particular, I admired a group of carrier girls, striding with baskets on their heads down a jungle path. They were fine Amazonian creatures, with bright blouses and vivid turbans, but they seemed colorless and dwarfed against the rich green background of the forest.

He smiled when I told him that.

"I only put them in there as a measuring-rod. My father used to say about the Bible, 'It may not be the word of God, but the word of God is in it.' That picture may not be the forest, but the forest's in it. At least, I hope it is."

He spoke unaffectedly about his work. "I care as much about my painting as I ever did. But I don't seem to care what other people think about it any longer. I'd just as soon not sell my pictures. I like to have them round me."

I had expected to find in him a certain sourness, a certain acidity; certainly an attitude of contentiousness. I didn't. Apart from the charm of his manner, which was very real, apart from an inherited and inherent air of ease and breeding, what struck me most about him was the sense he gave of distance, of seeing the human scene in focus.

I asked him the inevitable question. What was it that had brought him here? He smiled at that.

"You know the old beachcomber story of a man seeing a pretty native girl on a veranda and letting his ship sail on without him. It was a mango tree that brought me here. Its native owner was about to cut it down; the only way to save it was to buy the ground it stood on."

"I'd like to see that tree," I said.

He pointed across the valley. There it stood in all its majesty, spreading its branches to the sunlight. It was not yet the mango season. I pictured it as it would be in a few weeks' time, heavy with swelling fruit.

"Why on earth did they want to cut it down?" I asked.

He laughed.

"It wasn't any use to them. I didn't know it at the time, but mangoes won't bear above fifteen hundred feet. We're over two thousand here. They'd have sold it as firewood. Charcoal fetches a good price. They were quite right, of course. I see that now." He paused, then smiled. "I felt rather cheated when I found it out. As a man might who gives up his career for a girl who turns out worthless. But that's nearly twenty years ago. I don't feel that way now. They were right, but so was I, though I didn't know it then. I'm glad I spared it. It's enough to be beautiful; there's no need to bear fruit as well."

All Dominica is in that comment. [*If Dominica is now definitely in the black, it will probably lose its attraction for "the misfit."*]

Envoi

WRITTEN IN 1955

"I suppose," a friend said to me last October, "that you'll be going there again this winter." I did not need to ask him what he meant by "there." "There" is the Caribbean. Since I first saw the West Indies in 1927, I have spent as many winters among those favored islands as I have in London and New York.

I love it there. I love everything about it. I love the climate. It is hot, but except in Trinidad, not humid. The trade-wind is always blowing from the East; you can take enough exercise to keep in health. You can get a proper sleep at night. The wind is too strong for the mosquitoes, so that if your bungalow is on a hill, you can sit on the veranda after sundown. There is plenty of rain, but the showers if violent are brief.

I love the beauty of the islands, the long white beaches with the coconut palms fringing them; the high-peaked mountains with the fields of sugar cane winding like broad, green rivers along their valleys. I love their drowsy little towns and their fishing villages, haphazard collections of shingle huts perched on boulders, straggling on either side of a shallow stream that, when the rains are heavy, will become a torrent, with children and chickens and pigs tumbling over one another under the shade of breadfruit trees, with nets hung out to dry along the beach.

I love the sense of history that you feel there—the stone-built forts that in the days of battle guarded the harbors, the towers of abandoned windmills that dot the hills and the old estate houses, many of them now in ruins, that recall the rich plantation days. Finally I love the West Indians themselves. You could not find a more diverse group. Their complexions range from white to ebony. There are wide mouths and flattened nostrils—aquiline noses and thin lips. The hair may be short and curly or straight and black. They are sorted into innumerable social strata. There are the descendants of the old feudal families in whose houses, particularly in Barbados, the traditions of eighteenth-century hospitality survive. There are the white-collar professional classes— ninety-nine per cent of them are partly or wholly of African descent—who are taking over stage by stage the administration of the islands.

Lastly there is the grinning chattering proletariat. I am sometimes infuriated by their casual, lazy improvidence, but it is impossible to be angry with them for long. They are basically so good-natured, always ready to dance and sing and laugh; they are born comics. They contribute immensely to the visitor's enjoyment.

And every island is different from its neighbors. That is one of the great charms of the Caribbean. People who have not been to the West Indies speak of them as though they were a single place. A friend said to me last March: "What, going to the West Indies? Then you'll run into Billy Collins. Give him my love, won't you?" The gentleman in question was going to Jamaica. I was going to Trinidad, and when I first went to the islands, before air travel, a journey from Trinidad to Jamaica took seven days by boat. We novelists are mainly to blame, I fancy, for this misconception. We have to be on our guard against libel actions, so when we write stories with a West Indian background, we invent an island to which we attribute features that we have found in half a dozen islands. The reader is consequently presented with a composite picture of mountains, beaches, palms, and a lush luxuriant undergrowth. Actually, though you will find all those things in the West Indies, you will rarely find all of them in one island.

Barbados and Antigua, for instance, have superb beaches, but they are not mountainous, Barbados being for the most part flat. Trinidad is mountainous but the bathing is poor. Dominica is mountainous but it has no sand beaches that are safe for bathing. St. Thomas has magnificent beaches and it is mountainous but its soil is dry. Grenada is the one small island that provides, within each reach, everything that a preconceived picture of the tropics has led the visitor to expect.

History as well as geology has helped to make these islands different. In the eighteenth century the Caribbean was the focal point of European foreign policy. The islands were constantly changing hands. The Stars and Stripes now fly over St. Thomas and St. Croix, but the churchyards of Charlotte Amalie and Frederiksted contain not only Danish but French and British headstones. The French Revolution affected not only Haiti where the slaves became the masters, not only the French island of Guadeloupe where the guillotine was set up in the market square, but British islands like St. Lucia and Grenada which were plundered by the revolutionaries. The present day social life of these islands has been determined by the historical events of a century and a half ago. And it is fascinating for the twentieth-century visitor to note where and how the caprice of history has made Trinidad different from Jamaica and St. Thomas from St. Croix.

There it stretches, the Archipelago of the Antilles, in an arc from Florida to Venezuela, the summits of a submerged mountain range. From a ship, as you see them shadowy on the horizon, the separate islands look very like each other. When you first land, you are inclined to say, "Yes, but I've seen this before. St. Vincent looked just like this."

It may have done, but there'll be differences—socially and geologically. That is one of the great charms of the Caribbean. As long as there is one island still untouched, their whole story is not yours.